SAME FAMILY, DIFFERENT COLORS

SAME FAMILY, DIFFERENT COLORS

Confronting Colorism in America's Diverse Families

LORI L. THARPS

BEACON PRESS
BOSTON

Beacon Press
Boston, Massachusetts
www.beacon.org

Beacon Press books
are published under the auspices of
the Unitarian Universalist Association of Congregations.

19 18 17 16   8 7 6 5 4 3 2 1

This book is printed on acid-free paper that meets the uncoated paper ANSI/NISO
specifications for permanence as revised in 1992.

Text design by Ruth Maassen

Some names and identifying characteristics of people mentioned in this work have been
changed to protect their identities.

Library of Congress Cataloging-in-Publication Data

Names: Tharps, Lori L., author.
Title: Same family, different colors : confronting colorism in America's
  diverse families / Lori L. Tharps.
Description: Boston, Massachusetts : Beacon Press, [2016] | Includes
  bibliographical references and index.
Identifiers: LCCN 2015048421 (print) | LCCN 2016004100 (ebook) | ISBN
  9780807076781 (hardback) | ISBN 9780807076798 (ebook)
Subjects: LCSH: Colorism—United States. | Racially mixed families—United
  States. | BISAC: SOCIAL SCIENCE / Ethnic Studies / General. | FAMILY &
  RELATIONSHIPS / Parenting / General. | SOCIAL SCIENCE / Discrimination &
  Race Relations.
Classification: LCC E185.62 .T468 2016 (print) | LCC E185.62 (ebook) | DDC
  305.800973—dc23
LC record available at http://lccn.loc.gov/2015048421

"Oh boy . . . God's not black. He's not white. He's a spirit."
"Does he like black or white people better?"
"He loves all people. He's a spirit."
"What's a spirit?"
"A spirit's a spirit."
"What color is God's spirit?"
"It doesn't have a color," she said. "God is the color of water."

—JAMES MCBRIDE, *The Color of Water:
A Black Man's Tribute to His White Mother*

For my original rainbow coalition:
Manuel, Esai, Addai, and Aida

CONTENTS

Author's Note   xi

Introduction   1

ONE   The Darker the Berry: African Americans and Color   19

TWO   *Mejorando la Raza*: Latinos and Color   65

THREE   Fair Enough: Asian Americans and Color   97

FOUR   Beige Is the New Black: Mixed-Race Americans and Color   129

Conclusion   163

Acknowledgments   179

Sources   183

Index   193

AUTHOR'S NOTE

Talking about color is hard. Admitting you and the people you love have been affected by colorism is even harder. Understandably, some of the people I interviewed for this book did not want their real names used for fear of hurting others, as well as for their own protection. I had no problem honoring their wishes. However, my manuscript started to look quite messy with all of the asterisks and explanations of which names were real and which were actually pseudonyms.

To make it easier on everyone, I have changed all names and identifying details of the people I interviewed for this book, with the exception of the public figures. I define public figures as authors, academics, celebrities, journalists, and activists. In other words, I used the real names of all of the people I interviewed for their expert opinion on colorism and pseudonyms for those who were generous enough to share their stories about living in a home of many colors. In two or three cases these categories overlapped and I chose—with permission—to use real names.

INTRODUCTION

The first difference which strikes us is that of colour.
—THOMAS JEFFERSON, *Notes on the State of Virginia*

"I spy something white!"

The game was getting good. It was 2012 and I was sitting in the dimly lit hallway of the Settlement Music School in the Germantown section of Philadelphia. To pass the time while waiting for my son to finish his guitar lesson, I was playing I Spy with an adorable five-year-old Black girl whose beaded cornrows were keeping my daughter Aida entertained. The little girl's father smiled at me in gratitude for keeping his child occupied while he attempted to read the newspaper. It was a win-win situation for everyone.

"So, I'm looking for something white," I repeated, scanning the dull-green walls, sandy-brown carpet, and dark wooden benches lining the hallway. I didn't see anything light, bright, or remotely white in the vicinity. Since the girl was only five and on a previous turn had "spied" an invisible purple horse, I began to guess some imaginary white objects she may have "seen."

"Is it a snowflake?" I asked.

"No," she giggled.

"Is it a giant marshmallow man?"

"Uh-uh," she shook her head and her braids made a delightful tinkling sound. Aida reached for them in awe with her pudgy little fingers.

"Is it a flying white unicorn with glitter on her wings?" I tried.

"No!" The girl screeched with laughter. "It's her," she declared as she pointed directly at my daughter with a challenge in her eye and an accusation in her tone. "She's white!"

I opened my mouth to respond, but no words came out. A five-year-old had rendered me speechless. Before I could figure out how to, or even if I should, correct the little girl's erroneous assumption, her father yanked her to her feet, mumbled an embarrassed apology to me, and dragged the girl toward the downstairs waiting area. I could hear her protests as he ushered her to the steps, "But she is white, Daddy. She is!"

Aida climbed up on the bench next to me and started playing with my hair instead. My dreadlocks didn't have any fancy beads, but they could still be pulled and tugged for entertainment. I hauled my child on to my lap and took a good look. Indeed, even in the windowless light of the music school, my sixteen-month-old daughter looked like a little white girl. Her round, cherubic face was all strawberries and cream, and her jet-black hair hung straight to her shoulders with just the hint of a wave at the ends. I sighed. Children don't lie. That little girl had only said aloud what most people probably thought when they saw my daughter anyway. She's white. But I'm Black. So, how did that happen?

From a biological perspective it's an easy question to answer. There are more than one hundred different genes that influence skin pigmentation. Scientists haven't even begun to isolate all of them yet. The variations of human skin color range from the deepest midnight black to an almost translucent, ethereal white. In between are unlimited varieties of brown, beige, copper, and cream. When two people of the same ethnic heritage with similar skin tones reproduce, it is expected that the offspring will share the same skin color as their similarly colored parents.

Of course, my situation, like that of a number of Americans nowadays, isn't so black and white.

I am a Black American woman with medium-brown skin, and my husband is a Spaniard with a milky-white complexion. Using both logic and some creative form of math and science, one would expect our children to exhibit a skin tone somewhere between chocolate brown and milky white. But when it comes to skin color and genetics, it's not such a simple equation. In my case, our three children are three distinctly different colors. One is almost as dark as I am, one is almost as pale as my husband, and one is the color of sand. As Nina Jablonski, the prominent anthropologist known for her work on the evolution of human skin color, explained when I asked her about the variations in skin tone of mixed-race kids, "When it comes to predicting the skin color of the offspring of interracial couples, it's like playing genetic roulette. You never know what you're going to get."

It's not like I didn't know that marrying a white European would increase my chances of having children with skin lighter than mine, but I never thought of Manuel as "white," meaning he's not an Anglo-Saxon. He's Spanish. From the south of Spain, specifically, where the people have both Arab and African ancestors tangled in their DNA and skin colors in a single family can range from pure white to toasty brown.

Manuel and I met during my junior year of college, which I spent studying at the Universidad de Salamanca, situated about ninety miles northwest of Madrid. Manuel's parents had sent him up north for college because they wanted him to experience another part of the country besides the sleepy Andalusian town where he'd been born and raised. By the time we met, Manuel wanted to see even more of the world, and it didn't take much for him to decide to follow me across the ocean and start a new life in the United States. It took us seven more years to get married, but we were pretty sure by then that our relationship would last. What we had in common was a love and respect for family, food, and literature and a certain fascination with the sea. In our early years we plotted a life that included bilingual children, a transatlantic lifestyle, and possibly a small café that specialized in fusion Spanish soul food.

By the time Manuel and I decided we wanted to start a family, we'd been together for almost a decade. As is probably the case with most expectant parents, we spent a lot of time imagining what our future child would look like. Like his parents and three siblings, Manuel's pale skin warms up to a nice shade of brown in the sun. His thick dark hair is naturally curly and, in his youth, grew up and out like some sort of loose, Spanish Afro. His eyes are brown with specks of green that sparkle when the light hits them just the right way. My jet-black hair is thick and kinky. My skin is medium brown and darkens easily in the sun, and my eyes are also brown. Given Manuel's potential African or Arabic ancestry and the fact that my physical appearance betrayed little evidence of any recent Caucasian ancestors, we were confident that our biracial kids would be on the browner side of the spectrum. Even though some people might assume I married a European man because I wanted my children to be lighter than me, nothing could be further from the truth. Like most people, I wanted my children to look like *me* and to be unquestioned members of my tribe. Quite simply, to be Black like me. Manuel, on the other hand, wanted his children to be darker than he was, simply because he disliked being so pale and had always felt an affinity for skin with more color.

Esai was born in 2001 with his eyes wide open. He was such a pretty baby that he was often mistaken for a girl. And he was such a pale baby, with thick, straight, black hair, that I was often mistaken for his nanny. Given that we were living in Brooklyn, New York, in the early 2000s, I looked like any other Black domestic worker caring for a white child. But a funny thing happened to Esai. When he was about eighteen months old, we took him to Spain to visit his paternal grandparents. While we were there, we spent a lot of time at the beach. Esai developed a beautiful sun-kissed tan that just never went away. His skin, the formerly pale version, was replaced with skin the color of cinnamon. And his loose black curls tightened up and lightened up into a kinky brown Afro. So, of course, when I gave birth three years later to another milky-white baby boy with straight black hair, we assumed he too would go through a similar skin and hair transformation—but he didn't. Not really. By age three, Addai's skin color had barely made it from white to beige, and his dark hair curled but never transitioned all the way to kinky.

Even though I didn't think of my children as two different colors, the rest of the world took great delight in pointing out that I had one Black son and one white. Some people even found it fitting to point out—in inappropriate public spaces, no less—that it made sense, since one child resembled his pale father and one his dark mommy. The only thing is, Addai looks more like me, with his broad shoulders, long arms, and almond shaped eyes, and Esai is a clone of his tall, lanky father, simply with darker skin. Most of the time I try to ignore other people's issues with my children's skin color, but sometimes it really bothers me. And sometimes it just hurts.

There was the time, soon after we moved from New York to Philadelphia, when the difference in skin color between my sons created an uncomfortable situation for Manuel. He'd started using a corner dry cleaner recommended by our neighbors. The shop was close enough to our home that Manuel could easily walk there on Saturday mornings. He would take both boys with him, Esai walking and Addai in the stroller. The Asian shopkeeper always greeted Manuel with a smile and a friendly word, but she literally gushed over two-year-old Addai. She always told Manuel how cute Addai was, and she'd always find a piece of candy to give him. Always. She barely registered Esai's existence.

At first when Manuel mentioned this to me, I brushed it off, thinking he was probably reading too much into the woman's actions. Addai was still technically a baby, and people like babies more than five-year-old kids, I reasoned. But Manuel wasn't convinced, and it kept happening. He told me the woman was blatant with her favoritism toward Addai and he was sure it was because Addai looked white and Esai looked Black. Although he never confronted the woman about her behavior, Manuel did something more significant. He found a new dry cleaner. When I asked him why he was willing to travel farther and actually pay more money to have his shirts laundered, his response was quite emphatic. He said he never wanted Esai to feel that his brother received preferential treatment for having lighter skin even if that wasn't the case with the dry cleaner. "He may be oblivious right now to how's he being treated and why," Manuel said. "But soon enough he's going to pick up on those kind of things and I don't want him to grow up with a complex."

Ten years after Esai was born, Aida entered the world looking just like her brothers. Pale skin, straight black hair. During the first year of her life, I was asked any number of questions regarding her "true heritage." Some asked why I had adopted a baby from China. Others wanted to know whose baby I was caring for, because clearly she wasn't mine. As we watch Aida mature from baby to young child, her melanin production has increased. While she could still easily pass for white, her skin has developed a warm almond undertone and her straight, shiny black hair has been replaced by a frizzy, unruly hodgepodge of curls that refuse to be defined. It is clearly not the white-girl hair she had for the first eighteen months of her life. Because of her hair, the questions about her connection to me have diminished, but we still get the stares when we go out. People have to look twice to decode our relationship. And it's pretty much the same for our entire family. We don't match. We don't share the same colors. Recently Esai said to me, "When I'm out with Papi, people think I'm adopted." I tried to tell him he was wrong, thinking it was my duty to assuage any feelings of racial angst he may be having. But the truth is, people do think that. Manuel has told me. It happens all the time.

Same Family, Different Colors

Many challenges come with being a family with different skin colors, challenges that range from the practical to the political. Everything from selecting different SPF levels of sunscreen for each member of the family to training one son to be prepared for a society that will perceive him as a threat while teaching the other not to take advantage of his light-skin privilege. And these aren't issues felt only by families like mine where one parent is Black and the other white. In Black families, Latino families, and Asian American families, skin colors can vary in microscopic gradients or in obvious shades of difference. And those differences—whether glaring or minute—can impact everything from interactions among family members, parenting practices, and sibling relationships to racial identity formation. Outside of the house, siblings who are light and dark may be treated differently, and of course they bring those lived experiences back into the home.

The truth is, even in the twenty-first century, the general public does not understand families that don't match. Witness the ugly online comments that were made when General Mills put out a Cheerios commercial in 2013 featuring an interracial family. The advertisement featured a family with a white mother, a Black father, and their adorable, chubby-cheeked daughter. In the thirty-second commercial, the mother and father aren't even in the same room together, yet so many people posted offensive comments—the commercial was "disgusting" and it "made them want to vomit," among other things—General Mills shut down the comments section on the commercial's YouTube page.

The response to the Cheerios commercial could be blamed on ignorance or racism, or perhaps a toxic combination of the two, but the end result is devastatingly familiar. The public fears what they do not understand and that fear can be twisted and transformed into something that resembles anger, hostility, and violence. Imagine that anger or hostility directed toward your family. Imagine what it's like to have your closest relationships misunderstood. In September 2015, police in Snellville, Georgia, received a 911 call from a concerned citizen who saw a white baby in a car with a Black family. Admittedly, the child did not look to be in any kind of danger, but the "concerned citizen" thought it looked "odd"—odd enough to place an emergency call to the police. Clearly, the baby could have been adopted, or the "white" baby could have been Black like my daughter, or someone could have just been babysitting. But to a stranger, that white baby did not belong with the Black family, because they didn't match. Because they weren't the same color. This is just another example that demonstrates that Americans do not have a language or a framework with which to understand a child who is lighter than her mother, or a father who is darker than his son.

The issue cannot be overstated: people expect families to match, despite the fact that interracial marriage has been legal in all fifty states since 1967 and despite the fact that Black people, Asians, and Latinos come in a multitude of shades and colors and always have. There's something about the concept of family that demands a sense of uniformity, of sameness—same race, religion, class, and, yes, skin color. And when that sameness does not manifest, some sort of disruption occurs. Of course, with class and religion, differences can be kept private, but skin-color differences are always open to public scrutiny. From the minor aggravation of being stared at in public to the very real fear of having your most valued relationships challenged by those in power, being a family of different colors can produce a never-ending roller coaster ride of trials and tribulations. And while it may seem unbelievable that something as innocuous as skin color—not necessarily "race"—could have such a significant impact on family life, the reality is that color matters. It matters a lot.

Color Matters

Skin color matters because we are a visual species and we respond to one another based on the way we physically present. Add to that the "like belongs with like" beliefs most people harbor, and the race-based prejudices human beings have attached to certain skin colors, and we come to present-day society, where skin color becomes a loaded signifier of identity and value. In the United States in particular, where we have an extremely diverse population, yes, race still matters, but color matters too.

I would argue that in the twenty-first century, as America becomes less white and the multiracial community—formed by interracial unions and immigration—continues to expand, color will be even more significant than race in both public and private interactions. Why? Because a person's skin color is an irrefutable visual fact that is impossible to hide, whereas race is a constructed, quasi-scientific classification that is often only visible on a government form. The fact is, our limited official racial categories in the United States—Black, white, American Indian, Asian, and Native Hawaiian—are already straining under the weight of our multi-hued, ethnically diverse, phenotypically ambiguous population.

(And where do Latinos fit in here anyway?) A conversation about "race" is no longer sufficient when our first Black president has a white mother, and record-setting golfer Tiger Woods is a "Cablinasian," and, in 2015, a white woman named Rachel Dolezal feels justified in claiming a Black identity without having any African ancestry. The discussion has to get more nuanced and categories beyond Black and white must be introduced. And I'm not the only one who feels this way. In early 2016, *New York Times* columnist and author Kwame Anthony Appiah wrote about the dubious nature of what we Americans call race. He said, "The fact is that our system of racial classifications is based, as I've suggested, on a mélange of falsehood and ignorance—with, no doubt, an occasional admixture of truth. It presupposes an extremely oversimplified picture of the relationship among ancestry, appearance, biology and culture."

I think it is as clear as glass that Americans are on a collision course with a future in which the word "race" gets redefined or perhaps even retired from official government use. But in the meantime, skin color will continue to serve as the most obvious criterion in determining how a person will be evaluated and judged. In this country, because of deeply entrenched racism, we already know that dark skin is demonized and light skin wins the prize. And that occurs precisely because this country was built upon principles of racism. It cannot be overstated that if racism didn't exist, a discussion about skin hues would simply be a conversation about aesthetics. But that's not the case. This privileging of light skin over dark is at the root of an ill known as colorism. And colorism is like a parasite feeding off the blood of racism.

The curious thing is that the word "colorism" doesn't even exist. Not officially. It autocorrects on my computer screen. It does not appear in the dictionary. So, how does one begin to unpack a societal ill that doesn't have a name? It's like trying to wrap your hands around a ghost. However, according to Thomas Morton, a sociolinguist at Temple University, words do not require validation from a dictionary to have a place in the world. "A word exists as soon as two or more people know what it refers to," he said. "And just because [the word] colorism is not in the dictionary does not mean it has no meaning when used orally."

The author and activist Alice Walker is the person most often credited with first using the word colorism, out loud and in print. In an essay that appeared in her 1983 book *In Search of Our Mothers' Gardens,*

Walker defined colorism in the African American community as "prejudicial or preferential treatment of same-race people based solely on their color" and noted that "preferential treatment" was regularly reserved for light-skinned Blacks. A preference for light skin had been common in Black America for generations, but Walker gave it a name and marked it as a trend that must be stopped in order for African Americans to progress as a people. But Black Americans are not the only people privileging and lusting after light skin. Colorism is a problem felt in many places all around the world, including Latin America, East and Southeast Asia, the Caribbean, and Africa. As a nation of immigrants, many of our ethnic communities import their native colorism to this country, adding to its entrenchment in our melting pot American culture. But it is important to note that, contrary to Walker's belief that colorism is practiced by "same-race people," colorism is an equal opportunity form of discrimination. White Americans, for example, are just as likely to show preferential treatment toward light-skinned Blacks and Latinos as are other Blacks and Latinos. In other words, colorism is both an interracial *and* an intra-racial phenomenon, which simply makes it twice as insidious as previously thought.

A group of researchers from Harvard University, the University of Washington, and the University of Virginia has been trying since 1998 to quantify just how much skin color matters to Americans of all ethnic backgrounds with the creation of the Implicit Association Test (IAT). The test, administered anonymously online, highlights the hidden biases people harbor, based not just on skin color and race, but also on gender, sexuality, and self-esteem. However, the results so far regarding color in particular are beyond troubling. In reporting on the scale of the light-skin bias across cultures, journalist Achal Mehra wrote, "The implicit bias for lighter skin tone is consistent across all US racial groups." He continued, "But more significant than the fact that almost 70 percent of the millions of people who have taken the IAT demonstrate at least some preference for light skin is the real world impact of such biases. There is mounting evidence of the social, economic, and political disparities that colorism engenders, often as striking as disparities based on race."

Shankar Vedantam is the author of the 2010 book *The Hidden Brain: How Our Unconscious Minds Elect Presidents, Control Markets, Wage Wars, and Save Our Lives*. A science reporter for the *Washington Post*, Vedantam's research touched on color and how even the most liberal-minded progressive thinkers still display a bias toward light skin. In an opinion piece in the *New York Times*, he wrote, "Dozens of research studies have shown that skin tone and other racial features play powerful roles in who gets ahead and who does not. These factors regularly determine who gets hired, who gets convicted and who gets elected."

Vedantam is correct, and despite the fact that the word doesn't exist, researchers and scholars are now systematically tracking colorism's existence and multifaceted effects. A 2006 University of Georgia study found that employers of any race prefer light-skinned Black men to dark-skinned Black men regardless of their qualifications. Sociologist Margaret Hunter writes in her book *Race, Gender, and the Politics of Skin Tone* that Mexican Americans with light skin "earn more money, complete more years of education, live in more integrated neighborhoods, and have better mental health than do darker-skinned . . . Mexican Americans." In 2013, researchers Lance Hannon, Robert DeFina, and Sarah Bruch found that Black female students with dark skin were three times more likely to be suspended from school than their light-skinned African American counterparts. In 2015 I heard economist Joni Hersch, from Vanderbilt University Law School, present her research on the economic disparities between light- and dark-skinned legal immigrants in the United States. She found that immigrants with the lightest skin earned between 8 and 15 percent more than immigrants with the same qualifications but with darker skin. This was true across all immigrant ethnic groups. Hersch was quoted in the *New York Times* as saying, "On average, being one shade lighter has about the same effect as having an additional year of education." As Hersch said in her presentation, "In other words, light-skinned immigrants are at an advantage." An advantage based on color.

Like racism and sexism, colorism is a key component of America's social landscape. Some scholars even argue that the United States, like many of her Latin American cousins, operates as a pigmentocracy where those with light skin are privileged above those with darker skin and light outranks dark in all areas of society, from religion to the criminal justice system. Statistics show that one's health, wealth, and opportunity for success in this country will be impacted by the color of one's skin, sometimes irrespective of one's racial background. Even darker-hued white Americans have different experiences than their lighter-hued Caucasian counterparts when it comes to access to resources and overall treatment in society.

An extreme case from history—but one that exemplifies how one white family found itself on the wrong side of the color line—was reported in a 1955 issue of *Ebony* magazine. Under the headline "Florida Sheriff Calls White Family Black," the article depicts the harrowing story of how Florida sheriff Willis V. McCall stormed into the home of a white family in the middle of the night, after he'd gotten word that some of the children "looked liked Negros." The Platt family claimed to be white, of Irish and Native American descent, and indeed both parents look white enough in photos that appeared in the magazine. But then there were the children. Of the seven children pictured, most have thick, curly hair and some have a skin color that truly looks closer to brown than white. (Note: Not that this had any bearing on the case, but I did find it ironic that the Platt boy with the darkest skin and kinkiest hair was named Denzell. If that's not a Black child giveaway, I don't know what is.) The youngest child, however, had light skin and light eyes. Regardless of the presence of some paleness in the family, Sheriff McCall wanted answers about this working-class family of orange pickers.

According to the *Ebony* article, during his middle-of-the-night raid, the sheriff lined up the seven Platt children, took their pictures, and subjected them to his own brand of a racial purity test. They didn't pass. "I don't like the shape of that one's nose," he reportedly said of one of the Platt girls, and he found five of the children's complexions too "dusky" and hair texture too Negro-like. That's all it took to turn a white family Black. The darker children were subsequently barred from their whites-only school, and the landlord evicted the family from their house. The Platts were forced to move out and were shunned by the community and taunted with racial slurs and threats of violence. Even after they moved, their new house was set on fire. Eventually the family took their case to the courts to prove that they were indeed white, and while, technically, justice was served, when the courts could not prove that the Platts carried Negro blood in their veins, Mr. Platt never got over the experience. Many years later, at the age of eighty-three, he told a reporter for the *Orlando Sentinel*, "I wouldn't have treated a dog the way they treated me."

What happened to the Platt family seems unbelievable, but they weren't the only white family with "dusky" skin that faced discrimination because of colorism. And it is that same colorism that is plaguing our country today, more than sixty years later—even though the word itself still doesn't exist. And the reason it doesn't exist probably has to do with the fact that few people outside of academia are talking specifically about colorism, despite its ubiquitous presence throughout the country. For various reasons that will be explained in later chapters, colorism is still a taboo topic in practically every community. What's more, as a country, we've staked our claim on racism as the form of discrimination we can all collectively agree to fight. Racism is our historical legacy, our cause célèbre of the civil rights movement; most importantly, racism offers a documented and defined explanation of both its truth and its consequences. Colorism, on the other hand, requires a more nuanced approach to discrimination, a parsing of shades of skin color, grades of hair, and keenness of features. It requires a knowledge of ethnic histories, beauty standards, and identity politics. Because of the lack of official documentation and statistics, until very recently, the consequences of colorism were difficult to prove. And because there is little public recognition of colorism as a national issue, and given the lack of language surrounding skin-color politics, the pain it causes is difficult to talk about.

As the mother of three children with three different skin colors, and as a journalist keeping track of the trends in identity politics, I want to talk about colorism. I want to talk about it until colorism comes out of the closet and becomes as recognized as racism as a form of discrimination that troubles this nation. The two—racism and colorism—are inextricably intertwined, but if we're not acknowledging colorism's unique existence, then we'll never reach a place where we can talk about solutions.

Family Matters

I had a simple goal and clear agenda when I started writing this book. My goal was to jump-start an accessible conversation about colorism in the United States by focusing on the family. Many writers have utilized the American family to examine social trends because the family is so influential in both human development and social progress. Plus, it is an institution that is both personal and political, public and private. By exploring colorism through the prism of the family, I felt I could contextualize a complicated issue in a familiar framework for a diverse audience. My agenda, therefore, was to investigate how skin-color differences in a nuclear family affect family dynamics. I wanted to see if the skin-color hierarchy present in American society at large is replicated in the home, and if so, what are the implications? Since colorism is an equal opportunity issue, I've sought to have an inclusive narrative, including families of diverse ethnic backgrounds, specifically, African American, Latino, Asian American, and interracial families. This book argues that colorism is not native to the African American community and that if we ever hope to eradicate this insidious disease of color bias, we must acknowledge that colorism is everybody's problem.

By examining the ways different families from different ethnic groups confront and deal with skin-color differences in the intimate space of the home, we can see where, when, how, and why color bias begins or ends and why it takes hold of some people while others are able to shrug it off like yesterday's news. We can see why a dark child in a Latino family scrubs herself with bleach every night so people understand she is her mother's child. We can see why a blond-haired, blue-eyed, biracial girl covers her face with her Black mother's makeup so people recognize she is *her* mother's child. Colorism isn't just public statistics; it is also private agony that influences identity formation, self-esteem, and personal relationships. Old and young, dark and light, male and female—colorism has a wide reach and America's families can give us an entrée into understanding this world of color bias, providing a microcosm of the wider society where color politics are seen in full effect. When you think about it, it is indeed the multi-hued American family that is the real expert, living on, in between, and tangled up in the color line. In the following chapters, I've collected the incredibly personal stories of a diverse group of people who shared with me their experiences living in a family of different colors.

Inspired by Andrew Solomon's book *Far from the Tree*, in which he profiled families dealing with children who have radically different identities than their parents, my methodology for researching the ways that skin-color differences affect family dynamics was simple. I interviewed as many people as possible—in the African American, Latino, and Asian American communities—who came from nuclear families whose members were the same race but different colors. I also interviewed interracial families where mom and dad were different races but the children, obviously, were the same mixed-race combination. I did not include transracial families formed through adoption for the simple reason that the added issue of adoption would transform this discussion into one where skin color was no longer the most significant identity difference between family members. But adoptive families will likely relate to many of the stories chronicled here. My guess is that many people will find these stories relatable, if not wholly familiar. After interviewing dozens of people from across the country and from multiple ethnic communities within it, I was surprised at how similarly skin-color politics played out in every family. For every African American girl hiding from the sun under her mother's strict orders, there is a Korean American girl playing in the shadows as well.

I do not claim to have written the definitive account of how colorism affects the American family, nor was that my intention. Instead I have captured snapshots of individual lives to demonstrate the impact colorism can have on a person. If what social scientist Frank Sulloway wrote is true—that "no social injustice is felt more deeply than that suffered within one's own family"—then the family is the perfect institution in which to focus this study on colorism. But it is not all doom and gloom. Some people I interviewed provided a blueprint for dismantling colorism, and many others proved that colorism could be overcome in one generation. While statistics show that colorism stands in the way of equality for those with darker skin in this country, the stories I collected tell a fuller story. As Solomon wrote in his introduction to *Far from the Tree*, "Numbers imply trends while stories acknowledge chaos." And chaos I did find, but it wasn't the only narrative I heard.

In the following four chapters, I chronicle stories from Americans of various ethnic backgrounds, ages, and classes, although the majority of the people I spoke with are solidly middle class. The stories are poignant and deeply personal, and I was often amazed that people were willing to share so much with me, a curious journalist. I've come to believe that part of the reason for their willingness to be vulnerable is because they haven't had the opportunity or perhaps the permission to discuss colorism, and I suspect many others feel the same way.

Some of my interviews were done in person, and others were conducted over the phone and via the miracle of Skype. Because I was interested solely in how colorism manifests in our uniquely race-obsessed American culture, my criteria for subjects were that they had to currently live in the United States and had to have spent a significant part of their childhood here as well. Also, I only interviewed people over age eighteen because I wanted my subjects to have the maturity to reflect on their upbringing and/or current family life.

Each chapter of the book focuses on a specific cultural community—African American, Latino, Asian American, and interracial—and begins with a brief historical summary of the skin-color politics in that community in order to provide context to the stories my subjects tell. Clearly, condensing hundreds of years of history into a few short pages leaves room for omissions and alternate interpretations, but my aim was not to provide a comprehensive history lesson but rather a historical primer for the current perspectives on color in each community.

Within each chapter, the personal stories are organized around common themes. Also included are the voices of noted experts who underscore the importance of the issues being raised, even beyond the private space of home. My own story is woven throughout these pages as well, since it influenced and inspired many of the questions I asked of both my subjects and the experts. These experts—academics, artists, and activists—already engaged in colorism work, also address possible solutions to this endemic problem. Still, this is neither a self-help book nor a parenting manual, although I entered into this project looking for answers relevant to my own unique parenting journey. What I ended up writing, however, is a book that lays bare the lie that race is our country's biggest social issue. Yes, racism is still a gargantuan problem in the United States, particularly as it corrupts most of our institutions. But if we did away with racial categories because they can no longer contain our increasingly diverse population, as is the case in many South American countries, a powerful social hierarchy would still exist. And that hierarchy would be based on color. In other words, even if by some miracle we managed to fix our racism problem, colorism would still be present. Indeed it is on that color line, which W. E. B. Du Bois lamented, that our biggest problem truly rests. But the color line does not simply divide Black and white. The color line we must figure out how to dismantle also traverses all the shades in between. And maybe, just maybe, the solution to the problem lies within the American family.

Sidebar: The Color Complex

The story of our skin starts a long time ago. Thankfully, the anthropologist Nina Jablonski has already taken the time to research that history and write about it extensively. "Our skin is the meeting place of biology and everyday experience, a product of human evolution that is perceived within the context of human culture," Jablonski gracefully begins her book *Living Color: The Biological and Social Meaning of Skin Color*. In it she tackles the evolution of skin color from our earliest human ancestors, as well as the reasons certain prejudices were attached to particular skin colors. While it would be impossible to summarize 197 pages of dense science into a single paragraph, we can conclude that the development of different skin pigmentations evolved as a means of adaptation to different environments. As humans moved away from places where the sun's rays were strongest, the amount of melanin in our skin—melanin being the chemical that gives our skin color—decreased. So, as humankind spread all over the globe, skin colors adjusted accordingly. But somehow we forgot what these skin-color differences actually meant. What was simply an evolutionary adaptation became the basis for one of the worst forms of discrimination that ravage this planet. And racism and colorism were born.

Obviously, one person cannot be credited with inventing skin-color prejudice. Yet Jablonski highlighted the work of eighteenth-century German philosopher Immanuel Kant during a 2014 lecture I attended where she spoke about her research. In her book, *Living Color*, Jablonski elaborates on this point: "Kant was convinced that skin color denoted qualities of personality and morality." Not surprisingly, he believed that Africans, with their dark skin color, were inferior to lighter-hued Europeans. Because of his influential status in society, Kant's beliefs were disseminated widely. "Kant's views were readily embraced by the intelligentsia of Western Europe and eventually by the general populace because they supported existing stereotypes and long- and widely held Judeo-Christian religious beliefs," Jablonski writes. One of Kant's biggest fans was our third president, Thomas Jefferson. Considering that Jefferson helped draft our nation's creed of independence, along with others who shared his beliefs, the institutional racism endemic to our nation is understandable.

Although many the world over now believe that skin color is a key marker of difference between human populations, Jablonski said clearly in her lecture that, in fact, "skin color is a very poor classifier of groups," reiterating the point that skin color is truly only a biological response to one's environment—nothing more and nothing less. In her book Jablonski writes, "The association of color with character and the ranking of people according to color stands out as humanity's most momentous logical fallacy." Before people like Kant popularized the concept of separating humans into hierarchal groups based on their physical characteristics, according to Jablonski, skin color didn't really matter in human interactions. "Only recently have we become color obsessed," she said, keeping in mind that "recently" is relative in terms of humankind's two million years on the planet. Jablonski covers this topic in her book: "We have no evidence that when people of different skin colors first met in the regions surrounding the Mediterranean Sea their relationships or business transactions were affected by skin color." For Jablonski, this means there is still hope that humanity can be cured of this disease. "[Colorism] isn't inherent to the human condition," she said. But it has been around for a really long time.

Regardless of whether we're talking about people, places or things, Westerners seemed to have always had an issue with color. "In the West, since Antiquity, colour has been systematically marginalized, reviled, diminished and degraded," argues artist and writer David Batchelor in his book *Chromophobia*, an interesting tome that dissects the complex relationship Westerners have with color. "Generations of philosophers, artists, art historians and cultural theorists of one stripe or another have kept this prejudice alive, warm, fed and groomed." Historically, white symbolized purity, refinement, and civilization, while color, according to Batchelor, represented "the mythical savage state out of which civilization, the nobility of the human spirit, slowly, heroically, has lifted itself—but back into which it could always slide." Batchelor is commenting on color itself, particularly in art, but it is hard not to infer that the fear of color contamination can be likened to skin color as well, to a fear of colored people. From their earliest experiences on this land we now call America, white Europeans have feared contamination of their pure white blood. And yet, simultaneously, they have been attracted to color as well. "This mutual attraction and repulsion to color has centuries-old roots, bound up in a colonial past and fears of the unknown," wrote historian Carolyn Purnell. Even today, the relationship Americans have with color, with dark colors, with dark people, is complicated and complex.

From beauty culture to religious beliefs, the ranking of dark and light is ubiquitous across cultures here in the United States. Blame it on chromophobia—the fear of color—or garden-variety racism, but skin-color differences get tangled up in our collective ignorance and historical legacies of lies about the significance of skin color in determining a person's worth. And if we continue on this path of segregation based on pigmentation, even though science tells us that skin color is a poor evaluator of human value, then it seems safe to say that true progress for our nation, nay, our world, will never be achieved.

ONE

THE DARKER THE BERRY
African Americans and Color

If you're Black, stay back;
If you're brown, stick around;
If you're yellow, you're mellow;
If you're white, you're all right.
—Popular refrain in Black America

The Truth of the Matter

Many people assume that the colorism in contemporary African American society is a result of a perceived animosity between house slaves and field slaves in antebellum America, but this is a gross oversimplification of a complex problem. Even worse, this assumption makes it easy for people to believe that Black people themselves created colorism in a bid for power on massa's plantation. But the truth is, colorism—or the privileging of light skin over dark—was first implemented and continuously reinforced by the white Europeans in power who, for various reasons, considered light-skinned Black people more valuable than their dark-skinned counterparts. This was the case in the colonial era and it continues in the twenty-first century. Like racism, colorism in America involves both prejudice and power. And since white people have consistently held tight the reins of power, it seems fair to say that it was they who not only established the concept of colorism in the United States, but institutionalized it as well.

Over the years, however, Black people have been complicit in reinforcing colorist ideals, favoring those with light skin over dark, establishing communities, organizations, and institutions meant exclusively for those with light skin, and, worst of all, buying into the idea that dark skin somehow signifies an inferior status. But still, all of these skin-color machinations performed in the Black community are done within the boundaries of a racist society where whiteness is the standard for all things. Until the power structure is no longer ruled by white men and beauty ideals are no longer based on white women, it seems perfectly reasonable—if not tragically sad—to assume that Black America will continue to operate under the rules of colorism. But skin-color politics in the Black community aren't only about demonizing Black and celebrating white. There are nuances and distinctions that have to be accounted for when discussing color politics in Black America. To understand it all, it's necessary to go back to the beginning.

Light and Free

Before we delve into the horrors of slavery, consider that there was a time in our colonial history where Black Africans were brought to this country and given the status of indentured servant. The first such servants to arrive in the original thirteen British colonies were a group of city-dwelling Angolans who had been kidnapped by Portuguese slave traders. As the concept of race-based slavery had yet to take off in the colonies, these Angolans were made to work, alongside other (white) indentured servants, for seven years and were then granted their freedom. In actuality, the concept of race didn't even really exist at this time. The British didn't conceive of themselves as white, and Africans weren't categorized as Blacks. The division between people was still mostly based on class—the two predominant ones in the colonies being owners and servants.

And so it passed for the next twenty-plus years. Black Africans were brought to the colonies to work as servants, but when they had served out their time, they were considered free and often afforded the same rewards—land, corn, arms, livestock, and clothing—as their European counterparts. During this period, Blacks and poor whites worked in servitude side by side and many interracial relationships occurred, thus producing a class of individuals who were neither fully Black nor fully white but would eventually be free. So, in addition to free Black Africans, there was also a new generation of free mixed-race people of color as early citizens of the colonies. But this system didn't last very long.

Soon enough the ruling class in the colonies began to realize that their need for cheap labor was not going to be met by poor Europeans willing to sell themselves for ship passage to the New World, especially as the British economy was improving. With demand for tobacco rising and their labor supply shrinking, the British colonists gradually started to change their laws, turning servitude into slavery when it came to African people. Beginning in 1639, when the colony of Maryland decided that baptism was not enough to make a slave free, more and more laws were enacted that made it legal to enslave a person for life based on the color of their skin and their heathen—read non-Christian—status. Massachusetts legalized slavery in 1641. In a reversal of British tradition, Virginia issued a law in 1663 that said children would inherit the legal status of the mother instead of the father, in order to guarantee that any slave impregnated by a free white man would give birth to a slave, not a free person with brown skin.

The colonists also started making laws that restricted marriage between the races. While many servant-class white men were willing and eager to marry African or Native women, given the massive shortage of white women in the colonies, the ruling elite couldn't abide it; if the law sanctioned marriage to an African, the implication would be that Africans were human and worthy not only of a white person's love but also of the approval of the Christian church. And that, of course, would not allow the ruling male elites to downgrade Africans to subhuman status and enslave them for life. So, laws and sanctions continued to appear that not only forbade interracial relations but also severely punished any man or woman involved in such relations and any child born of such a union. (Of course these punitive laws did nothing to curtail the rampant rape and abuse of Black women—both enslaved and free—by white men.)

But regardless of the best attempts of the law, Black people and white people continued to procreate together in combinations of free and enslaved. And more often than not, it was a result of proximity and availability. In the North, white indentured servants continued to arrive upon these shores and often the only women a white male servant would know were Black slaves. In the South, especially in the more desolate plantations, the only option for female companionship for a white plantation owner was a female slave. And while many plantation owners simply raped and abused their female slaves, there were others—not many—who married them and subsequently educated and freed their biracial children. In the book *The Color Complex*, the authors note, "Mulattoes in the Deep South . . . were often the beloved progeny of the finest families and typically not the descendants of lower-class servants and slaves, as was the case in the North."

And so it came to pass that these "mulatto offspring" of numerous combinations of Black and white became a separate entity of free people of color, straddling a world of Black and white. In the South, especially in the cities of New Orleans and Charleston, North Carolina, these privileged free people of color came to be known as Creoles or Coloreds.

Creole Culture

Ironically, the Portuguese and Spanish first used the noun *creole* in the sixteenth century to refer to a "slave that was born in the master's house." In colonial America, particularly in the Southeast, the word was used to identify a hodgepodge of different people. From a European born in the Caribbean to a person of mixed African and European ancestry, "Creole" meant many different things to many different people. In Louisiana, Mississippi, and parts of Alabama, the Creole community, also known as the free people of color, enjoyed a level of freedoms and privileges only a step below that of many whites. And the telltale sign of a Creole was his light skin.

All told, the Creole population in New Orleans and its environs held a very privileged status throughout the eighteenth century. New Orleans boasted a great number of doctors, lawyers, and business professionals who were Creole. The Creole population maintained a precarious but special place in society, firmly wedged between the Black slaves at the bottom and the white ruling class at the top. For over one hundred years the Creole and Colored population in the South continued to grow and prosper as a distinct population, separate from both whites and Blacks. An influx of new Creoles arrived in New Orleans after the violent rebellions on the islands of Haiti and what is now the Dominican Republic, causing their numbers to swell even more. The light-skinned Creoles fleeing these rebellions often brought with them great wealth and a sense of class superiority. Many of them had owned land, were educated— some in Europe—and were part of a professional class of people.

So, this golden age of the Creole class served to establish a clear-cut color code. Whether or not individuals dressed a certain way, or lived in a certain neighborhood, the Creole population was defined primarily by their skin tone and hair texture. A Creole was identifiable by her light-brown complexion, such that in places like Louisiana, a light-skinned person was presumed free and a dark-skinned person was presumed a slave. This de facto visual proof of status could be advantageous for enslaved people who had light skin, as they could try to pass into the Creole class, which many of them did.

And it wasn't just in the South that a light-skinned, free Black population existed. Pockets of a colored class with privileges and wealth also lived up north and in the Middle West. In 1841, a member of Philadelphia's light-skinned Black elite community, Joseph Wilson, wrote an article in which he stated that the price of admission to the community, in addition to wealth and education, was "a light complexion." A directory called *The Colored Aristocracy of St. Louis* was published in 1858. Written by a man named Cyrian Clamorgan, himself of African and French background, the directory listed the names, professions, and accomplishments of St. Louis's wealthy light-skinned, free Black elite.

But not every Black person with light skin was free.

House Slaves vs. Field Slaves

Even though light-skinned Blacks held a privileged place in many parts of antebellum America, far more light-skinned Blacks were slaves than were free. According to the authors of *The Color Complex*, "Approximately 10 percent of the more than 400,000 slaves in the South before 1860 had some degree of White blood." So, besides separating Blacks into two camps—free and enslaved—the light skin versus dark skin dichotomy also manifested within the structure of slavery. For various reasons, light-skinned slaves enjoyed an elevated status within the cruel system.

Once slavery had become an entrenched institution in the United States, certain rules and practices become common—including preferential treatment for light-skinned slaves. Light-skinned slaves were generally preferred for indoor assignments, such as cook, driver, seamstress, and other more specialized positions that were preferable to the backbreaking labor in the plantation fields. One could argue that some of the jobs in the big house were equally labor intensive and demeaning, but the fact is that slaves who worked in the master's house had certain life-changing advantages. "It was far more likely that the house slave would learn to read, be introduced to upper-class white traditions, be permitted to play or interact with white family members than would a field slave. In fact, slave-owning families found they could run their homes more efficiently when their house slaves were more knowledge-able and educated," noted historian Adele Logan Alexander.

The reasons why light-skinned slaves were preferred over their darker-skinned brethren are numerous. Often times, these light-skinned slaves were the master's progeny and he simply wanted to keep them close. Light-skinned slaves were also favored because the vast majority of white Americans believed that racial superiority was biological. In other words, white people believed that the more white blood a Black person had in him, the greater his intellectual capacity and the likeli-hood he would be "civilized." Eventually, the reasons didn't matter. The belief that light-skinned slaves were more intelligent, more skilled, and easier to "train" in the ways of respectable society simply became a self-perpetuating myth. As such, light-skinned slaves were more valuable commodities when bought and sold at auction, which eventually led the slaves themselves to buy into a color-based hierarchy.

"It did not take long for the lighter-skinned house slaves to internal-ize certain assumptions about themselves, and more than a few did begin to internalize this sense of superiority about themselves relative to their darker-skinned compatriots," write the authors of *The Color Complex*. Likewise, a resentment and distrust of the light-skinned slaves grew within the ranks of darker field slaves. From a slave owner's perspective, it was to his advantage that the slaves distrusted one another because they would be less likely to band together to revolt. Therefore, whether it was intentional or not, white slave owners reinforced divisions among slaves, and skin-color differences were an easy mark of distinction.

It is important to note, however, that the real number of plantations with big houses where a distinction was made between field slaves and house slaves was relatively small. In the South, where slavery was most predominant, only 25 percent of Southern whites actually owned slaves, and of those 25 percent, only 12 percent owned more than twenty slaves. That is to say, there weren't a whole lot of "big houses" in the South. Instead, the average slave owner had a few slaves who might work in the house, on the farm and/or as some sort of skilled worker. If there was work to be done, either inside or outside, nobody cared what color a slave's skin was—the work just had to get done. In other words, the field slave versus house slave conflict, while undeniably real, has been widely exaggerated as the main reason light-skinned and dark-skinned Blacks have a contentious relationship today.

Likewise, the Willie Lynch letter, a mythical eighteenth-century document that was supposedly the transcribed text of a speech given by a Caribbean slave owner named Willie Lynch, has been proven to be a hoax. In the speech Lynch supposedly made to American slaveholders, he offered up his foolproof methods for keeping slaves under tight control, one of them being to exploit any differences between the slaves, including differences of complexion and hair texture. Because the Willie Lynch letter has been widely disseminated online and is often quoted by public figures in the African American community as the source of skincolor prejudice within Black America, many people assume it to be a real document and a legitimate theory. But neither assumption is true. Scholars say the letter is peppered with language and vocabulary not in use in the early eighteenth century and that the concepts Lynch supposedly spoke of are out of sync with the social thought of the time.

The Rise and Fall of the Mulatto Elite

Before the first shot of the Civil War had been fired, a change was already under way. In response to the North's demands to end slavery, the Southern states dug in their heels. Unwilling to give up their way of life, meaning their free source of labor, legislators enacted harsher and more entrenched slave laws. In addition, states like Louisiana and South Carolina, with significant and established Creole populations, swiftly revoked the privileged status of the light-skinned elite, dismantling the three-tiered social structure of white, mulatto, and Black. Now subject to the "one-drop rule," Creoles and Coloreds simply became categorized as Black and therefore subjected to the same ill treatment and discrimination as their brown-skinned brothers. Still, refusing to lose all they had established over the previous century, the free light-skinned community fought to keep what was theirs and to hold on to their most precious commodity—their light skin color.

Fully aware that this was their badge of distinction, the light-skinned elite knew they needed to keep that physical mark of their superiority alive. And they did so through extreme and exclusionary tactics. The most important of these was to marry only other light-skinned individuals to keep their light-skin genes untainted by a darker hue. In a practice known as "complexion homogamy," the light-skinned Negro Elite, as they were dubbed, were quite systematic in finding suitable romantic partners and potential mates, often traveling across state lines and using complex networks to find just the right husband or wife. In a 2014 article that explored the economic consequences of "complexion homogamy," Howard Bodenhorn wrote, "The impulse toward conformity among light-complected blacks was so strong that selection of a spouse was less a matter of the heart than one of familial obligation." Not only did this group of light-skinned wealthy Blacks stick to their own kind when it came to romance, but they literally created an entire social, religious, and professional community for those Black people fortunate enough to be born with light skin.

From social groups like the Bon Ton Society of Washington, DC, and the Blue Vein Society of Nashville to neighborhoods—Harlem's Sugar Hill and Chicago's East Hyde Park—and professional organizations, this privileged group established many institutions still in use today. It may be surprising to know that many historically Black colleges and universities, including Howard University and Spellman College, had unofficial but well-known admission preferences for light-skinned students who came from wealthy, professional families. According to the authors of *The Color Complex*, estimates show that, by 1916, some 80 percent of the students at historically Black colleges and university's were considered light skinned. Darker-skinned students, then, often found that vocational schools like the Tuskegee Institute or the Hampton Normal and Agricultural Institute were the only options available to them for higher education.

Tragically, not even churches provided sanctuary from the color wars. Many Black churches instituted demeaning skin-color requirements, such as the paper-bag test or the door test, for spiritual seekers searching for a home. That is, if a person's skin was darker than a brown paper bag or darker than the light-brown paint on the church's front door, they were denied entry. In 1870, the influential African Methodist Episcopal (AME) Church split into two factions. While official records do not address the claim that colorism was the reason for the split, it has been suggested in various documents that light-skinned worshipers wanted their own, more refined houses of worship and thus created the Colored Methodist Episcopal (CME) Church, while dark-skinned worshipers remained in the AME. Not until 1954 did the CME change the word "Colored" to "Christian" in its name.

By the turn of the century, the idea that Black people with darker skin were inferior to those with lighter skin continued to prevail. It was a concept that whites perpetuated without much thought and that Blacks struggled with in theory but also continued to accept in practice. For some intellectuals, artists, and writers within the Black community, the dark skin versus light skin conflict—as well as the increasingly popular trend of using skin-lightening creams—was quite troubling. "With the rise of new movements for racial solidarity in the 1910s and 1920s, skin color and hair texture—and the use of cosmetics to alter them became even more charged political issues," writes Kathy Peiss in *Hope in a Jar*. "A newly assertive political leadership pointed to the use of straighteners and bleaches as ipso facto evidence of self-loathing and the desire to appear and be white," she notes.

Novels such as Wallace Thurman's *The Blacker the Berry*, published in 1929, and George Schyler's *Black No More*, from 1931, explored the absurdity and pain caused by colorism in the Black community. Several "race men and women" penned scathing articles in the Negro press imploring Black Americans to take pride in their African features. "What every woman who bleaches and straightens [her hair] needs is not her appearance changed but her mind. She has a false notion as to the value of color and hair in solving the problems of her life. Why does she wish to improve her appearance? Why not improve her real self?" wrote civil rights activist Nannie Burroughs. But despite the rising calls for an end to colorist thinking and dangerous cosmetic habits, the Black community still adhered to a belief system that glorified light skin and denigrated those of a darker hue. In her 2015 memoir, *Negroland*, cultural critic Margo Jefferson explains the importance of skin color in pre–civil rights America:

Ivory, cream, beige, wheat, tan, moccasin, fawn, café au lait, and the paler shades of honey, amber, and bronze are best. Sienna, chocolate, saddle brown, umber (burnt or raw), and mahogany work best with decent-to-good hair and even-to-keen features. In these cases, the woman's wardrobe must feature subdued tones. Bright colors suggest that she is flaunting herself. Generally, for women, the dark skin shades like walnut, chocolate brown, black, and black with blue undertones are off-limits. Dark skin often suggests aggressive, indiscriminate sexual readiness. At the very least it calls instant attention to your race and can incite demeaning associations.

All areas of society, from employment practices to romantic entanglements, continued to uphold the division between dark and light. Within the Black community, certain jobs were available only to women with light skin, certain clubs—Harlem's famed Cotton Club, for example—only allowed chorus girls with light skin to hit the stage, and, perhaps most importantly, the majority of the thought leaders and power brokers—including Du Bois and Walter White, both influential leaders of the NAACP—had light skin. Known as the Talented Tenth, this group of businessmen, race men, and Negro intellectuals were often accused of replicating the pigmentocracy imposed by white America where light skin had simply replaced white skin in matters of money and power. Of course there were exceptions to these rules, as nothing is ever purely Black or white, but colorist thinking had been entrenched in the Black community for more than three hundred years. If change was going to come, it had to be singing a new song.

Say It Loud, I'm Black and I'm Proud

With the advent of the civil rights movement came a very clear message about Black identity: Black is beautiful. Along with a cry for equal rights and an end to segregation came a push for self-acceptance and recognition of the natural beauty of Black people. Dark skin, kinky hair, full lips, and broad noses were all being celebrated in a very public way. James Brown's "Say It Loud, I'm Black and I'm Proud" became the popular anthem for this part of the movement, perfectly encapsulating the pride Black people were feeling for the first time about their distinctly African features. The Black Is Beautiful message persuaded a lot of young Black men and women to throw away their bottles of bleaching cream, stop straightening their hair, and embrace their dark skin. And in turn, many light-skinned Blacks made additional efforts to make sure their Afros were extra big and their politics extra fierce so they too could feel part of this celebration of Black identity. It was a turning point for many, but for many others the message wasn't loud enough to drown out history's anti-Black brainwashing.

In her dissertation on contemporary colorism in the twenty-first century, JeffriAnne Wilder wrote that the "political and ideological shifts of the 1970s were neither all encompassing nor long lasting." Yes, the Black Is Beautiful mantra was a positive and effective one, but did it really just add a funky soundtrack and a more public voice to a message that had been percolating in the Black community since the early 1900s? The Black Is Beautiful message encouraged Black people to find the inherent beauty in themselves and stop looking to the European major-ity for validation. It was an empowering message, and the visual and aesthetic symbols were powerful too, with kinky hair and dark skin fi-nally being showcased on the covers of magazines, on billboards, and on TV. But at the same time, ads for bleaching creams and hair straighten-ers continued to run in those same magazines. Clearly, not everybody was on the same page in terms of eradicating colorism. "We went a certain distance with the Black Power movement, but you still didn't want to be too dark," said Marita Golden, sixty-four, activist and award-winning author of several fiction and nonfiction books, including a memoir about colorism, *Don't Play in the Sun*. "Dealing with colorism is going to be the unfinished psychological work of the civil rights move-ment," she said. "It's going to be the work we didn't do then. Now it's time to finish it."

Colorism and the Black American Family

Black family parenting might look different than white family parent-ing. Because the United States is a country still grappling with the very real effects of institutionalized and aggressive racism, raising Black chil-dren adds an additional layer of responsibility for parents. Sociologists say that in addition to teaching their children to look out for cars when they cross the street and to respect their elders, for example, Black par-ents must also racially socialize their children. Black parents generally expose their children to Black society, but they also have to prepare them for instances of racism and bias. This often leads them to instill in their children some degree of mistrust for institutions, authority, and even the law. While much of this training is done almost through osmo-sis—meaning most children simply pick up on the opinions and attitudes of their parents—some of the lessons they learn are more overt. "I think there are some mothers with dark-skinned daughters, for example, who may be dark themselves who think they are teaching their daughters something. 'Don't wear red, don't wear bright colors, you don't want to draw attention to yourself, you're already dark,'" said Yaba Blay, an author, colorism activist, and professor. Sociologist JeffriAnne Wilder has an explanation for this type of lesson. "If you think about it, in a larger context of racism and black families socializing their children with a race consciousness, it's the same thought process," she said. "Parents don't teach their children about racism to make them scared but to help them be prepared. In the same vein, parents teach their children about colorism to help them be prepared for the world as opposed to being fearful." Like a daily dose of cod-liver oil, colorism lessons are bitter pills to swallow, but Black parents may think they're doing the right thing by feeding them to their children. Of course, not all colorism lessons are the same, and not every child learns the same way.

Dark Dad and Light Mom

It seems improbable that a parent would purposefully teach a child to engage in colorist thinking, but even without overt discussion of the idea that light skin is good and dark skin is flawed, these lessons can be learned through mere observation. If a parent treats one child differently because of the shade of their skin, the other children will surely notice and put two and two together. But what happens when it's not the children who are different colors, but mom and dad? If a parent feels uncomfortable in their own skin, it's possible they will pass those feelings on to their children. If there is jealousy between mom and dad, based on who got the better deal in the skin-color department, surely that affects their relationship, not to mention the dynamics in the home.

I spoke to three different women who grew up with a dark father and a light mother, and their unique stories indicate the wide variety of experiences a person can have when mom and dad are the same race but different colors.

"Color didn't really come up," is how my friend Sarah Johnson answered my question. We were sitting in her home in the Overbrook neighborhood of Philadelphia. At fifty-two, Sarah is one of those women who makes ageing look graceful. Her makeup-free face is more bronze than brown, with an olive undertone and a smattering of freckles across her cheeks. She wears her thick, naturally curly hair loose in a wild Afro, her shiny black ringlets tangled with gray. Mostly it's because of her hair and sun-kissed skin tone that people often mistake Sarah for Latina or biracial. But in her own words, she's "just Black."

I visited Sarah on a Sunday, so she still had on her fancy church dress, but the fact that she was wearing furry, black bedroom slippers on her stocking feet let me know she was ready to relax and tell her story.

Sarah grew up in the suburbs of Detroit. Hers was the first Black family in her neighborhood, but the area grew increasingly more integrated, such that by the time Sarah was in high school there were at least ten Black families living nearby. Sarah is the oldest of three children, two girls and a boy, two years between each. "We're all the same color," Sarah said of herself and her siblings. But her parents, on the other hand, were two extremes. "My mother was so fair skinned, many people thought she was white," Sarah said. "My father," Sarah paused, as she thought of the best way to describe him, "was richly melanated. Some people would say he was dark skinned."

According to Sarah, living with two parents whose skin colors represented the opposite ends of the color spectrum didn't really matter that much in the day-to-day life of her family. It wasn't a defining aspect of her childhood. Sarah paused to gather some pictures of her family members to show me. Her "richly melanated" father looks debonair in a sepia-toned head shot, and her mother smiles into the camera holding a chubby baby version of Sarah. It's true that the two look like an interracial couple, not a Black couple. But in another picture, with the two of them together with their three children in front of a white picket fence, they just look like a typical family. Their different skin tones seem inconsequential.

Of course there were a few key times when color came up. For instance, Sarah recalled stories her mother would tell of being in places where white people would be speaking in a derogatory fashion about Blacks and her mother would have to "announce" that she was Black. "White people were always confused about my mother's identity and didn't understand why she identified as Black," Sarah said. For a while, when she was younger, Sarah herself even thought her mother was white. "I remember hearing a radio program about interracial families and thinking, 'Oh yes, that's us,'" Sarah recalled.

"My mother was surprised that I thought she was white, so she had to have a conversation with me to tell me that that's not how she sees herself," Sarah said. "It never occurred to her that she needed to tell us, her children, that she was Black." According to Sarah, who spent a lot of time in her late teens and early twenties researching her family history, the reason her mother was so light skinned is because she had a lot of racial mixing in her gene pool. "My mother's side of the family has many generations of interracial people," Sarah explained. "Some of my ancestors migrated from slave states to a free community in Indiana that was composed of mixed-race people."

With her father, Sarah said color came up only once: The day she grabbed his hand when she was no more than eight or nine years old and said, "Daddy, your hand looks like chocolate cake." He pulled away and said, "That's not nice," and they never spoke about it again. "It hurt my feelings," Sarah remembered. "I didn't know what I'd said or done, but we didn't talk about it."

When Sarah's mother died, Sarah was by her bedside at the hospital. Her father had already passed a couple of years before. While her mother lay dying, a nurse came in the room and questioned Sarah's relationship to this white patient. That hurt. As did the death certificate that identified Sarah's mother as Caucasian.

As Sarah finished her story, I found myself feeling skeptical. Growing up in the 1960s and '70s, with a light-skinned mother and a dark-skinned father, color difference wasn't a regular topic of conversation in their house? "In our home, color wasn't really discussed," Sarah reiterated. "It was just irrelevant. It wasn't like people were avoiding it, it was just, 'This is who lives here,' 'This is what we look like.' 'This is us!'" She did acknowledge that being one of only a few Black families in her neighborhood might have contributed to the lack of importance placed on color inside the house, since outside the house, as Sarah says, "We were just *that* Black family." Sarah also said her parents were very deliberate in teaching their children not to think of themselves as better than anyone else because of their middle-class status or for any other reason, color included. Despite living in the suburbs, Sarah said her parents would put her on the bus to take tennis lessons in the inner city just so she wouldn't look down on or be afraid of low-income people.

"The bottom line is that I think because my family didn't conform to all of those norms around light skin and dark skin, I don't," Sarah concluded. "I'm an outlier, because in a way, my parents were too."

Today, Sarah lives in accord with her parents' example. "I have friends across the color spectrum," she said. "I don't participate in activities that exclude people. I just don't do any of those games around skin color and class." Clearly Sarah's experience of growing up with two parents who were very intentional in not making distinctions about skin color gave her a solid sense of equality and justice for all people. Despite the fact that Sarah's mother could pass for white, the only real lesson Sarah learned about light skin was that her mother's skin color brought her no advantages in life, only a continuous questioning of her identity, not to mention a disconnect with her own nuclear family that followed her to her deathbed. And from her father, though they never spoke of it, Sarah learned there was a sensitivity and vulnerability in being the color of "chocolate cake." The end result? A child who doesn't buy into any color rules.

On a cold, snowy day in January, I drove twenty miles outside of Philadelphia to interview a woman named Lauren Walker, who grew up in a family structure similar to Sarah's. But unlike Sarah's experience, color talk had been a regular part of Lauren's home life.

Lauren, fifty-nine, grew up in Washington, DC. Like Sarah's, her father was, in Lauren's words, "a dark chocolate handsome man" and her mother was "very fair." Lauren was the oldest of four children who ranged in color from light to dark. Lauren said she was the one with the lightest skin, but the difference in color among her siblings wasn't very dramatic. Indeed, when she showed me a black-and-white photograph of her family, the difference in skin tone between the children was hard to detect at first glance. Lauren clarified that what set her apart from her two sisters was not the shade of her skin as much as the fact that she had the kinkiest hair. "I had one aunt who would always say to me, 'When the Lord was passing out the good hair, you must have been hiding behind the door.'"

Today Lauren is a successful corporate attorney, happily married to her second husband and mother to two adult children. Just barely five feet tall, with caramel-colored skin and light brown dreadlocks, Lauren was dressed in casual head-to-toe black for our interview, with bare feet and toes sparkling with blue nail polish. Her home radiated color and warmth, defying the cold winter day outside. We settled in her living room to talk about her family, which seemed an ideal location as almost every surface was covered with framed photographs of relatives, close and distant. When I asked how and when color came up in her home while growing up, Lauren said it was a very common theme in her house. She recalled many admonitions not to bring home any boys darker than a paper bag, and when she dared to date dark-skinned boys, her aunt would caution, "I know they say the darker the berry the sweeter the juice, but don't get diabetes."

Growing up in a tight-knit African American community in the 1950s and '60s, Lauren said, it was impossible not to hear conversations about color all the time, but she never took the warnings to stay away from darker people to heart. In fact, she dated several boys and young men in her youth that her aunt would surely have worried could induce diabetes. But the relationship with her siblings, she claimed, was never affected by their subtle shade differences. And yet, a strain of color consciousness clouded her otherwise happy childhood memories. Lauren's father was destroyed by colorism and that pain was always present.

"My father was always angry, and because he was so angry, he wasn't a great dad," Lauren said. He suffered greatly while growing up in Washington, DC, in the 1930s and '40s, said Lauren, not only because he was Black but also because he was darker-than-a-paper-bag Black. "One of the stories my dad used to tell us," Lauren recalled, "was that when he was in elementary school, the fair-skinned kids got to sit in the front of the classroom and the dark-skinned kids had to sit in the back." At that young age, Lauren said, her father already had a plan for his future. "He said he was going to marry one of those light-skinned girls so his kids would never have sit in the back." She shook her head at the memory. "I clearly remember him saying that, and he was this really handsome, really bright guy but because of his color there were a lot of opportunities that were closed to him." After elementary school, Lauren's father discovered that Washington's famed Dunbar High School for African American students, with its reputation for excellence and for graduating college-bound scholars, was an institution for the light-skinned elite. "My dad used to say that Dunbar was for the fairer-skinned or wealthy students and Armstrong was for the darker or poorer Black students," she said. Lauren's dad went to Armstrong. Her mother went to Dunbar.

Lauren's father did in fact end up marrying a fair-skinned woman, and three out of four of his children ended up lighter than he was, but he still viewed the sum total of his life as a series of stolen opportunities and overt discrimination. He never got over the way society treated him and he never felt comfortable in his own brown skin. "I remember finding bleaching cream in his medicine cabinet when I was a teenager," Lauren said. "I was shocked, but I also realized he never got over his issues with color. He was a broken man."

Lauren said she has since forgiven her father for his anger and subsequent abuse because she couldn't even imagine the degradation and frustration he had to live through as a Black man with dark skin at that point in time. What's more, Lauren did not inherit or internalize any of her father's anger or any desire to lighten her future offspring. In fact, her husband is several shades darker than she is and he sports long, manicured dreadlocks. When asked why she is attracted to people with more melanin, Walker shrugged her tiny shoulders and said, "I feel just the opposite of the way my parents were raised to believe. I think color is better. It's more beautiful. It's a gift. To be pale and devoid of color, I feel sorry for you."

Later, I couldn't help comparing Lauren's and Sarah's different experiences growing up and then wondering how they had arrived at the same place as adults. Sarah's family avoided all talk of color and demonstrated love to all Black people in the same way. As a result, Sarah is an adult with zero obvious hang-ups about color. Lauren, on the other hand, was raised to believe dark skin was a curse and a crime, yet she too, like Sarah, has no obvious prejudices against those with dark skin and in fact feels a greater affinity for those with more melanin than for those with less. So, two different parenting styles engendered similar results—and positive ones at that. Sarah, it seemed, was a product of her parents' positive energy. Lauren, on the other hand, like many children, rejected her parents' lessons completely in order to free herself from their pain.

Linda Green is another woman who is the product of a light-skinned mother and a darker father. Now sixty-eight, and in contrast to Lauren Walker, it has taken Linda many years to appreciate "color" in herself or anyone else. Colorism contributed to the failure of her parents' marriage and it also caused her to doubt her own self-worth. Today Linda lives in a small town in upstate New York, but she grew up in rural North Carolina. I met her through a friend when we both lived in New York City in the 1990s. I telephoned Linda in the fall to talk about her life in color.

Linda is the youngest of seven children who grew up working-class with a father who was a sharecropper before he found a job as a factory worker. She described her mother as "paper-bag tan" and her father as "dark skinned." Two of her siblings, Linda said, were light like their mother; the rest, including Linda, were brown. "My dad said we were 'shit color,'" Linda laughed. "And that was considered a good thing in the South."

Growing up, Linda said, she was always aware of the importance of skin color. "I played out in the sun a lot and my mom was constantly saying, 'Get out of the sun, you're getting Black.'" And she knew that Black was not something she wanted to be. "I would hear my father always saying he thought my mother was absolutely beautiful because her skin was light and she had long hair. He always talked about that." And it wasn't just her father who fawned over her mother's pale complexion. Linda remembered stories her mother would tell about neighbors coming over every time a child was born to check whether the baby had inherited their mother's color or their father's. Disappointment was always shown if the baby seemed to have dad's dark coloring and kinky hair. While she wasn't as dark as her father, Linda did inherit his kinky hair. "Sometimes I would say to my mother out of frustration, 'Why did you have to marry him? Why didn't you marry someone who looked like you, who had hair like you?'" Her mother would smile and say, "Honey baby, I loved him. That's why I married him." Linda said she thought that was a poor excuse. "All I could think was, if only she'd married someone with good hair, I could have good hair too." Throughout her childhood and teen years, Linda said, she was never praised for her beauty and that hurt. "I looked like my father growing up and I never wanted to look like my father, I wanted to look like my mother."

Linda's older sister, Angel, had the light skin and straight hair Linda craved, but she didn't lead a charmed existence. Despite the fact that their father fawned openly over Angel's looks, and that she was known around town as the family beauty, her brothers and sisters, Linda included, used Angel's color as a way to tease her. "We would say things like, 'Look at you, you're red and we're not red. We think you're adopted.' And she would cry and cry because she was so sensitive," Linda said. Tragically, Angel died in an accident at age twenty-five. And even in death, her skin color was an issue. "I actually heard some women at the funeral whispering that God took Angel first because my father preferred her, because she had light skin." Linda's reaction to hearing that was telling. "When I heard that, I had to think to myself, 'Did he like Angel better? Does he like me even though I'm darker?'"

Linda's parents' relationship didn't last, and Linda believes color differences played a part in its unraveling. "I think my father felt inadequate in a lot of ways," Linda said. "My father was illiterate, so my mother took care of the affairs of the family, and she was light skinned and beautiful." Even though Linda said her mother never flaunted her education or her complexion, her father could not handle the perceived inequity. "She was educated, he was not. She was light skinned, he was not. That's what he saw every day," Linda said. On the other hand, Linda said her mother didn't seem to care one way or the other that her husband had darker skin, and she worked very hard at promoting his best qualities to the children. But apparently it wasn't enough. "My father couldn't appreciate the woman he was married to," Linda said with a sigh.

After school, Linda moved to New York City and started her adult life. During the 1960s she was heavily involved in the Black Power movement and, despite her mother's warnings to stay away from men who were "too Black," she dated dark men. "I was so attracted to Black men," Linda said. "I was Miss Black Panther and I liked the dark guys." While it would appear that Linda, like Lauren Walker, didn't fall prey to her parents' belief system around color, Linda realized that dating men in the movement didn't mean she hadn't inherited some serious issues.

Linda said when she was around thirty years old, she met a woman named Carol whom she described as having "jet-black skin." Carol was a new coworker, and she exuded self-confidence and was known for being fashion-conscious and very stylish. "She would walk around the office and say things like, 'I know I'm beautiful,'" Linda said. "And I would think, 'Oh my God, she really thinks she's beautiful.'" And that's when Linda had her epiphany. "I thought, here I am thinking I'm Ms. Black Militant when deep down inside I thought Black was ugly. 'Say It Loud, I'm Black and I'm Proud' hadn't reached the core of my being," Linda said. "I really had to switch everything in my thinking to see Carol as beautiful because I did not grow up feeling [her type of features] were beautiful."

Today Linda is retired and spends a lot of time with friends, doing community service, and, most importantly, playing with her two young granddaughters. Color sometimes comes up during playtime conversations because even though her granddaughters are both 100 percent African American, one is so light that she is often mistaken for Puerto Rican or biracial. But even at age five, the little girl proudly tells anyone who questions her identity that she is Black. "I was just thinking growing up how I didn't want to be Black," Linda said as she talked about her granddaughter with pride. And even today, although she feels perfectly comfortable in her "shit brown" skin, Linda admitted she has still not healed completely. "At my age, when I go home to family reunions and people say, 'Oh my God, you look just like your mother,' even to this day I feel proud. At sixty-eight years old, for me, somewhere in my being, that means I'm not ugly."

The Darkest One in the House

Kia Walker, forty-two, grew up in the 1970s and '80s, a period less racially charged than the turbulent '50s and '60s. Kia was raised in Brooklyn, in a neighborhood that was mostly Black, although her social circles were quite diverse. She describes herself as having brown skin, and as for how she fit in with the rest of her immediate family, she said, "My mother and brother are both lighter than me." Because her parents divorced when Kia was five and she lived exclusively with her mother and younger brother after that, she was effectively the darkest one in the house.

I've met Kia's mom, and it is undeniable that she would be classified as fair skinned. Her skin is the color of butterscotch and her hair, though aided by the bottle, looks natural with its blond highlights. Kia's brother's skin, though not as light as his mother's, is golden brown. Make no mistake, Kia would never be classified as dark skinned, but when compared to her mother, the stark difference is impossible not to notice. In addition, Kia's very light-skinned maternal grandparents lived in a nearby brownstone and were an integral part of her upbringing, which made me

assume Kia must have had to struggle with her identity. But she didn't.
According to Kia, color has always been a non-issue for her.

"If color did come up, it was in a not-very-spectacular way. Like if
we were talking about sunscreen, my mother and brother had to use
more because they were so light," Kia told me in a conversation over the
phone. "But it's not like we had a lot of conversations about sunscreen."
An advertising executive with a live-in boyfriend, Kia now lives a life in
Harlem that most people would associate with an HBO series featuring
glamorous people and beautiful lives. Talking about color bias is something Kia has only agreed to because we're friends; her initial instinct
was to deny my request. Not because her past was too painful to discuss,
but because she said skin color was a non-issue in her home. She didn't
think she had anything worthwhile to share. But the fact that Kia is so
confident about her own beauty and brown skin made me want to hear
her story even more.

I asked Kia in any number of ways if she ever felt "less than" because
her mother was not only lighter than she was but also quite beautiful.
But Kia denied ever being hurt or even worried about her brown skin.
The only incident involving color that she could recall from her childhood came from outside her home, not from within. "There was this
boy I went to grade school with who was white," Kia recalled. "It was a
very racially diverse school, but when this kid saw my mother and little
brother one day on the playground waiting for me, he asked if I was
adopted." Kia was confused by the question and asked the boy why he
thought she was adopted. "He said, 'You don't look anything like your
mother and brother. You're brown and they're not.'" Rather than shaking her sense of self or identity, Kia shrugged off the incident. "I just
thought it was rude to say something like that, to say that I was adopted," Kia said.

Other than that one experience, Kia couldn't come up with any
other moment from her childhood or teen years where color had been
an issue. Not a single one. "I never had one day of wanting to be lighter
than I am. I knew that I was brown-skinned, like I knew I was short and
skinny with long hair. I didn't rank any of those things as better or
worse, and no one in my household did either," she said. Kia added that
her parents didn't spend significant amounts of time praising her beauty
or self-worth either. In fact, upon reflection, Kia could not recall one

time her father had ever told her she was pretty. "My dad is not the kind of person to walk around and say, 'You're so beautiful.' That's not his style," she said. On the other hand, Kia's dad is an artist and he would often paint Kia, which she said made her feel beautiful.

"So, what do you think made you so comfortable in your own skin?" I asked her.

Kia paused to consider her answer. "I just really love how brown skin looks," she said. "It wasn't learned or encouraged. I just like looking at people with brown skin because it looks like their skin has a lot of depth to it." I couldn't argue with that, but I still had one more question for Kia. I wanted to know how she maintained her love of brown skin, especially in a city as focused on image as New York and in a visual industry like advertising. Kia answered, "By the time I was out in the world and freely experiencing that people could think there was something wrong with brown skin, it couldn't affect me. It's like my parents had given me this built-in immunity, because it wasn't an issue for them and they never passed it along as an issue for me."

Kia's story was illuminating. Her parents had raised her without any suggestion that her brown skin could be interpreted as any type of defect. She was the darkest child in the family and yet felt no shame or pain around this fact. Could the answer to raising Black children who are immune to the disease of colorism really be in our parenting practices? Margaret Beale Spencer thinks so. She's the Marshall Field IV Professor of Urban Education and Human Development at the University of Chicago, and I heard her speak at a conference on this topic, so I decided to call her to find out more. When we spoke on the telephone, Spencer was unequivocal in her belief that proper parenting can protect a child from the pain inflicted by colorism in the outside world. "It's a question of how effective the parents have been in their parenting efforts," she said. "If you've done your job, then kids know how to externalize ignorance and internalize self-celebration." And how does one do this "job"? How do parents teach their children to "externalize ignorance"? According to Spencer, the lessons begin at birth and continue in perpetuity. And the lessons are twofold: You love your child and celebrate his physical attributes, whatever they may be, and you contextualize the concept of difference without an accompanying hierarchy. "If you've done your work, the first six years of the child's life, the kid knows that no matter what they look like they're wonderful," Spencer explained. "And if you've done the work around observed differences, using examples like flowers in a garden that are all different but they're all beautiful, then if anyone says anything different to your child, he thinks that person isn't very smart. That's how socialization and explanation helps kids push back."

Home as the Site of Resistance

Elizabeth Hordge-Freeman is an assistant professor of sociology at the University of South Florida. A specialist in race, gender, and family dynamics, Hordge-Freeman has been studying colorism in the African diaspora since 2008. Her book, *The Color of Love*, explores the role colorism plays in Afro-Brazilian families, yet Hordge-Freeman is currently expanding her research on colorism to draw out the connections between what she witnessed in Brazil and what goes on in other Black communities elsewhere in Latin America and in the United States. One thing she believes quite strongly is that the solution to colorism does *not* lie in the home.

"I really try to push against this idea that the solution is the family," Hordge-Freeman told me from her office in Florida. "In fact, I argue that's not the solution. The solution is in society." Hordge-Freeman uses words like "insidious" and "dangerous" to describe the reality of colorism in modern society and she bristles at the idea that colorism is nothing more than name-calling or a beauty-image issue. "This is what people don't get," she said. "This is about understanding how since the beginning of this country people were organized and given access to resources based on this [color] hierarchy." In other words, my friend Kia may feel confident about herself and move through life undeterred by society's constant favoring of light skin, but that doesn't solve the problems of inequity and access that we know occur based on skin color. So, while Kia may be okay, our institutions remain broken.

"The conversation has to move from talking about colorism as an idea to talking about colorism and the structural implication of that," Hordge-Freeman explained. "I want to talk about people's access to resources and people's life chances being shaped by an idea and a structure. The conversation about colorism can't just be about people's personal experiences." The studies that show light-skinned Black people experience a higher quality of life in so many situations make it impossible to disagree with Hordge-Freeman's opinions. According to scholars Jennifer L. Hochschild and Vesla Weaver, "Relative to their lighter-skinned counterparts, dark-skinned Blacks have lower levels of education, income and job staus; they are less likely to own homes or to marry," so colorism can't simply be a conversation about personal feelings when dark-skinned Black people are at a disadvantage in society, everywhere from the classroom to death row. But still, I push the idea that individuals create society. And we as individuals bring our personal experiences to the table when we create policy, or when we enforce laws, so doesn't the personal influence the public and the political? Doesn't what starts in the home eventually leak into society? Or, as Marita Golden so eloquently suggested, couldn't the home "be an important incubator to inoculate people against the virus that is colorism"?

Hordge-Freeman was willing to consider this mode of thinking. "It's true in terms of internalizing these ideas [about color], families can have a really important impact, and I love the idea of families being a site of resistance because it provides hope that things can change little by little," she said. But even with a family that preaches a positive message inside the home, Hordge-Freeman countered, "You will always have that person that had other experiences outside of the family that in some way contradicted the positive association that the family conveyed about Blackness."

Brothers and Sisters in Dark and Light

Everyone understands the concept of sibling rivalry and people expect certain personality traits to shine through based on birth order. The independent only child who doesn't like to share, the bossy older child, the forgotten middle child. Likewise, people expect siblings to clash based on these personality types—the younger brother fights to be seen outside of his big brother's shadow, the older sister wants to be free of the responsibility of caring for her younger siblings. While every family experience is different, there has been enough scholarship on the subject— not to mention the stereotypes thrown around in popular culture—for parents to expect certain behaviors and conflicts based on birth order. And they have the choice to do something about preventing those conflicts or not. What if the same were true about skin-color differences?

Many parents, especially African American parents, know that the world treats people differently based on skin color, so if one's children are born in variations of dark and light, those differences may need to be addressed in the home, and possibly even compensated for in some way. Of course, most parents don't sort their own children into separate categories of dark and light, but considering the pervasiveness of colorism, it should come as no surprise that some parents perpetuate a skin-color hierarchy in the home. In his autobiography, written with Alex Haley, Malcolm X said that his dark-skinned father favored his lighter children over the darker ones. "I actually believe that as anti-white as my father was, he was subconsciously so afflicted with the white man's brainwashing of Negroes that he inclined to favor the light ones, and I was his lightest child." On the other hand, Malcolm's light-skinned mother flipped the paradigm on its head. "Just as my father favored me for being lighter than the other children, my mother gave me more hell for the same reason. She was very light herself but she favored the ones who were darker . . . . I remember that she would tell me to get out of the house and 'let the sun shine on you so you can get some color,'" he said. And while the example of Malcolm X is pulled from history, that type of parental favoritism, ranking one child above another, tragically still exists.

Not surprisingly, I did not find any parents who wanted to admit that they consciously favored one child over another because of the color of their skin, but I did find a few examples of dark and light siblings with parents who tried their best to offset society's skin-color stereotypes.

Michael Eric Dyson is a well-known author, professor, and cultural critic who grew up in Detroit. A self-described "light-skinned" man, Dyson has written about a childhood filled with barbecues, soul music, Sunday school, and go-carts built by his father. Dyson's brother Everett was a part of that same childhood, yet their lives ended up being very different. After a stint in the military, Everett Dyson—whom Michael has described as a "deep-chocolate Black man"—turned to a life of crime and was eventually sentenced to life in prison. While Michael Eric Dyson admits that his brother's own choices ultimately landed him in prison, he also believes that color played a part in both his own success and his brother's failures.

"I am not suggesting that the mere difference in shade has led to his brutal circumstances and my rise. I am arguing, however, that the persistence of colorism—a sometimes subtle hierarchy of social standing historically dictated in part by darkness or lightness of one's skin, measuring the proximity to, or distance from, the vaunted white ideal—affected how he was viewed as a developing youth, impacting the view of what gifts he might possess while shaping the presence or absence of social opportunities open to him," Dyson wrote for CNN.com. It's clear that he doesn't blame his parents for his brother's situation, but rather looks at society's limited expectations for "deep-chocolate" men in the world. Dyson suggests that he himself was given more opportunities in society when he was younger because he looked the part, while his brother, simply because of his darker skin, wasn't expected to possess the same potential.

After hearing Dyson's story, one imagines how hard it must be to raise two children of two different hues when one child benefits from his appearance in the outside world and the other suffers for the same reason. I spoke to two sisters who grew up in similar circumstances, where both mom and dad tried to assuage their darker daughter's pain, but to no avail. She suffered greatly as a child but ultimately found a way to love her complexion.

I took the train to Brooklyn to spend some time with the two sisters, who had contacted me via Twitter. Thanks to the January premier of the film *Light Girls*, on Oprah Winfrey's OWN network, there was a lot of online chatter about colorism in early 2015. I added my voice to the conversation occasionally and mentioned that I was working on this book. That's why Lana Davis reached out to me. Lana and I had never met in person, but I knew her older sister, Asha, from college. Asha is a year younger than me, and we've maintained contact mostly through Facebook and an occasional in-person reunion. But it was Lana who sent the message insisting that I come hear their story. So, I hopped on a train and went to hear what they had to say.

Asha is forty-one and Lana is thirty-nine. Asha proudly claims that she is a real African American because their mother is Eritrean and their father is Black American. Although their mother came to the United States as an adult and still speaks with a heavy accent, the sisters both say their childhood in Brooklyn felt very American. They lived in a brownstone on the same block their father grew up on, and their grandparents lived around the corner. It is at that house that I arrived on a Wednesday morning to conduct the interview. Asha let me in, wearing jeans and a navy blue T-shirt, despite the cold outside. Lana arrived a few minutes later, having walked from her apartment a few blocks down, wearing sweatpants and a blue hoodie with "Martha's Vineyard" emblazoned on the front. Asha settled on the sofa and wrapped herself up in a blanket while Lana settled herself on the floor in front of her. Before I asked a single question, I tried to guess how color played a role in this family. Asha, whom I'd never thought of as particularly light skinned before now, took on a new hue as I compared her to her dark brown sister, Lana. And that's what their life was about, that's what made it difficult. The comparisons.

"When Asha was born she looked like she could be Asian American," Lana began the story. "She was the color of milk and had straight hair. When I was born I looked like a chocolate drop." And while she of course doesn't remember this, there's an oft-repeated story in the family about Lana's birth that she shared. "When I was presented to my mother, they say she said, 'My God, that child is Black.'"

Both Asha and Lana said that the difference in their coloring was obvious and spoken of freely in the family. In addition to the fact that their father was lighter than their mother, there was a family legend on their mother's side that every family member got one dark child who carried the mark of the family patriarch, who happened to be quite dark. Lana was heralded as that child and she took solace in the connection. "Because my grandfather was a very respected man, it was seen as a good thing to be his descendant," she said. In addition to that genetic honor, Lana said she had fond memories of her father always telling her she was beautiful and bestowing her with the pet name "Chocolate Drop." For her part, her mother would rub Lana's cheeks almost daily and ask if she could have some of that beautiful color.

"My dad was really intentional with telling my sister how beautiful she was," Asha said. And as an adult she gets why he did it but she also remembers feeling left out of her father's favor. "I remember very clearly asking him, 'Well, am I pretty?' and he said, 'You're pretty in a typical way.'" I asked Asha how she had felt about that response. "I'm not saying it necessarily hurt, but it stung a little bit," she admitted. But it's clear throughout the interview that Asha adores her father and harbors no ill will toward him for trying to give her little sister a healthy dose of self-esteem. And in a lot of ways it worked. But in a lot of ways it didn't.

"I remember you could be light skinned in the '80s and not be attractive, but you were always better looking than a brown-skinned person who was beautiful," Lana said as she started to recall her difficult teen years. "I remember sitting in school and just feeling so out of place and I remember praying to God to just make me light skinned. Just make me light and then the boys will like me and I'll be friends with the cool girls. I'd just sit there and look out the window and say, 'God, that's all I need.'" At this point, Lana's voice broke and she had to stop talking because the memories became too painful. She took off her glasses to wipe away the tears streaming down her face, and a full minute passed before she could finish her story. When she continued, it was to say that even while she was going through that pain, she knew she was smart and even pretty but felt her dark skin was what was holding her back. "I remember thinking, 'I just need to get that skin tone thing figured out and I'll be fine,'" she said.

I asked Asha if she knew her sister was going through such distress, and she shook her head no. "I guess maybe I was delusional in thinking that having my dad tell her she was beautiful would be enough. I had no idea," she said. " But also," she added, "Lana has never been one to seem lacking in self-esteem. She always seemed confident in herself." Lana credits her parents for that, but said it wasn't enough. "Having my mom and dad tell me that I was beautiful helped me to not lose my mind, but it was still tough," she said.

Outside of the house it was impossible not to be aware of how the rest of the world fixated on the color difference between the sisters. "People who didn't know our family would assume we weren't even related," Asha said. "I don't remember people treating us differently but I do remember people being really surprised that we were sisters." Lana jumped in here with a story to prove the point.

"When I was in middle school, there were people who knew Asha and knew we were sisters and they would still ask me, 'Is she Puerto Rican?' And I would say, 'But you know we are sisters. Why would you ask me that?' But they could not believe we were related because we looked so different."

Asha said this type of encounter happened so often that their mother would get offended when she was out with her daughters and people would ask whose child Asha was since obviously a dark mother matched a dark daughter, but not a light one. "She'd always snap, 'They're both mine,' and leave it at that," Asha said.

Ironically, as the two sisters got older, they started looking more alike, partially due to the fact that Asha, in her own words, "browned up." There's still a noticeable difference in skin color, but it's not as extreme as it was when they were children. In fact, both sisters said they've been mistaken for each other and a few times have even been mistaken for twins! Their relationship has also evolved, from a typical older sister/younger sister rivalry to one of real friendship. Although both women said color didn't cloud their relationship with each other when they were younger, Lana admitted she had been jealous of her older sister's popularity. And Asha admitted she had been a typical self-centered teen who never paid too much attention to her little sister's world.

Seeing how the sisters interact with each other now and knowing how much they truly care about each other, I believed them when they said that their relationship today is solid and positive, without traces of color damage. Lana said she has come to a healthy place with her identity. "I love my skin color and I wouldn't change it for anything," she said with a genuine smile. But she did admit that she would never stop noticing other people's skin color and wondering what their experience in the world is like. "Even if I made the conscious effort, I don't think I can break myself out of that habit. It's so ingrained in me to notice these things," she said. "But I don't consider myself bad for noticing skin color. I consider myself a modern-day anthropologist."

On the other hand, Asha said she would change her skin color if she could. She would like her skin to be a little darker and every summer she does her best to darken up in the sun. "I find that I'm trying to get away from that ['light skin' label] like it's a bad thing. So, I'm still struggling with that," she said. "I just think, let me just get a little browner and everyone will leave me alone. It's not something I obsess over, but I do think about it." Another thing Asha thinks about is how these color issues manifest in today's young children. As a speech therapist, she works in a lot of public schools in the city of New York and continues to see and hear a lot of insults and injuries stemming from the legacy of colorism. "I just wish we could celebrate this range of beauty and make all little girls, whether they are butterscotch or dark chocolate, feel good about their skin color," she said.

Dark Mom, Light Dad

This is my story. Actually, it's my parents' story. They grew up thinking of themselves in categories of dark and light. My father saw himself as light skinned and my mother grew up believing she was dark. So, how did that influence their children? How did their own trauma around color influence their parenting? Thankfully, not at all. In fact, before writing this book, I never heard any of these stories I'm about to share about my own parents.

The truth is, I don't have one single memory of a conversation about color bias or colorism during my entire childhood. Like me, my older sister and younger brother are also medium brown. When it came to discussing skin color in my childhood, the only two colors that really mattered were Black and white. I grew up in Milwaukee, Wisconsin, a city that stubbornly refused to abandon its top-tier status in any "most segregated cities in America" ranking. But despite the almost institutionalized segregation in all of Milwaukee's neighborhoods, my family always managed to move to a block where no other Black person had lived before. No crosses were ever burned on our manicured lawns, however, and no racist graffiti ever appeared on our two-car-garage doors. Suffice it to say, the world of my childhood was almost uniformly devoid of color. So, when it came to noticing color differences, I was only too keenly aware that my skin was brown and everybody else's wasn't. While this colorless upbringing left some things to be desired in terms of my racial identity formation, it also freed me from ever falling down the rabbit hole of colorist thinking. So, with their decision to raise us in majority-white Milwaukee, my parents liberated their children from their own color-coded past. Before I asked them to sit down for an interview for this book, I'd had no idea that colorism had touched their lives.

I now know that, growing up with ten sisters and one brother, my mother—raised in Milwaukee, but born in Egypt, Mississippi—believed she was the "dark" one in her family. My mother's family had been part of the second wave of the Great Migration. My grandfather arrived in Milwaukee in 1949, having been recruited by the Milprint printing company to work in their factory. As soon as he was settled, he sent for his wife and growing brood. There were only nine children at the time, but two more would join the clan up north within three years.

With eleven girls and one boy to raise, my grandmother did an excellent job, I'm told, of honoring each child's unique qualities. They were not one indistinguishable mass of mouths to feed; rather, there was this one who did well in school, this one was a great cook, this one loved to make her own clothes. Depending on whom you ask, my mother was the smart one, or at least one of the smart ones, and apparently she could always make her mother laugh. But my grandmother also had another way to single my mother out and that was by her color. Looking at my mother today and comparing her complexion to that of her sisters, it is fair to say she is darker than some but no darker than others. The thing is, some of her sisters had really light skin, while my mother is the color of roasted coffee beans. So, comparisons were easy to make. What's worse, my mother has vivid memories of her own mother calling her names like "ink spot," "ace of spades," and "Black gal," in times of anger.

Today, my mother says she is not defined by her complexion, nor does she feel in any way inferior, but there were times growing up when her skin color, in contrast to that of her honey-colored sisters, made her feel more vulnerable to critiques of her appearance. It would be impossible not to feel physically inferior or unattractive, even if she hadn't come of age in the 1950s and '60s in a world where the Black community was unapologetically color-coded. But my mother is quick to clarify that, despite her harsh words, my grandmother didn't favor certain children over others because of their color. "My sister Ruth was the lightest," my mother said, "and she was always getting into trouble, but she wasn't forgiven because she was light." On the other hand, praise was heaped on the girls who did well in school—including my mother. "I was always made to feel special," my mother recalled.

Deciphering attitudes about color—especially from a time when Black was considered anything but beautiful—is complicated. To me it sounds like my grandmother used my mother's complexion to wound her when she was angry. It might have been the easiest way to get my mother's attention. Or maybe she wasn't even aware of how hurtful the insults were to her daughter.

My grandmother died when my mother was only nineteen, but not before she had given my mother a few life lessons that pertained to someone of her particular hue. One, she should never wear red, lest she be mistaken for an organ grinder's monkey. And two, she must make sure to marry someone lighter than herself so her children wouldn't be too dark and hate her. To this day, my mother has very negative opinions about certain shades of red, she refers to her lighter sisters as the pretty ones, and, as I mentioned, my dad—who has been compared to both Lionel Richie and Colin Powell—qualifies as officially light skinned.

When my father was growing up in 1950s Baltimore, he says, they didn't talk about skin color, which is hard to believe considering his own nuclear family is completely split down the color line. My father's mother is even lighter than he is, with lavender eyes, but his father—my grandfather—was a deep, dark, ebony brown. My grandparents had four children, two boys and two girls; two were dark and two were light. The boys have light skin while the girls favor their father. I bet if I were to ask my aunts whether color was ever an issue for them growing up, they would have more memories to share than my father, but theirs aren't my stories to tell. According to my father, the color differences in his family were obvious but never spoken of out loud.

My father says it was the same with his friends. They didn't talk specifically about color preferences or about feeling a sense of superiority, yet his two best friends—Herman and Charlie—also had light skin and dated only light-skinned girls throughout high school. "We were the three musketeers," my father recalled with a chuckle. He also remembered, without a hint of laughter, that he would sometimes use bleaching cream on his skin to lighten up what was already closer to white than Black. And yet, my father never questioned the creams, or his choice of friends, or the girls he courted. It was just the way things were in his world. That is, until the Black Is Beautiful messages of the civil rights movement made him reconsider his sense of self.

In the late 1960s, my father was in the Navy and stationed in Sheboygan, Wisconsin. Everything and everyone around him was white, but for the first time my father felt proud of everything about himself that was Black. "It was a whole shift in mindset," my father said about the pride he had finally felt in his identity as a Black man in America. And with that change came the realization that he wanted something different in a woman. He wanted to be with someone who physically embodied the Black aesthetic the movement lifted up. My mother fit the bill. It's not like they didn't have anything else in common or that he approached her only because she was darker than him, but my father freely admits that he was looking for a darker-skinned woman when he met my mother at a fraternity party in Milwaukee in 1967. "It was my way of acknowledging that Blacker is better," he admitted. My father wasn't being political in choosing my mother; it was more like he was being saved. "I don't think we were ever taught that we were beautiful.

We were always told we had to emulate whiteness," he told me, some forty years later, his voice laced with regret. For my father, the Black Is Beautiful message was like a balm to a wound he didn't even know he had.

When I asked my mother if she had worried about the shade of skin her children would turn out to have, she waved away my question with a derisive sniff. "I didn't care what color my kids were," my mother answered. And while I'll never know if this is really true, my mother never instilled in me a sense of color consciousness. Still, when I look back at my childhood now, I recall comments from my mother about my skin getting dark after days in the sun. She never explicitly said that getting "dark" was bad or limited my time outdoors in any way, but still, it wasn't until I started spending summers in the south of Spain as an adult that I learned to glory in the deepening of my skin's color. To see its darkness as beautiful and not a burden. But my mother was masterful at making me feel like a gift filled with endless potential. Like I said, overt colorism plays no part in my childhood memoires. And I don't blame my mother for trying to protect me from what her mother had drilled into her: dark skin was a curse that only the careful cultivation of a good mind and a light-skinned husband could fix.

Light-Skin Isolation

The thing about color bias or colorism is that light skin isn't always the preferred shade, despite the seemingly overwhelming evidence to the contrary. Not all Black Americans want to be lighter. Not everybody considers white to be right. Particularly in the Black community, having light skin can often be a very lonely experience, one in which a person's loyalty to the race—or even membership in the group at all—is called into question. "Light-skin isolation" is how author and advocate asha bandele, forty-eight, terms it, and she speaks from experience. Today she has to watch her own fourteen-year-old daughter, who also has light skin and long, loosely curled hair, deal with the same trauma bandele herself did more than twenty years ago. Watching her daughter struggle through this issue breaks her heart. "To see my child in any kind of pain is just devastating to me," said bandele. "Black is who she is. She's never known anything else and the idea that anybody would think of her as not Black drops you into Neverland."

Bandele notes that, as a community, Black Americans are well versed in speaking about light-skin privilege, whether one claims it or not. "But we don't talk much about light-skin isolation," she said. "It's one of the most painful things to think that the people you are born into, and that you love so much and whose history courses through your blood, do not recognize you." Bandele and others lament not only the isolation that often comes with light skin, but also the rejection from the Black community. Bandele recalled her own youth, when people constantly asked her that vexing question—"What are you?"—because they didn't believe she was African American. And that still happens and it still stings, especially because bandele has dedicated her life to activism work within the Black community. "Hopefully, for all of us, the measure of who we are becomes what we've done and not what we look like," she said.

For Christopher James, light-skin isolation was only too real when he was growing up, but his parents didn't know how to talk about it. In fact, their response to the problem was to ignore it.

Christopher, forty-eight, was raised in the suburbs of Washington, DC. The baby of the family, Christopher grew up with an older sister and his two parents. His mother was a second-grade teacher and his father was a bus driver for the city. The neighborhood where Christopher grew up was mostly Black, although a handful of white families lived in the area as well. Christopher says conversations about color in his household were nonexistent, despite the fact that the range in skin tones within the family of four would make anybody seeing them all together do a double take. "My mother is light complected," Christopher said, offering that on a scale of one to ten, where one is the lightest, his mother would rate a two. His father, on the other hand, Christopher said, was a solid eight. Predictably, his sister fell right in the middle with a four, but Christopher himself is the lightest in the family. "I'd say I was a two, but some people would say I'm a one," he admitted.

It's true. I met Christopher through a friend who introduced us because she knew Christopher's story and knew I was working on this book. When I walked into the restaurant where we'd agreed to meet, the first thing I noticed about Christopher was his extremely pale skin and clear blue eyes. Imagining this man standing next to a dark brown father, I found it hard to believe that color never came up.

Christopher immediately corrected me. Color didn't come up *in* the home, he said, meaning his family members didn't talk about their color differences. But outside the house was a different story. "The first time we talked about color at home was when I got suspended from school for fighting because someone called me 'white boy,'" Christopher said, fidgeting with his coffee cup. "I was eight or nine years old." When I asked how his parents responded to this episode, he shrugged. "They were more dismissive of it than anything else," he said. "They told me, 'God made you the way you are. If [other people] have a problem with it, that's their problem.'"

Sadly, it wasn't a problem that left Christopher alone. He said he spent a lot of his childhood fighting anyone who questioned his Blackness. "I probably spent an inordinate amount of time and energy trying to be Black," Christopher said, mentioning the amount of hairspray he had to use to get his non-nappy hair to stay in a respectable Afro. "I hated being so white. I would try to get tan in the summer so I could be darker." For Christopher, the essence of wanting to be perceived as Black came from wanting to be an unquestioned member of his tribe. "Like anybody, I wanted to fit in," he said. "Your family is Black, your friends are Black, and the people you hang out with are Black. You want to be Black," he explained. Not fitting in with the kids at school was one thing, but not fitting in with your own family was another. "Growing up, if it was just my dad and me out somewhere, and my father would say, 'This is my son,' the reaction on people's faces was always like, 'How does a fairly dark man have a fair-skinned kid with blue eyes? Your mom must have been messing with the milkman.'" For Christopher, having light skin felt like a curse, not a blessing. "I never saw any privileges that came with it," he said. "Perhaps there were some, but I never saw any."

Even Christopher's romantic encounters were affected by his skin color. "Growing up, even in high school, I never had a girlfriend because even when a girl liked me, it would eventually come back to 'you're too light,'" he said. "I had a problem with being light for a long time."

As an adult, it is clear Christopher has finally made peace with his painful past. But it hasn't been an easy journey. He joined the army and traveled around the world, and having different types of people appreciate his skin color and his unusual blue eyes gave him some perspective. But he never had a truly revelatory conversation with his parents about why they had avoided the color conversation when it so obviously troubled him. "I don't think they understood what I was going through," Christopher surmised. After his father passed away, in 2013, Christopher finally mustered up the courage to ask his mother why she had never addressed his pain around his skin color during his childhood. "She said the reason she never brought it up or talked about race or color was because of the way her family treated my father because he had dark skin," Christopher said, noting that his mother's family hadn't wanted her to marry his father. "My mother's father was very cruel to my father. He would call him 'spook' and all kind of things like that," Christopher said, shaking his head. "So, I think my mother was just trying to spare my father's feelings." But that costly decision left Christopher to fend for himself.

Today Christopher is divorced but he has a serious girlfriend. At forty-eight, he said, kids aren't in his future, but I asked him anyway what color he'd want his kids to be if he did have them. "If they were biologically mine, I wouldn't care what color they were," Christopher said. "I would only hope that they wouldn't care about my color. I would just want them to have a good character and be oblivious to all that skin-color nonsense."

I was surprised to hear Christopher say that he would hope his own children "wouldn't care about his color," as if he still saw his light skin as a flaw. So, while he may be happy with his life now, he may be forever scarred by his childhood. Light-skin isolation is obviously very real. How people handle it varies widely. As with any other unresolved issue a person might have, feeling unhappy in one's own skin can be passed on to future generations, as evidenced by the next person I interviewed.

If Christopher James had a psychic twin it would be Lisa Washington. Lisa grew up in Chicago in the 1970s and '80s. A light-skinned Black girl whose own family members jokingly referred to her as "yellow" when she was a child, because she was the lightest in their family of four, today, Lisa, forty-three, is the mother of three children who range in color from almost-white to milk-chocolate brown. Unlike Christopher James, Lisa isn't hoping that her children grow up oblivious to color. Instead, her dream is that they embrace color and love the melanin in their skin. Of course, that becomes complicated when the melanin is in short supply.

Lisa and her family live in Jacksonville, Florida. Both she and her husband are teachers at a private school; Lisa teaches art and her husband teaches high school biology. Besides sharing a profession, Lisa and her husband also share a similar ache, much like Christopher James, from growing up with light-skin and struggling socially to prove they were "Black enough." When the two decided to start a family, they assumed, because they both have light skin, that their child would be similarly shaded, so they agreed to give her a name that would clearly identify her as Black. "Some Black couples want it the other way around, but we wanted it to be clear that our child was Black," Lisa told me in the first of our two telephone interviews that ended up lasting way into the night. They named their first daughter Kenya. In terms of color, Kenya looks just like her light-skinned mother, but with her Afrocentric name, she isn't often mistaken for anything but Black.

Three years later, Lisa gave birth to a boy. This child was born with such pale skin and loosely curled hair that he is often mistaken for white. Lisa said that by the time Colin was born, however, she and her husband weren't so caught up in skin color and naming. "We were more concerned about whether we could provide for two kids," she said. They named him Colin after Lisa's husband's father. Fifteen months after Colin joined the family, and as a bit of a surprise, Lisa gave birth to their third and final child, a girl born via cesarean section. "They took my daughter out," Lisa recalled of that day in the delivery room, "and my husband saw her and he leaned into me and said, 'She's absolutely gorgeous!' And I looked over and there was the most beautiful baby I'd ever seen. She was browner than both of us, and we felt like this was such a huge victory. We didn't expect it, but we were thrilled. I know that's probably wrong, but yeah, she was the most beautiful baby we'd ever seen, and we were really happy that she was brown."

When I interviewed Lisa, right before Thanksgiving, her children were twelve, nine, and seven. And while she said that their household—with two working parents and three kids—is often chaotic and busy, it is one filled with love and laughter. She also said that color isn't a constant source of worry or strain in the house, but it is almost impossible to ignore that their family is one of different colors. "I'm very cognizant that we are all different skin tones because outside of our home we are treated differently based on our complexion sometimes," Lisa said. "But within our home, we're just a family."

As an example, Lisa told me of an incident that had occurred the previous summer when her husband went to pick up their youngest daughter from day camp. Given her daughter's "healthy caramel complexion," and

her husband's pale skin, the other kids at the camp questioned their relationship. "One kid said to my daughter, 'Is that your dad?' and another
one said, 'Wait a minute, are you adopted?' They just assumed there was
no possible way they could be related. She came home very hurt and upset
by this." Lisa said this was the first time she and her husband sat all three
kids down for a conversation about color and colorism. "We told them
that in African American culture there are many different shades on the
spectrum that you'll see within a family, and our family is like that."

What was interesting about my conversation with Lisa was that,
prior to actually sitting down and thinking about these issues, she hadn't
really considered how the fact that her children were three different
colors was affecting her habits and practices as a parent. But once she
started to consider it, she realized that she was indeed doing things differently for her kids depending on the shade of each one's skin. At first,
she recalled a funny story where she realized that her younger daughter
needed to have lotion applied to her skin far more frequently than her
lighter-skinned siblings after a teacher pointed out that her daughter
looked "ashy" on her first day of kindergarten. But then Lisa realized
things went much deeper.

"I affirm my younger daughter Isabel's beauty regularly, more than I
do for Kenya. I think they're both beautiful, but I know society is harder
on darker women," Lisa began. "I don't want Isabel to go through life
feeling like she's less than because of her complexion, especially having
grown up in a family where she's the darkest person." However, despite
her best efforts, Lisa has already heard her youngest daughter express
feelings of inferiority. "Sometimes Isabel says things like, 'Everybody
else has hair that just lies down. I wish I had hair that lies down. Why
can't I be regular? Why can't I be normal?'" Ironically, Lisa said this is
exactly how she'd felt as a child—but wishing she were darker, like the
rest of her immediate family.

One thing Lisa is confident about is that the difference in skin colors
hasn't negatively affected her children's relationships with one another. "I
just see brothers and sisters who adore each other and fight. But their
fights are about regular sibling things," she said. And in some ways, the fact
that her two youngest are so opposite in color, which causes a lot of double
takes and questions outside the home, is something that bonds them together when they stand up to those who question their familial ties.

One week after our first interview, Lisa called me back because she had more to tell me. When we spoke on the phone this time, Lisa revealed that our previous conversation had really made her reflect on her own history of not feeling authentically Black because she was so light in a family of brown-skinned people. And now those feelings were bleeding into her children's lives.

In a soft voice, Lisa said she'd been helping twelve-year-old Kenya pick out an outfit to wear to school the previous morning when Kenya made a devastating confession. Devastating to Lisa, that is. "She said, 'I have an awkward color. I wish I were darker. I don't like my skin color,'" Lisa said. I could feel Lisa's pain and regret through the phone. She sighed heavily, and then out came a mea culpa of guilt and despair as she tried to figure out how she'd done this to her child. "I don't think I've taught her to not like her complexion, but I realize she has a lot of the same feelings that I had. I also realize that probably it is a lot of my being so excited to have a brown-skinned child, because on some level it validates my Blackness. I'm sure that seems really obvious from everything we've talked about, but I've never really thought about it."

Lisa walked back through her own childhood experiences remembering how she was accused of acting white, looking white, and talking white back in Chicago and all of the efforts she made to try to fit in with the Black kids at her school, to no avail. And now Lisa now feels she has passed her own trauma on to her daughter without meaning to. But as a parent of two girls, one dark and one light, she had really thought it was her darker child who would need more uplift. And many of her friends reinforced her beliefs.

"I have a friend who told me not to worry about Kenya because society is going to reaffirm her beauty and worth anyway," Lisa said. "She actually said, 'I wouldn't even tell her she's cute because everyone is going to give her that attention anyway. You need to be more concerned about Isabel because it's going to be harder for her,'" Lisa recalled. "This was advice from a trusted friend with a PhD in African American studies," she added. "For the record, my husband thinks that friend is crazy."

Lisa's situation, in which she is parenting her children differently based on their color, is not unusual. Research shows that color does affect how Black people parent their children. In her dissertation study on the impact of skin tone on parenting practices in African American families,

Antoinette Landor of the University of Missouri found that the shade of the skin can determine the quality of the parenting. Landor's results indicated that lighter-skinned daughters received a higher quality of parenting, a trend she attributed to the historical preference for lighter skin in women. But surprisingly, there was also a higher quality of parenting noted for darker-skinned sons—something Landor surmised was due to the family's "attempt to counter discrimination or protect their sons from it." (This is what Lisa and her husband found themselves doing with their youngest daughter, Isabel.) These darker sons also tended to receive more "racial socialization messages" from parents, messages that were meant, Landor concluded, "to help prepare their sons for possible negative race- and skin-related experiences given that darker skin males receive fewer advantages than their lighter skin peers." While Landor's findings do not speak to Lisa Washington's particular family dynamic, they do underscore the reality that Black parents treat their children differently based on the shade of their skin.

As for Lisa, she plans to keep talking to her children to make sure she puts an end to the "light-skin isolation" both she and her husband felt as children and any feelings of inferiority based on color. "These situations are going to keep coming up and we have to figure out how to react," she said, admitting that they are clearly going to have to do something differently. "I needed to talk about this," she said as we ended our interview. "And this conversation has to be ongoing."

Margaret Beale Spencer of the University of Chicago would agree. For parents who have inadvertently given their kids the wrong message about their skin color, or who have yet to get over their own past wounds, she said, transparency is key. "You've got to come clean," Spencer said. "You've got to communicate with your children that 'Mommy messed up,' 'Mommy didn't have enough information to ensure that you are clear about how wonderful you are and how dangerous the world can be.'" According to Spencer, it is never too late to give children the information they need, even if it means admitting you made a mistake. "The most effective strategy [in this situation] is to come clean with how this has affected you, so much so it may have silenced the truth," she said.

What Do We Talk About When We Talk About Color?

Most experts agree that people in the African American community are finally talking about color. In public. Which is definitely a sign of progress. From Bill Dukes's 2014 and 2015 documentaries that aired on cable TV—*Dark Girls* and *Light Girls*, respectively—to a seemingly ongoing social media discussion with the hashtags #teamdarkskin and #teamlightskin, the talk about color can now be heard both online and IRL (in real life). "We now have a vigorous continuing conversation about colorism that was unimaginable, say, twenty or thirty years ago, and it's being kept alive by a whole group of young image activists," said activist and author Marita Golden. "We're now in a space where colorism, for the first time I can remember, is actively and consistently challenged in the cultural and intellectual space." Golden went on to discuss recent magazine spreads and album covers where certain celebrities appeared to have been lightened and the almost immediate pushback from online activists and social media personalities. Further, dark-skinned actresses such as Gabourey Sidibe, Viola Davis, and Lupita Nyong'o have very publicly laid bare the issues faced by Black women with dark skin in Hollywood.

Of course, not all of the experts agree that this chatter circulating around the entertainment industry and via social media means progress is occurring in the real world.

Yaba Blay proudly claims the title of colorism activist, and much of her work is meant to dismantle the idea that light skin is the ideal for Black beauty. "I think in terms of progress being made, we are definitely having more conversations, but my fear is that we continue to talk about colorism in the same way," she said. "Most people still want to refer back to the plantation and the house Negro versus the field Negro, and about dark skin as disadvantaged and light skin as privileged. I still have yet to read [about] people really attempting to think through solutions."

JeffriAnne Wilder, an associate professor of sociology at the University of North Florida, who has been researching colorism in the Black community for almost twenty years, agrees. "We don't really have any concrete strategies for dismantling colorism because we don't have a concrete strategy for dismantling racism," she said. "One isn't going to disappear before the other one does." But that doesn't mean we are doomed to live with colorism. Wilder believes the conversations taking place *are* part of the solution. "The more people talk about it and acknowledge it, the better people will be equipped to deal with it. And because the public discourse attached to colorism is so loud now, I think young women are more equipped to dismantle the negative messages they receive," she said. "They are definitely more empowered than their mothers were." Like most of the other experts I interviewed, Wilder admits that the media and entertainment industries continue to have a light-skin bias. Still, she sees progress. "Now if women are hearing or seeing these ideas and images in the media, they have more space to work through that and not internalize it and they can process it differently than they did before. People are now being called out for being colorist when before that didn't happen," said Wilder.

Golden agrees. "For the first time, a whole generation of enlightened public intellectuals and cultural advocates are taking on this issue so that whenever there is a blatant colorist incident, there will be pushback," she said. But the "pushback" in the public arena, Golden acknowledged, isn't necessarily being felt in the home. "You have that contradiction, that the impact of the cultural activists and public intellectuals has not yet trickled down into the private lives of African Americans," she said. "In our families, we're still having issues talking about it." Golden likened the progressive public and online discussions about colorism to the civil rights movement and its effect on individuals. "We had to have the civil rights movement so that Black people could say to a white person, 'You can't call me nigger!'" Golden explained. "That change in consciousness for all Black people wasn't going to happen until that movement trickled down, and I think that's where we are now."

Same Difference

The last person I interviewed for this first section of the book is the future. Cassidy Thomas is a single mother of two. At twenty-six, she seems far more accomplished than most young women her age—understandably, as she has to juggle her career as a nurse and caring for her daughters, ages five and nine. I "met" Cassidy on a website for a picture book about colorism. She'd left a comment that the book was a blessing and that she regularly read it to her daughters, one dark and the other light. It turned out Cassidy lived in Philadelphia, so I tracked her down via e-mail and she agreed to be interviewed.

Cassidy arrived at my office out of breath, still in her scrubs from her afternoon shift at the hospital. She had precisely one hour to sit with me before she had to pick up her daughters from after-school care. I wasn't exactly sure what the color situation was in her family, so I just asked.

"My eldest daughter, Tiffany, is the more darker-skinned one; my youngest daughter, Asia, is the lightest, and I fall in between," she said. "Plus, my youngest and I have hazel eyes. My eldest does not." She didn't have to explain further. Looking at those eyes, I could already imagine what torment little Tiffany must go through. Those eyes are the first things you notice when you see Cassidy. Her skin is the color of toffee and her almond-shaped eyes are green and catlike, giving her an exotic look that most people would probably attribute to a European or Latin relative, but Cassidy is quick to clarify that she is just Black. Nobody knows where the eyes came from, but Cassidy, her sister, and her mom all have them. And now so does one daughter, but not the other.

"People always comment on my younger daughter's eyes and tell her she's beautiful, and then they'll turn to my older daughter like an afterthought and say, 'Oh, you're cute too,'" Cassidy said. She went on to explain that Tiffany very quickly internalized the message that her sister was pretty and she wasn't. "Sometimes she would get very emotional about the fact that she wanted to look like me and her sister. 'You all have these eyes and you all are lighter,' she would say," Cassidy recalled. When she realized the toll this was taking on Tiffany's self-esteem, she knew she was going to have to do some things differently.

"I became more vocal when dealing with strangers who would walk up and make comments about my girls. I had to be more assertive and make sure people knew there were two girls here who were both beautiful. And I will say that out loud because Tiffany needed to hear Mommy say it. I want my daughter to always look at me as her protector."

Thinking about Lisa Washington and her dilemma praising her darker daughter at the expense of her lighter daughter, I asked Cassidy how she made sure that both of her girls would feel comfortable in their own skin and not covet each other's. I wanted to know how she made sure they each felt equally loved and appreciated in their own skin.

Cassidy had obviously been thinking about this. Her response made a lot of sense. "One thing I have made a priority for both of my daughters is that I love them both greatly, but they require different kinds of love from Mommy," she began. "I told them, 'I love you both the same, but I have to extend my love to you and show my love to you ladies in different ways.'" With her younger daughter, who has been told since birth that she's beautiful, Cassidy is working on teaching her about internal beauty.

And with Tiffany, she's working on confidence. "I've had to focus on two different things with them, but what I make sure to do is have key moments where that happens with them both in the room," Cassidy said, "because I don't want it to seem like there is any secrecy or shame in the difference."

It's funny: *Same Difference* is the name of the book Cassidy had left the comment about. A beautifully rendered picture book by Calida Rawles, *Same Difference* is about two cousins, one dark and one light, who realize they are different but the same. "*Same Difference* has been the greatest tool I've ever come across," Cassidy gushed. "At least for my older daughter. It really did a lot for her to understand we're the same and we've got our differences, but 'that's my sister' at the end of the day. I had to get her to the point where she could realize it's not a competition between the two of them. It's not about who is more beautiful or who is enough. You're sisters and that is what matters."

Soon after, Cassidy had to go as our hour was up. I wished her well and then wished I had a crystal ball to see if her life lessons would work for her daughters or, as with Lisa Washington, would one daughter still feel slighted or envious of her sister? The fact is, with parenting there are no guarantees and it's hard. Parenting Black children in America is really hard. Parenting Black children who are two different colors adds an additional layer of complexity to this already complicated task. But Black people have been doing it for years, and the existence of racism and colorism has not diminished the joy and love found in the Black American family.

Thankfully, colorism is being publicly discussed in multiple forums and formats in the Black community. And while we may still be waiting for it to trickle down to the family unit en masse, I think we're witnessing the change that Marita Golden described as the unfinished business of the civil rights movement.

Sidebar: Black America's Skin-Color Glossary

Black Americans are known for having created many elements of American popular culture, from musical genres like R&B and hip-hop to fashion trends like diamond-encrusted fingernails and sneakers without shoelaces. One of the areas of modern popular culture in which Black people have arguably had the most influence, however, is in the American lingua franca. From "boo" to "bae" to "bling," Black people have invented an untold number of words and phrases that have entered the American lexicon—and not just as slang but also as certifiable *Webster's Dictionary* entries.

But not all Black language inventions are meant for public consumption. Some of Black America's most colorful linguistic creations are used solely within safe Black spaces. These are words and phrases that generally refer to people, places, and things within a Black world and therefore have not migrated to mainstream society. One category of such "Black-only" terminology is the one that is used to describe the skin colors of other Black people.

Perhaps because a large majority of white people pay little attention to the myriad shades of color Black people actually come in—Aren't Black people just black?—these colorful terms used to distinguish a light-skinned Black person from, say, a brown-skinned Black person have remained cloistered within the Black community, even though these labels have been in existence for years. In 1946, sociologist Charles Parrish identified twenty-five unique "nicknames" referring to skin shades in the African American community, names ranging from "sexy chocolate" to "tar baby." Some years later, Howard University professor Curtis Banks expanded that list to a total of 140 different skin-color labels. Far from innocent, most of these "nicknames," as Parrish referred to them, were accompanied by stereotypes, many of them negative.

Today, many of the same color names Parrish uncovered in 1946 are still in play and still carry the same stigma or shame. But it is a shame that remains hidden in Black America. Much like that offensive yet ubiquitous N-word, these color terms are often tossed around the Black community by Black people, but it would not be okay for someone outside the tribe, particularly a white person, to use these names, at least not without fear of serious repercussions.

The following is a list that is neither exhaustive nor scientific in its creation. These are terms I've heard simply because I'm Black, I have ears, and I've been writing a book about colorism for the last two years and gathered these along the way. Within three categories—light, medium, and dark—the terms are listed in alphabetical order.

Labels for Light Skin
Browning (popular in the Caribbean)
Caramel
Coolie
Creole
High Yellow
Light Bright
Light Skinned
Red-Bone
Yellow

Labels for Medium Skin
Brown
Brown Skin
Chocolate Brown
Shit Brown

Labels for Dark Skin
Ace of Spades
Black Black
Blue Black
Dark Skinned
Ink Spot
Jigaboo
Skillet (as in, as Black as a . . .)
Sudanese Black
Tar Baby

TWO

MEJORANDO LA RAZA
Latinos and Color

"If we were a rainbow family of different shades, why was the black shade relegated to behind the ears, like dirt that wasn't supposed to show? Wasn't it clear that the pot of gold was clearly toward that lighter end of the rainbow?"
—JULIA ALVAREZ, *Black Behind the Ears*

The United States government defines Latinos as "persons who trace their origin or descent to Mexico, Puerto Rico, Cuba, Central and South America, and other Spanish cultures." The key word in that definition is "Spanish" in that the common cultural elements among different Latino cultures can generally be traced back to the motherland that is Spain. In addition to the language—Spanish—and the religion—Catholic—the other cultural element shared by many Latinos is a strong anti-Black sentiment when it comes to skin color and identity. Throughout the Spanish-speaking world, one of the least popular identity categories is *negro*, the Spanish word for Black. Because a large portion of the Spanish-speaking world has African roots, however, this anti-Black sentiment sets the stage for some serious identity issues, which impact not only the larger society but the family as well.

So, while it wouldn't be entirely fair to blame the Spanish colonizers for the color complex that continues to plague the Latino community today, a good place to begin any investigation of Latinos and colorism is in Spain.

New Colors in the New World
When the Spanish arrived in the so-called New World in 1492, they were looking for ways to increase their wealth. With visions of gold and silver in mind, the Spanish initially viewed the Native peoples they

encountered as minor impediments to that wealth, but they soon realized the Native Americans could also be put to good use. They could be potential vassals for Spain's growing kingdom, potential workers to exploit, and new believers for the Catholic church. So, with all of that potential just waiting to be tapped into, the Spanish got busy.

In very short order, the Spanish Conquistadors began enslaving the Native people all across the South American continent, as well as in the Caribbean, on the islands that would eventually come to be known as Cuba, the Dominican Republic, and Puerto Rico. They also brought their plundering ways to the southeastern and southwestern United States. In addition to enslaving many Natives, the Spanish also found time to baptize some of them and rape the women. In other words, both baptism and rape were premeditated methods by which the Spanish staked their claim in this new world. "Rape was a common form of Spanish social control in New Spain, and indigenous women were the most common victims," writes Margaret Hunter in her book *Race, Gender, and the Politics of Skin Tone*. Hunter notes that the Spanish were very deliberate in their choice of aggression, writing, "As was true for most European colonizers, the Spanish justified their pillaging of the land and people with an ideology portraying themselves as civilized Christians on a mission to save the savage and heathen dark Other." That is, raping the Natives was for their own good, as it might result in offspring that would carry the superior blood of a European.

The Spanish desire for even greater wealth and the seemingly endless opportunities presented in the New World—from silver mining to raising cash crops like tobacco and sugar—required a larger workforce than could be supplied by the indigenous people. The scale of production launched by the Spanish demanded an enormous labor force, which was complicated by the fact that European diseases decimated entire populations of Native Americans including, of course, potential laborers. So, the Spanish turned to the African continent and began importing massive numbers of African people to enslave. In fact, some historians estimate that nearly 90 percent of the Africans brought to the Americas via the transatlantic slave trade were bound for the Caribbean and Latin America.

Not surprisingly, it soon came to pass that the population in the Spanish colonies was made up almost entirely of people of color, a mixture of Native peoples and Africans. The Spanish themselves were a small but powerful minority. And due to their small numbers, but very real need for "intimate relations," interracial relationships were quite common in the Spanish colonies. "Catholicism in Portugal and Spain is usually taken to explain a supposedly greater frequency of sexual intercourse and intermarriage with local populations," wrote historian Francisco Bethencourt in *Racisms: From the Crusades to the Twentieth Century*. "The alleged promiscuity of Catholicism is opposed to British and Dutch Protestantism as cultures of sexual restraint and stricter rules concerning the choice of partners," Bethencourt noted. Whether these relationships were consensual or forced, the Spanish colonies were soon populated with a veritable rainbow of skin colors as a result, from the very dark to the very light. Given the circumstances, it became clear to the Spanish elite that something had to be done to maintain control over the multicolored citizens who greatly outnumbered them.

Castas: Art Imitates Life

Here we must go backward before we continue forward. The Spanish were already accustomed to living in a multiethnic society where different skin tones were well represented, particularly during the eight hundred years of Muslim rule. During that period, Spain was a country populated with Europeans, Arabs, Jews, and sub-Saharan Africans. After the Spanish *Reconquista*, things changed. For reasons ranging from economic necessity to the need to build cohesion among the fractured population, the Spanish monarchs slowly began forcing all of their citizens to either convert to Christianity or leave the country. Under the threat of expulsion, many of Spain's Muslims and Jews converted, so the country was soon left with a rainbow population of citizens who all claimed to be Spanish Catholics but looked nothing alike. Labels were given to these new converts—converted Jews were *conversos* and converted Muslims were *moriscos*—but these religious identity categories soon took on new meaning. They didn't simply signify a person's religious status; these terms came to serve as proxies for racial (im)purity.

By the mid-sixteenth century, *limpieza de sangre* (clean-blood) laws were enacted restricting certain positions in the government and church to those of pure Spanish blood, meaning *conversos* and *moriscos* need not apply. These laws effectively set up a social hierarchy in Spain theoretically based on purity of blood. However, phenotype, physical characteristics, mannerisms, and dress all became easy stand-ins when distinguishing a "real" Spaniard from a second-class citizen.

In the Americas, the Spanish continued to use their theories of blood purity to designate a social order and to create some kind of social hierarchy among the multiracial populations in their colonies. Based on what can only be described as a loose understanding of science and a combination of racism and cultural narcissism, the Spanish created a ranking of people based on their perceived ethnic makeup. This social hierarchy was then conceptualized in a visual framework by local artists of the day into what were known as *casta* (caste) paintings. These paintings, though not official government products, were often displayed in public spaces such as museums, universities, palaces, and government buildings, most notably in Mexico City and Peru.

The artist Juan Rodriguez is credited as the creator of the first casta painting in Mexico City, in the early 1700s. According to Bethencourt, "The purpose of [the *casta* painting] was to present a narrative, hierarchical vision of the process of racial mixing between the diametrically opposed types of Spaniards and 'savage' Indians . . . , spotlighting the triple mixture of Spaniards and Indians, Spaniards and black people, and Indians and black people." Despite its rather offensive purpose, the *casta* paintings offer beguiling renderings of individual families—a father, a mother, and a child—with captions depicting the "race" or "caste" of each individual and special emphasis on the new resulting race of the child. A typical *casta* painting featured sixteen different family renderings beginning with the basic, Spaniard plus Indian begets mestizo, and then Spaniard plus Black begets a mulatto, and ending with such complicated and convoluted mixtures that one new category of child is actually labeled *no te entiendo*. Translated literally, that means "I don't understand you." Can you imagine walking around with *no te entiendo* as your racial designation?

Far from innocent, the *casta* paintings present the families in descending order of social prestige to highlight the difference between the noble Spaniard and, as Bethancourt notes, "the 'savage' Indians living outside colonial society." Historians agree that the *casta* designations were never meant to serve as official government categories, but the words themselves became part of the local vernacular, and the people with the least amount of Spanish blood were treated the worst in society, paying higher taxes to the government and more money to the church, for example. One's location in this color-coded caste system also determined one's access to education and other key community resources.

In addition to labeling the offspring of every possible ethnic mix—and often likening lower castes to animals—the *casta* paintings served an additional purpose. They became an unofficial blueprint for society's strivers who wanted to move up the color/class hierarchy. Everyone knew that the lighter the skin, the more power and respect one achieved in society. And though people couldn't change their own skin color, they could procreate with someone of a lighter hue and achieve a higher status for their offspring. The paintings showed exactly the category of person someone would have to marry in order to create a child with a higher status. Of course, a child tainted with either Native American or African blood, even if the skin color "returned" to a milky white, could never achieve racial purity. For example, a Spaniard and a mulatto would create a *morisco*, and a *morisco* and a Spaniard would produce not a Spaniard—despite this child being more than three-quarters Spanish—but an "albino." Bethencourt explains the phenomenon of the albino designation: "In this case we do not have a return to pure Spaniard but instead an artificial and ambiguous . . . whiteness." Nonetheless, people could try to "pass" as Spanish—or at least partly Spanish—if their skin color was light enough, setting the stage for a culture obsessed with light, European skin.

As Spanish colonial society became more and more mixed, particularly in Mexico, the *casta* paintings expanded their labels with terms like *lobo* (Black/Indian), *chino* (Black/*lobo*), and *cambujo* (*chino*/Indian). These terms were insulting and derogatory and reflected the Spanish preoccupation both with their increasingly mixed-race society and with how to maintain some kind of hierarchy in terms of who would rule. And while the names of every single *casta* category may not have been memorized by the masses, it could be argued that the *casta* system is the reason why Latinos still have so many different classifications for skin color and retain a fear of falling into the lower castes of society.

Mejorando la Raza

The concept of "marrying up" didn't originate in colonial Spain, but the Spanish and the Portuguese certainly deserve credit for institutionalizing the concept in Latin America, beginning with the *casta* system. Both Spanish and Portuguese colonizers promoted the idea of *blanqueamiento*, or whitening up the population, by incentivizing white Europeans to immigrate to their colonies and by urging the dark-skinned masses to procreate with lighter partners. Men and women of darker hues were encouraged to bring forth lighter offspring for the sake of both the child and society. That way, they would be *mejoranado la raza*: improving the race. Meanwhile, white Spanish men (not the women, of course) were not explicitly encouraged to engage in rape and/or concubinage with women of color, but a blind eye was turned to the act because the resulting children would be lighter than their mothers. "In early 1800s Mexico, the people in power were actively trying to recruit European immigrants to breed the Blackness and indigenous element out of the population," explained Christina Sue, an associate professor of sociology at the University of Colorado, Boulder, who studies race and color politics in Latino culture. "These were active political government campaigns [intended] to whiten the population with European blood." By this time, the European populace—thanks to the scientific community and its burgeoning movement to classify the distinct human "races"—was officially on record with the belief that white Europeans were a superior race while Blacks and Native peoples languished at the bottom of the evolutionary ladder. The Spanish Crown could hardly be expected to support the development of a colony populated with low-level humans, thus *mejorando la raza* became everybody's responsibility.

Tanya Hernández, professor at Rutgers University Law School and author of the 2014 book *Racial Subordination in Latin America*, likened the *blanqueamiento* policies in postcolonial Brazil to Jim Crow laws in the United States. "This was state-sponsored whitening of the population," she explained to me. "The plan was to inundate the country with low-skilled white [Europeans]. And the work of breeding out Blackness was the work of lower-class white men, not the upper class and certainly not white women." Hernández noted that countries beyond Brazil, including Venezuela and even Cuba, enacted this method. "Other countries used immigration incentives and outreach to try to bring European immigrants, but [these countries] did not have sufficient economic resources to lure the Europeans to the extent that Argentina and Brazil had," she explained. But even those countries that didn't succeed in re-populating their shores with white people still managed to instill a clear idea that new, white European bodies had far more value than did the brown and Black bodies already in residence. "*Blanqueamiento* is a real economic, political and personal process; it is a dynamic that involves culture, identity and values," wrote Eduardo Bonilla-Silva and David Dietrich in their article "The Latin Americanization of US Race Relations: A New Pigmentocracy." "As a social practice, whitening is just not neutral mixture but hierarchical movement," they noted, "and the most valuable movement is upward."

Postcolonial Life

By 1898, the Spanish had relinquished or lost control of most of their former colonies, including Florida, parts of Louisiana, New Spain (what is present-day Mexico), and their islands in the Caribbean—Puerto Rico, Cuba, and the Dominican Republic. But by the time the Spanish officially retreated, their legacy of devaluing and debasing African and Native American ancestry was firmly planted in the culture they left behind. It was as intrinsic as the Spanish language and the Catholic faith. Each newly independent nation found its own way to deal with the *castas*-based social hierarchy that had essentially evolved into a color-coded ranking of the population. We can look at what happened in Mexico as an example of one country's approach to the situation.

Mexico

Absent the presence of Spanish rulers, the new leadership in Mexico had to deal with the fact that the citizens of their newly independent country did not all look alike. Taking stock of their population, Mexico's leaders realized that white skin was in short supply, while the brown-skinned mestizos were numerous. They feared Mexico would be seen as an uncivilized nation by the rest of the world. As the European and American scientific communities continued on with their race theories, trying to prove with science that certain races—white ones—were biologically distinct and superior to others—dark ones—the Mexican government knew they had to do something to normalize their darker-hued population.

The Mexican philosopher José Vasconcelos is credited with developing the theory of *La raza cósmica*, which basically stipulated that mixed-race individuals represent the best sum of all of their parts, and therefore that a mix of races is superior to any single race. Essentially, Vasconcelos made a case for the Darwinian concept of hybrid vigor. His championing of the mestizo eventually came to be known simply as *La raza* and brought the Mexican people a great deal of pride in their mixed-race heritage. Some scholars assert that for Afro-Mexicanos and those of in-digenous descent, embracing the mestizo identity offered an escape from discrimination. "Afro-descendants and indigenous people subscribed to mestizaje; albeit, for different reasons than their White oppressors. Mes-tizaje was their feeble attempt to deny their racist ideologies and to 'erase' the public discourse about their inferiority," wrote social scientists Nayeli Chavez-Dueñas, Hector Adames, and Kurt Organista.

Other countries that found themselves newly independent after Spain's retreat and populated by multi-hued citizens, such as Cuba and Colombia, went through similar social growing pains and had to strug-gle with nationwide identity issues. Most Latin American leaders came to the same decision, to deracialize their national identity and instead claim that all people are equal, at least on paper. Of course, in practice, what occurred was an unofficial skin-color hierarchy, or pigmentocracy, which privileged those with light skin and European heritage and con-demned those with African or Native American blood. A clear legacy from colonial rule, a small minority of light-skinned elites reigned over the brown-skinned masses. "Pigmentocracy has been central to the maintenance of White power in Latin America because it has fostered (1) divisions among all those in secondary racial positions, (2) divisions within racial strata limiting the likelihood of within-stratum unity, (3) mobility viewed as individual and conditional upon whitening, and (4) white elites being regarded as legitimate representatives of the 'nation' even though they do not look like the average member of the nation," wrote Bonilla-Silva and Dietrich. And in most countries, the concepts of *blanqueamiento, mejorando la raza,* or what was termed "progressive mix-ture"—progress resulting from mixing with someone lighter—continued unabated as everyone saw the benefits of lightening up.

The Dominican Republic

The Dominican Republic has the distinction of being the only nation in Latin America that never secured its independence from Spain. Instead, its fight for freedom was with Haiti. The Haitians expelled the French in their own revolution in 1795 and declared independence; eventually, in 1822, they took control of the entire island of Hispaniola. It wasn't until 1844 that the Dominican Republic became an independent nation, after launching its own fight for freedom. The result of that twenty-two-year occupation by Haiti is a palpable anti-Haiti sentiment in the minds and memories of the Dominican people that continues to this day. And what's more, that anti-Haiti vitriol has evolved into a pervasive anti-Black sentiment, such that many Dominicans—even though more than 85 percent of them have some African ancestry—would rather go to their grave than check any Black identity box. Of course, not every Dominican feels this way, but as evidenced by the continuing persecution of Haitians in the Domincan Republic in 2015, it is still an unresolved issue.

Coming to America

The three largest ethnic groups in the United States today from former Spanish colonies are Mexicans, Puerto Ricans, and Cubans, in that order. Dominicans are close behind. As stated, these nations were all colonized with a clear concept of a color hierarchy. The sad fact is that the color consciousness long embedded in those countries is often brought to the United States and augmented with our own brand of white-versus-Black racism.

In terms of size, Mexicans were the first significant Latino population to come to the United States. For many Mexicans, this came about not because they moved but because their country, once a part of New Spain, seemingly overnight became part of the United States through treaties, wars, and relinquishments. For many Mexicans, the opportunity to be a citizen of this new, growing nation known as the United States seemed like a great opportunity, but for the US government it was a problem. Why? Officials didn't know how to categorize these new citizens because they didn't fit easily into a Black or white box. In the 1800s, the US government classified Mexicans as whites. But increasingly, an argument was made to include a separate Mexican "race" category on the census to separate Mexicans from other, European immigrants. On the 1930 census, "Mexican" was included among the racial options, but the census director noted a discrepancy in how people defined themselves, saying, "The wealthier class of Mexican call themselves white, whereas the class of peons will [call themselves] Mexican." By 1936, all Mexicans were officially classified as white again. This back-and-forth change in categorization and its accompanying confusion would continue to plague Mexicans and other racially diverse newcomers from the Caribbean and

Latin America who did not fit into America's simple binary racial categories. Eventually, in 1970, the term "Hispanic" was added to the census,
whereas Latino didn't appear until 2000.

Although categorizing Mexican Americans proved to be a challenge
to the Census Bureau, in the late nineteenth and early twentieth centuries, it soon became very apparent that how people looked would determine their level of success. Mexicans with lighter skin and more European
features fared far better than those with darker skin and obvious Native
American or African features. This was true for both Mexican men and
women. And no attempt was really made to deny the trend. In fact, a
robust cosmetics industry blatantly capitalized on the fact that Mexicans
with light skin were doing better overall. According to Margaret Hunter,
"Many advertising campaigns of major cosmetic companies told Mexican American women, 'Those with lighter, more healthy skin tones will
become much more successful in business, love, and society.'"

Brown Pride

Like the Black thought leaders of the Harlem Renaissance and beyond,
Latino activists advocated for Brown Pride, that is, for new Latino immigrants to hold on to their heritage and stop coveting the ways of the
white man—*los gringos*. Accelerating in energy alongside the Black Power
movement of the 1960s and '70s, the Brown Power movement, or the
Chicano movement, put a very public face on Mexican American rights
in the United States. While the activism mainly concerned labor, education, and police brutality, movement leaders also pushed an element of
ethnic pride. In her book, *Latining America: Black-Brown Passages and the
Coloring of Latino/a Studies*, Claudia Milian writes, "The Chicano movement also worked constantly, creatively, and self-consciously to fashion a
new racial identity. . . . Those of Mexican descent [were] to express pride
in their ethnic origins rather than try to blend into a homogenous white
mainstream." Unfortunately, while the Brown Pride movement challenged the "white is right" ideals of identity, much like the Black Is Beautiful movement, its effects were neither wide ranging nor long lasting.

New Immigrant Groups

It doesn't take much for a newly arrived immigrant to pick up on the fact
that Black people are the victims of systemic racial discrimination in the

United States and that white people hold the reins of power in almost every realm of society. Thus, the negative perceptions of Blackness that many Latino immigrants learn in their home countries are simply reinforced when they arrive in the United States. Needless to say, little progress—if any—is made toward unpacking the years of brainwashing experienced in their native lands. Instead of embracing their Blackness or indigenous roots, many Latinos quickly learn upon arrival in the United States that they should not associate themselves with Black Americans and should take pains to diminish any of their own physical characteristics that might be associated with negritude, like dark skin and kinky hair. Researchers have shown, in fact, that immigrant Latinos tend to have more negative views of American Blacks than do US-born Latinos. From embracing the concept of *blanqueamiento* to slathering on bleaching creams and straightening their hair, many Latino immigrants make vigorous efforts to erase any aspect of Blackness from their own identity. Sometimes the efforts to lighten up go too far.

In February 2012, Fox News Latino reported on an outbreak of mercury poisoning caused by illegal bleaching creams smuggled into the United States from Mexico. With outbreaks in immigrant communities in California, Virginia, and Minnesota, the cases were so worrisome that the Centers for Disease Control issued a special report about the dangers of mercury poisoning, which include kidney damage, skin rashes, nerve damage, and psychosis. It was discovered that some women had even used the creams on their babies, with the hope that lighter skin would help their children get ahead in their new life in America. They believed that lightening their children's skin with chemicals would give them a leg up in this society where white people hold all the power.

While slathering illegal bleaching cream on a child may seem outrageous to some, the truth is that Latino success does look light and bright. Just look at the entertainment industry and witness a blinding swath of light-skinned Latinas, from Cameron Diaz to Arianna Grande to Salma Hayek. And the statistics tell a fuller and more depressing story. According to a 2003 study by John R. Logan for the Lewis Mumford Center for Comparative Urban and Regional Research, Latinos who identified as Black had lower median household income and higher unemployment and poverty rates than non-Black Latinos. Light-skinned Latinos fare better in employment opportunities and housing options. The numbers don't lie, and popular culture reinforces the idea that Latinos with pale skin are more desirable, are more attractive, are more popular, and have more money. Is it any wonder then that Latino mothers warn their children to stay out of the sun, that is, *pa que no se oscure* (so you don't get dark)?

Black Behind the Ears

In the midst of my looking for families to interview for this chapter on Latinos and their unique skin-color issues, an incident happened that perfectly exemplifies the Latino perspective on Blackness. On March 11, 2015, Rodner Figueroa, an Emmy Award–winning personality on the Univision TV network in the United States, said First Lady Michelle Obama "looks like she's part of the cast of *Planet of the Apes.*" He said this live, on television, and even when one of his show co-hosts tried to jump in and save him by insisting that Mrs. Obama is actually quite attractive, Figueroa didn't change his stance. It didn't take long for the Interwebs to explode, for Univision to offer a sincere apology, and for Figueroa to find himself out of job. Not for nothing, it also didn't take long for Figueroa to launch his public apology tour, beg Univision for his job back, and proclaim to the world that he could not be racist because not only is he gay but his father is "Afro-Latino." And there it is in a nutshell. The paradox of being Black and Latino. Even though an overwhelming number of Latinos in the United States have some African ancestry, they can still find a way to separate themselves from and/or disparage Blackness.

Before I started talking to individuals about skin-color differences in their families, I really wanted to understand this disdain for Blackness—Black skin, kinky hair, African features (whatever that means exactly)—which seems to be universal in a community as diverse and heterogeneous as this loosely formed group we call Latinos.

One of the first people I knew I wanted to speak with was Dash Harris, a documentary filmmaker, journalist, and educator who graduated from Temple University's School of Media and Communication. I was interested in her opinion because every time I Googled the words "Black identity" and "Latinos" together, her name appeared in the results due to her critically acclaimed docu-series about Black identity in Latin American culture, *Negro.*

I wished I could have interviewed Harris in person in her native Panama, where she now lives, though she grew up mostly in the United States. Instead, I spoke to her via Skype in the spring. She sat in her sunny apartment, often gazing out past palm trees to the ocean as she contemplated her answers, while I drew my woolen shawl closer around my shoulders in my cold, drafty office in Philadelphia.

What made you decide to make this documentary? I asked her. Why *Negro*? Harris paused before answering. Her answer was deeply personal. "Back when I was in elementary school I started questioning my parents about why certain Latin Americans denied their Blackness when we were [being] raised with an astounding pride in it," Harris began. "It was never an issue for us, but it was an issue for so many other Latin Americans and I didn't understand why." That lack of understanding never left her, and once she became equipped with the skills of a journalist and found herself constantly confronting the same anti-Black sentiment in so many Latin American people, she decided to answer her own questions.

The *Negro* documentary is primarily in English and is intended for a North American audience. "I just felt that the monolithic view that the US has of Latin Americans is completely detrimental. For Latin Americans themselves, for the Latinos born in the US, and for the US," she explained. "My larger statement is that the complexities in Latin American identity have been so muted that we've been objectified to a mythic bubble and we've been oversimplified to the point where we don't matter."

Harris interviewed Latinos in the United States, various countries in South and Central America, and the Caribbean, asking them what it meant to be Black in their country of origin. She found overwhelmingly that Blackness was something deemed almost universally unappealing. "White supremacy is still rampant," Harris said with a sigh. "Even though it's not in the law or policy, it's in practice, and it's in social interactions, and it's manifesting the same ways as it did in colonial times."

As someone who identifies as Afro-Panamanian, Harris has been a witness to and victim of poor treatment, in both the United States and throughout Latin America, based on the color of her skin, which is a deep, rich brown. But, as she pointed out earlier, her parents were pro-Black before pro-Black was a thing, and thus her level of self-esteem and pride in her African heritage kept her grounded. On the other hand,

Harris discovered through filming that it was often family members who people pointed fingers at for instilling in them their ideas of anti-Blackness. "I've spoken to so many people," Harris said, "where the most hurtful colorism came from their own parents." She recalled stories of mothers telling children to stay out of the sun and fathers telling daughters to perm their hair because they had *pelo malo*—bad hair. "A stranger can say anything, but the most lasting effects are if your dad says you're too dark in a negative way," Harris said. "That's how legacies start."

Painful Family Values

The author and journalist Sandra Guzmán, fifty, perfectly exemplifies the type of painful legacy that Harris heard about when making her film. Born in Puerto Rico, Guzmán moved with her family to New Jersey when she was ten. One of five children, Guzmán fell in the middle of both the birth order and the color spectrum. With a father who was Black and a light-complected mother with indigenous and Spanish heritage, Guzmán and her siblings reflected a wide range of skin colors and hair textures. Guzmán described herself as having "African features, a flat nose, and curlier hair"—features inherited from her father's side of the family. Her eldest sister also took after their father's side, but her second sister inherited their mother's coloring, European features, and blond hair. Guzmán's two younger brothers were also divided along the color line, with one who was darker and the other one light. The phenotypic variation in the Guzmán home was far from unusual in Puerto Rican households, but that didn't mean it wasn't an issue. "Color was the elephant in the room in my family," Guzmán told me in a telephone interview.

I had reached out to Guzmán initially because I wanted to talk to her about colorism in the Latina community, as she is a former editor in chief of *Latina* magazine and the author of *The New Latina's Bible: The Modern Latina's Guide to Love, Spirituality, Family and La Vida*. Before I contacted her, I had no idea she'd had her own experiences living in a household where colorism was common. From seemingly minor things—like her eldest sister being nicknamed "Spring" because her kinky hair was so "springy," or Guzmán being told regularly that she should use a clothespin on her African nose to try to make it less flat—to dramatic instances of favoritism toward her lighter siblings, these slights wounded Guzmán terribly. "I always felt like if I were just a little blonder, if I just looked a little lighter skinned, maybe [my father] would love me more," Guzmán said.

For Guzmán and her eldest sister, what hurt the most was that it wasn't just in the outside world that their beauty wasn't honored; it was in the home, too. Guzmán's mother made no attempt to hide the fact that she found her light-skinned daughter more attractive than her other, darker girls. "My mother always thought that the most beautiful of her daughters is my sister who is blond, whom she named after her," Guzmán said, noting the favoritism in that act. "What my older sister and I looked like was not something that was celebrated as beautiful," she added. Even worse, Guzmán said she and her sister essentially suffered in silence, finding in neither their mother nor their father a champion for their darker skin. "We didn't have the language to discuss these issues when we were little girls," Guzmán said. "We knew that these issues existed and that it was something we had no control over. We knew that there was a disease; we just didn't know what the name of the disease was."

Interestingly, Guzmán said her brothers seemed unfazed by the cultural fawning over light skin and disparaging remarks about dark skin and African features. "For the boys, it was more about who's taller or who's stronger," Guzmán explained, noting that beauty in the Latino community is a female concern. And a big concern. "My sense of beauty was so warped I felt very much like Pecola in Toni Morrison's *The Bluest Eye*," Guzmán said, referring to the desperate young Black girl who tragically believed having blue eyes would solve all of her problems. In Guzmán's case, she didn't yearn for blue eyes; she wanted a permanent alteration to her body. "To be beautiful I wanted a different nose," she said. "My nose became the centerpiece of a conversation with myself for so long that I saved two thousand dollars and got a nose job right before I graduated from college."

So, with a new nose and straightened hair, Guzmán entered the world as an adult, but an adult who carried around these wounds for years. "[These issues] used to make me cry so much because I felt so slighted. I felt so cheated," Guzmán said, the raw emotion still present in her voice. She continued, "To grow up with a mother and an extended family that is so racist—" Guzmán stopped here to correct herself. "It's not racist exactly; it's just that they've been literally brainwashed to believe that they're not beautiful." Now, at age fifty, with a dedication to yoga, a lot of conversations with her mother and sisters, and a great hair-stylist who taught Guzmán how to embrace her natural beauty, Guzmán is on a healing journey. One of the things she learned from speaking with her older sister, whom she always considered to be privileged because of her light skin and blond hair, was that there was pain in her world too. "[During my childhood] I didn't have the lens to see not only how [our parents' behavior] affected us, the recipients of less love for what we looked like, but also the effect that it had on my sister who was getting extra love because of what she looked like," Guzmán explained. "I think it tormented her as much as it tormented me."

As a professional writer, Guzmán has put much of her energy into helping the next generation of Latinas embrace the full range of their beauty. As one of the early editors in chief of *Latina*, she insisted that the magazine include Latinas of every shade, even in the advertisements. "It was a mission of mine to represent Latinas in all of our diverse beauty," she said proudly. Today Guzmán sees progress in the Latino community when it comes to colorism in the family and in the culture at large, but she acknowledges that it's happening at a sluggish pace. "There are small pockets [of Latinos] who are saying, 'If you won't celebrate us, we will celebrate ourselves,'" she said. "So yes, there is progress, but it is still very slow."

Outliers in the Family: The Men Speak

Of course, not everyone in the Latino community who has dark skin identifies as Afro-Latino. But variations in pigmentation can still vary greatly within a nuclear family, which brings skin-color politics right to the kitchen table. "These politics of race and racism become enacted within families, pitting family members against each other," wrote Marta Cruz-Janzen in an article about color politics in the Latino community. Not surprisingly, it is often the darker-skinned family members who suffer the most in Latino families, say sociologists Eduardo Bonilla-Silva and David Dietrich. What might be surprising, though, is that men too can be victims of color politics in the family. Despite the fact that colorism may seem like a beauty issue to some, gender offers no protection from the color wars.

Charles Guevara, forty-one, teaches Italian at a small private high school in Long Island, New York. He currently lives in Brooklyn and was six months away from getting married when we spoke. I met Charles almost a decade ago when he was a colleague of my husband's. I got back in touch with him to see if he would mind being interviewed, because I remember my husband, Manuel, telling me that Charles's sisters looked so white he couldn't believe they were related to Charles. Charles, on the other hand, has brown skin the color of copper, dark eyes, and thick, shiny black hair that he often wears long enough for a ponytail. Though he works at a conservative private school, every time I ever saw him, Charles wore bright-colored clothing, sandals, and unbuttoned collars that showed just a pinch of dark chest hair. I have never met his sisters in person, but I've seen pictures, and they do indeed look like average white American girls.

We spoke on the phone for our interview, and the first thing Charles wanted me to know was that he was the darkest one in his nuclear family of five, a family that consisted of his two parents, his two sisters, and himself. He described his parents as "pretty standard Colombian-looking people, like a mestizo blend." And his sisters, he said, were both fair with light hair and green eyes. "I have the darkest eyes and hair and am the most Colombian-looking of all of us," Charles said. But in the next breath he clarified that these differences didn't cause much of a commotion in his household. "We never made distinctions about color in my nuclear family," he said. But when pressed he did admit that his mother made no secret about the fact that she did not like Black people, and when Charles would play outside in the summer and get tanned, his mother would make comments. "She'd say, 'You look Black,' in a way that wasn't exactly, 'Oh, look at your tan,' but rather, 'You're getting too dark.'"

On the other hand, Charles said, the difference in color between himself and his sisters couldn't be ignored outside of the house. "That came up quite a bit," he said, explaining how people initially would not believe that the two girls were his sisters. But more intriguing was how being the dark, obviously Latino child influenced Charles's sense of self and racial identity growing up in New York City, compared with his sisters' experience. "They never got the 'Where are you from?' 'Where are your parents from?' questions," Charles said. "They fit right in with our mostly Jewish and Italian neighbors because they didn't look much different than everyone else. I did. I was darker," he said. "I looked the most like an immigrant kid."

Today, Charles said, his relationship with his sisters is a loving one, and yet there are things they have just agreed to disagree on—the main one being race and all things related to race. He jokingly refers to one sister as "The White Lady" because she married a white American man, lives in the suburbs, and doesn't claim her Colombian heritage. She simply calls herself an American. The other sister, while not denying her origins, doesn't proudly raise her Colombian flag either. "[My sisters] don't have to live with [being Colombian] the same way I do," Charles said. He gave me an example of how, post-9/11, he cut his hair short and shaved off his beard because he looked "too ethnic." There are also the continuous questions he gets in his day-to-day life about where he is from. "No one ever accepts that I'm from New York, but when I go to Colombia, I'm not Colombian enough either." Perhaps that is why Charles spent much of his twenties traveling, learning Italian, and figuring out how to blend into any country he finds himself in. "I kind of think of myself as a lone wolf," he said. But at the same time, he has assigned himself the role of cultural teacher in his family. "I'm proud of being Colombian," he said, "and I like to educate my nieces, especially the blond ones, that we're all from Colombia."

From the darkest one in the family to the lightest, it's never easy to be the outlier. My next interview was with a young medical student named Enrique Martinez. A friend of a friend, Enrique is from Mexico but spent his high school and college years with his family in San Diego. Like most people, the first time I met Enrique I was shocked to discover he is Mexican. Why? Because he has milky-white skin and thick, flaming red hair that hangs just below his shoulders. As a journalist, a mother of mixed-race children, and an advocate for otherness, it pains me to acknowledge how deeply ingrained stereotypes are, because even after learning of his heritage, I grappled with reconciling Enrique's physical appearance with his Mexican identity. My vision and my knowledge refused to get in sync. When I discovered that Enrique was an anomaly not only in his culture, but also within his own nuclear family, I knew I wanted to talk to him for this book. Fortunately, he agreed to speak with me.

Enrique was born in Mexico and lived there until he was a young teen. He and his family moved to the United States so he could attend high school in San Diego. Enrique's parents were college professors and wanted their sons—Enrique has a younger brother—to attend school in the United States. And while technically they immigrated, his parents continued to teach in Mexico, crossing the border in reverse every morning.

Enrique came to my office in early March, bundled up the day after a snowstorm, and regaled me with his story of growing up with a mother whom he described as "Mediterranean white" and a brother and a father with brown skin and dark hair. "I am the weird one in the family," Enrique said, in accented English. "I am a little whiter than my mom, but my skin is white like Irish or Scottish white, and I have red, red hair." But he quickly points out, for the first of many times during our conversation, that his facial features are an exact blend of both of his parents.

Enrique told me that within his home, while living in Mexico and later in the United States, color never came up. "I don't know if my parents did that consciously or they just didn't think about it," Enrique said. He recalled one incident where he went on a swimming trip with a group of kids and his mother was there as a chaperone. Despite the fact that Enrique has really pale skin, she neglected to put any sunscreen on her son. "I burned so badly, I had enormous blisters on my shoulders and couldn't put a shirt on for a week," Enrique recalled, laughing as he remembered the pain. "I don't know if my mother didn't know any better or because she consciously didn't want to make the difference between my skin and the other kids' so obvious." Things changed after that. "Whenever we would go to the beach, my mom would say, 'Enrique, did you put on your sunscreen?' I didn't mind, even though my brother would just get to jump out of the car and run to the sea," he said.

As he looked back on his parents' decision not to speak about the dramatic difference in skin color between himself and his brother, Enrique was grateful. "Because we never talked about it, I never had this feeling to hate my skin color," he said. "In our house, my parents always tried to make us feel like it wasn't an issue. Of course, this changed as soon as someone outside the house had to meet me."

Like Christopher James and his experiences with his darker-hued father out in the world, Enrique said the public's reaction to him and his brother was always an issue. "Our skin color was always a shock to people," he said. From his upbringing in both Mexico and the United States, he could recall dozens of times when people couldn't or wouldn't accept that Enrique and his brother were in fact brothers. "There would

be many occasions when my father would introduce us and people
would say, 'Those are your children? No, you're kidding!'" He remembered a time when he wasn't allowed to collect his brother from school
because the teacher didn't believe the two were related. "Siblings that
look alike don't have these problems, but for us there was always this
need to justify that we were brothers," he said. "And that's when my alibi
about facial features started," something he only realized as he was re-
counting these memories. Enrique actually started anticipating people's
questioning of his connection to his family, thus the "alibi." Enrique
explained, "If people didn't believe we were brothers, I'd say, 'No, look
at our facial features. Look at us. We look exactly alike, we're just different colors.'"

Being different colors didn't only challenge outsiders' understanding of Enrique and his brother's relationship, but, much as it did with
Charles Guevara and his sisters, it influenced how they saw themselves
in the world and who they became as adults. From the time Enrique and
his family started crossing the border between Mexico and California to
go to school and visit family, Enrique was treated differently than his
brother and father. Even at a young age he winced when border control
accepted his declaration of US citizenship without hesitation, yet always
detained his brother and father a little longer in their questioning. "This
was when I started to realize that my skin color in the United States was
going to be very important in how people saw me," Enrique said.

Indeed, his skin color was an advantage. "For my brother, who is a
US citizen, his color was a negative," Enrique said. Although Enrique
can only speculate, he believes his brother's response to being perceived
as an immigrant was to distance himself from his culture. "I always felt
my brother was trying to prove something or deny something," Enrique
said, citing the fact that his brother attended a high school in San Diego
that was 97 percent Mexican and yet he managed not to have a single
Mexican friend. "My brother became very Americanized very quick,"
Enrique said. "That's the life he wants."

On the other hand, Enrique has become, like Charles Guevara, the
keeper of the culture. "I am the more politicized guy in the family," he
said proudly. "I keep these stories with me, these stories of crossing the
border and how they would question my brother and not me." For Enrique, being Mexican isn't an assumption the outside world makes about

him; on the contrary, he has to work overtime to prove who he really is. "Every single day I need to prove that I'm Latino or Mexican, whether it's in the Latino community or the American community. Why? Because people see you the way they see you," he said.

When Enrique was younger and people would challenge him about his Mexican heritage, invariably asking if he was from Scotland, Ireland, or Russia (and sometimes even wondering aloud if he was a Viking), he would get angry and frustrated. Today, as a twenty-nine-year-old married man who is contemplating starting a family of his own, he doesn't let other people's ignorance get to him. "Now that I'm older, I have fun with it," he said. "Ever since I moved to Philadelphia, I hang out with more modern youth and they're more sensitive. They don't just assume I'm from Ireland. Instead they ask nice questions like, 'Where are your ancestors from?'" Enrique laughed when he said this, as he realized that despite how annoying and sometimes deeply unsettling it is to be misjudged by the way one looks, his experiences have not really hurt him. "I have been discriminated against," he said. "But most of the time it has been in my favor."

It's interesting to note that having been the lightest and the darkest extremes in their respective families, Charles Guevara and Enrique Martinez both found themselves embracing their heritage as a means of self-preservation. For Charles, in response to the constant assumption that he was an immigrant, he embraced his Colombian heritage once he realized it was not likely he would ever be perceived otherwise. Rather than fight his reality, he embraced it with passion. Enrique, on the other hand, had to fight for recognition of his Mexican identity by both Mexicans and mainstream Americans. Even with his obvious Mexican accent, he cannot pass for what he truly is. He has to fight every day for the right to be seen as he sees himself. Like light-skinned Black Americans who face accusations of not being Black enough to earn their authentically Black membership card, Enrique deals with similar light-skin isolation.

As men, both Charles and Enrique admit that my probing questions were some of the first they had ever answered regarding these issues. Nobody in their professional or private lives had given them the opportunity to open up about their skin color and how it affected their sense of self. Both men also said that in their households, where the differences in siblings' skin colors were so pronounced, the subject had never come up. As a parent I found that mind-boggling, but in the Latino community, it may not be so unusual.

"For Latinos, depending on the group, of course, sometimes people don't want to talk about colorism or color differences because there's a very strong belief that everyone is the same," said sociologist Margaret Hunter when I called her to talk about skin-color politics in the Latino community. A sociology professor at Mills College in Oakland, California, Hunter writes frequently about race and gender issues in the Latino community and is a well-respected expert on Latinos and colorism. She continued, "Talking about color in an overt way feels like you're putting a United States paradigm on a Latin American experience." Hunter also said that some Latinos just don't want to admit that the kind of discrimination that happens in the United States also happens in their native countries and cultures. Not to mention in their homes.

Pretty Brown Girl Isn't Good Enough

Yvonne Latty, fifty-two, is a journalism professor at New York University, an author, and a documentary filmmaker. She grew up with a Dominican mother and a Jamaican father and, like Charles Guevara and Enrique Martinez, was the outlier in the family because of her color.

Despite the fact that Latty works in New York, she calls the City of Brotherly Love home, so it was easy to meet up with her at a café in South Philadelphia. It was officially spring and the weather was cooperating. Blue skies, brilliant sunshine, and temperatures that hinted at summer had brought everyone outside—and then, apparently, into the same café where we'd planned to meet. Latty apologized because, she said, the café was usually quiet, but on this day we had to find a table in the basement because the upstairs space was packed. Despite the dungeon-like ambiance, Latty and I both warmed up as we dissected her upbringing in Spanish Harlem.

"I was the darkest one in the family, followed by my dad," Latty began. Dressed in jeans, a pink and orange floral blouse, and a dark blazer, she began telling me her story, leaning back in her chair, legs crossed. "Then I would say it was a tie between my mother and my sister. My mom probably looks like a typical Latina with olive skin and my older sister was even lighter than her. When we went to the beach, my sister always had to be under the umbrella because she would burn." At this point, Latty paused to let me know that her sister died at age twenty-seven in a car accident.

Growing up, however, Latty, whose skin one would describe as medium brown with warm undertones, said color never really came up in her nuclear family. "My house was a safe place because my sister never made me feel dark. She didn't care," Latty said. She also noted that her parents never played favorites or seemed to favor one child over the other. In fact, Latty believes the color of their children's skin was the least of her parents' worries. "We were poor and in Catholic school. My parents had a lot of pressure on them," she said. For Latty, problems regarding her color really didn't start until she walked out the front door.

"Until I was eight everything felt fine," Latty began. "Then I had this incident at school when the Latino kids called me nigger and said I wasn't Hispanic and that I was adopted because I didn't look like my mom and my sister." That period of bullying went on for years, Latty recalled, and it really left her wounded. "I remember being eight years old and getting ready to get in the bathtub," Latty said. "And I remember thinking that if I scrubbed my skin very hard I would get lighter and look like my mom." Latty admitted to me that she had never told this story to anyone, not even her mother. But she said she thought it would be good to get it all out now and possibly help somebody else who is struggling. Those scrubbing baths continued, and she also prayed for her "real" father, a mythical white man, to come to her elementary school and claim her and tell the kids who she really was under her brown skin. Obviously, that didn't happen either.

Although the overt bullying eventually stopped, the years up to and including her teens were punctuated with incidents where Latty's Latino friends would remind her that her skin color kept her from being good enough, pretty enough, or just *enough*, period. Latty mentioned a Puerto Rican friend whose parents forbade their daughter from hanging out with "someone like her." And then there was another friend in high school, a Cuban girl, who got married at eighteen in a lavish ceremony. "I was her best friend, but I couldn't be in the wedding because her mother said I would ruin the pictures," Latty said, still incredulous after all these years. I was too.

Despite the fact that Latty's mother seemed unaware of her daughter's suffering, or at least didn't counter it head on, Latty gives her mother credit for saving her. "My mother thought I was very beautiful. She thought I was the most beautiful child and she would tell me that all the time," Latty said. "I could feel that she thought I was pretty so that helped me get through it all." Latty said it also helped that she had some Latina friends who, despite the bullying by others, remained her friend. But that didn't stop Latty from being jealous of her sister and desiring her caramel-colored skin, which would allow people to know, at first glance, that she was Latina.

"I never felt 100 percent like I belonged anywhere," Latty said. Too dark to be Latina, and too different to be African American. Today, Latty claims the title Afro-Latina. Ironically, Latty's sister admitted right before her death that she had always wanted darker skin. "She actually told me she wished she had my complexion," Latty said. "She thought I had perfect skin because she was always dealing with burning in the sun, plus she had eczema and allergies and I never had so much as a pimple." Moments like these, plus the gift of time and space away from the Latina community where she was reared, have given Latty the opportunity to make peace with her skin color and her identity. She admitted that at one point she had tried to reject her Latina identity, but it didn't work. "If I denied that I was Latina," Latty said, "then I was denying my mother, and how the hell could I deny her? The longest relationship I've had in my whole life is with my mother." Plus, being a mother herself, Latty realized that it was time to claim her origins.

"I think as an Afro-Latina at this point in time it's important to represent and be proud of who I am. We have to show the world that we're here and they can't sweep us away or call us the uglies. We are a beautiful culture and a beautiful people. Being Black is beautiful."

Latino Media Lighting the Way

All of the experts I interviewed about colorism in the Latino community were only cautiously optimistic about a future free of colorism in this community. And they all pointed to the media as one of the most significant obstacles in the way. "I think the [mainstream] media really misunderstands ethnicity and race," said journalist and author Soledad O'Brien when I asked her if she thought the media was guilty of perpetuating a light-skin stereotype of Latinos. In addition to a lack of knowledge about the history of the slave trade in Latin America, as well as a lack of Latino representation in American newsrooms, the media, in O'Brien's view, just hasn't tried very hard to put forth an accurate depiction of the diversity of Latinos in America. "Media-wise, we've done a poor job in how we think about Latinos," she said, adding, "In America, Latino is often code for Mexican." And for people like O'Brien, who claims an Afro-Latino identity, this always causes problems. "You're constantly fielding the 'but you're not really Latino' accusation because you don't match the picture in somebody's head, and that picture is a media creation," she explained.

"The mainstream media images in the United States reflect the value of whiteness," agreed Margaret Hunter when reflecting on Latinos visible on the big and small screen. "Look at the *telenovelas*," she offered as an example. "They are all about very white-looking Latinos, and maybe there's a maid and her family who are darker." Hunter said that not only are these media representations very limiting in their portrayal of Latino identity, but they are also making connections between color and class, given that dark-skinned Latinos are usually relegated to portraying subservient roles such as maids, gardeners, and sometimes criminals on these programs.

Hunter's assessment reminded me of a skin-color situation that the Walt Disney Company found itself embroiled in when it announced the arrival of its first Latina princess. In 2012, a Disney executive stated in an interview with *Entertainment Weekly* magazine that their newest princess character, Sofia the First, was Latina. News spread fast, but when folks saw pictures of the new cartoon character, they were none too pleased with her light skin, light-brown hair, and bright blue eyes. For all intents and purposes, Sofia the First looked like Cinderella's little sister. Most of the disgruntled women who complained publicly about Sofia's Anglo characteristics admitted that Latinas come in all shades and colors, but, considering the lack of representation of brown-skinned Latinas for young children, Disney could have done better. Said one Latina blogger, "She doesn't look like the majority of Latinas in the world. This was a great opportunity for Disney. . . . Instead they dropped the ball." In response, Disney cleared up the situation by backtracking on Sofia's Latin roots, instead leaving her origins up to our collective imagination. "What's important to know is that Sofia is a fairytale girl who lives in a fairytale world," said Nancy Kanter, general manager of

Disney Junior Worldwide, in a statement on the Sofia the First Facebook page. The irony here is that the fake "fairytale world" Sofia's parents are from is based on Spain and Scandinavia, which wouldn't make Sofia a Latina anyway. It would simply make her European.

Yvonne Latty, who researches media trends in her work, agreed that the ubiquitous portrayal of a light-skin Latino aesthetic in mainstream media in the United States is bad, but it's even worse on Latino television stations in the United States. "You put on Univision or Telemundo and every face is white," she said. "And that simply reinforces the idea that Afro-Latinos have no place in this culture and that we're not good enough." Latty's comments are supported by a quick Internet search: dozens of articles come up blasting Latino media stations here in the United States for whitewashing the Latino experience. One angry comment that struck me referred to Univision alternately as "Blancovision" or "Uniblanco."

As an example of the whitewashing she frequently sees, Latty sent me a music video by the Spanish pop singer Enrique Iglesias for his 2014 hit "Bailando." The American version features a posse of Afro-Latino dancers with big Afros and brown skin dancing around Iglesias. But in the version cut for the Latin American audience, all of those brown girls with the Afro hair had disappeared. Erased. Whitewashed out of existence.

This example brings us back to where this chapter started, with the Latino media and racism. When Univision host Rodner Figueroa made his tasteless remark about the First Lady, both the Latino and mainstream American media used the incident as an opportunity to examine race relations in Latino America. One New York City–based radio station hosted a program a week after the incident, inviting three Latina women representing three different cultures, to try to get at the root of the problem. I found it ironic that the show opened with the host exclaiming, "We have a deep dark secret in the Latino community. We're racist." After doing the research for this chapter, it doesn't seem to me that the racism in the Latino community is a secret as much as it is a taboo topic that is repeatedly denied and cleverly masked with language and selective historical amnesia. What's more, because "Latino" isn't a race but a geographical marker, the racism in the Latino community is actually based more on color than on race. And unlike the Black American community, which seems to be coming out of the closet with its colorist hang-ups—on social media, during conferences, via celebrity spokespeople—the Latino community isn't riding the same wave of enthusiasm. That is to say, discussions about color are happening, but not with the same level of urgency as we see in the Black community. "Current practices of denial, coupled with the legacy of our collective history, make it difficult for Latino/as to engage in [the] honest and self-critical dialogue regarding colorism needed to subvert this entrenched legacy," write Chavez-Dueñas, Adames, and Organista. Perhaps the Univision fiasco and other recent incidents will help jump-start the conversation.

Knowledge Is (Black) Power

I asked Christina Sue why she thought there seemed to be such a universal rejection of Black identity in the Latino community, and she had some interesting answers based on her research. "It's a mixture of explanations," Sue said, beginning with plain old racism. "The simple answer is that Blackness is stigmatized." But she also pointed to some key differences between the United States, where Black culture and history are celebrated and championed by Black Americans, and a country like Mexico, where the opposite is true. "If you go back in history there were active attempts by the Mexican government to erase [the African experience in Mexico]," Sue said, noting that in Mexican history books, "there's only a paragraph or two about slavery in Mexico." And Mexico isn't the only country guilty of whitewashing its history. "Concealment strategies were systematically used by white elites to provide misinformation to Latino/as relative to persons of indigenous and Afro-ancestry," wrote Chavez-Dueñas, Adames and Organista. These "concealment strategies" the authors refer to include the "omission of racist practices" from historical texts, normalizing racism and discrimination as natural phenomena, and justifying the violent behavior of the Spanish colonists toward the indigenous people and Afro-descendants as self-defense. In other words, not only is Blackness stigmatized, but there really is a dearth of facts and an abundance of false information about the Black experience in Latin America. "You need communities to keep that history alive and harp on the knowledge and have a strong sense of pride for one's ancestors," Sue said. So, if ignorance and racism are the reasons many Latinos shun their Blackness, then the solution to the color problem is knowledge and activism. Thankfully, in some ways that is already happening. In December 2015, for the first time, the Mexican government added an "Afro" category to the national census, formally recognizing the 1.38 million people in Mexico who claim African heritage. Clearly this is a step in the right direction toward acknowledging that Mexico is a country with Black citizens. Hopefully, with acknowledgement will come respect and representation.

Of all of the experts I spoke to, Dash Harris had the most optimistic outlook on where the Latino community was heading when it came to dealing with their perception of and appreciation of dark skin. Having seen burgeoning Afro-Latino pride movements led by youth in such countries as Cuba, Colombia, and Brazil, Harris sees possibilities for change. Closer to home—underscored by a reggaeton beat and led by the likes of musicians such as Tego Calderón—an Afro-Latino pride movement has been gaining ground in Puerto Rico and spilling into Puerto Rican communities in the United States.

Whether we are talking about Latinos in their home countries or here in the United States, Harris firmly believes that the change has to begin in the home. "Parents have to learn and unlearn the truth and then of course pass it along [to their kids]," she said. For her part, Margaret Hunter said she is "cautiously optimistic" about colorism decreasing in the Latino community. She credited the recent backlash toward Latino immigrants as a politicizing moment for a new generation of Latino youth, whom she believes are better prepared than their elders to combat both racism and colorism within the community. Citing youth activism, and a few media portrayals of more diverse Latino characters, Hunter said, "That's where my cautious optimism comes from, but it is cautious." But looking at the real numbers that show there is still a lot of inequality between light- and dark-skinned Latinos, Hunter said there is still a long way to go. "There is still a lot of inequality and I don't want people to overlook that just because J-Lo was on *American Idol*," she said.

Black Like Me

A month had passed since the whole Rodner Figueroa incident. Now another Latino man was making headlines, again because of a racially charged incident. This time it was the death of an unarmed African

American man in South Carolina. The man, Walter Scott, had been pulled over by the police for an alleged broken taillight in his car. What happened next was unclear, but initial reports from the police suggested the officer, acting in self-defense, shot and killed Scott. But then, seemingly out of nowhere, a video surfaced that showed what had really happened. And what had really happened was this: for some reason, Scott ran from the police officer, and in response the officer shot him in the back and then lied to cover up what he'd done. If it weren't for the video footage, Scott's death would have been just another police-justified killing. Instead, the officer was charged with homicide and Scott's death sparked outrage and resulted in the memorial he deserved.

But where did the video come from? Who recorded the video that changed the narrative for yet another Black man killed by the police? Who was the man who brought justice to this man's grieving family? The reluctant hero's name was Feidin Santana. A Dominican immigrant who admitted that he hadn't come forward right away because he feared retribution from the police, Santana eventually shared his video footage because he felt a sense of obligation and, he said, it wasn't right how Scott's case was being presented.

Santana worked as a barber and had kept a low profile before any of this happened, but he accepted his fleeting celebrity with grace, appearing on a slew of news programs to defend his actions. Sometimes he spoke with an interpreter, sometimes he figured out how to say in English what he needed to say. As a sign of the times, it didn't take long for a Feidin Santana Facebook fan page to appear. Santana didn't create it, but he took the time to post his thoughts on the page. He wrote, "We all equal, we all human, let's love each other and stop all this killings in our world."

Maybe Santana saw Walter Scott and realized it could have been him lying dead on the ground, with the rest of the world assuming the worst about him because of the color of his skin. In Scott, he didn't see someone beneath him. He saw someone who looked just like him. And that, my friends, is progress.

Sidebar: The Curious Case of Sammy Sosa

Samuel Kelvin Peralta Sosa was born poor and dark in the city of San Pedro de Macorís in the island nation known as the Dominican Republic. An unfortunate abundance of melanin and a lack of wealth, not to mention the early death of his father, had left the young Sosa facing a bleak future. Luckily for him, San Pedro de Macorís is a city known not only for its impressive history as a major sugar producer but also for producing baseball champions. And that's where Sammy Sosa, the famous Major League Baseball star, got his start.

By the time he was twelve years old, young Sammy was already attracting the attention of professional scouts. He arrived in the United States at age sixteen to play in the minor leagues, and he joined the major leagues three years later, playing for the Chicago White Sox. Ultimately he would play for a handful of different teams during his eighteen-year professional career, but the majority of those years were spent playing for the Chicago Cubs. As a Cub, Sosa led his team in hits and home runs and won the Most Valuable Player award in the National League more than once. Sosa's power, speed, and strength made him a popular player to watch and root for.

But it wasn't all peanuts and Cracker Jacks for Slammin' Sammy. His career was marked by controversy, from accusations that he used nonregulation baseball bats to persistent rumors that he boosted his strength with steroids. Through it all, Sosa proclaimed his innocence (even though it was discovered that he had failed a test for performance-enhancing drugs in 2003) and continued to play the game he loved. In June 2009, after a slow decline in performance, Sosa officially announced his retirement from baseball. Many assumed he would be inducted into the Baseball Hall of Fame based on his remarkable and record-breaking career, but because of the cloud of doubt around his alleged steroid use, that induction has yet to happen.

And while 2009 should have been the year that Sosa drifted off into the sunset, accepting his status as a has-been, he had one more game to play. In November 2009 he captured the public's attention again, but this time it had nothing to do with sports. In a bizarre form of alchemy, Sosa transformed himself from Black to white-ish. Appearing for the first time in public since announcing his retirement, Sosa and his wife, Sonia, were photographed on the red carpet at the Latin Grammy Awards. But Sosa was almost unrecognizable. His brown skin was now ghostly white, his brown eyes were now green, and his formerly kinky, curly hair now lay down straight upon his head in a slicked-back sheen.

Some people speculated that the former athlete was ill, while others believed these eerie physical changes were side effects of those steroids he might have been using. What everyone could agree on was that he looked dramatically different. With before-and-after pictures splashed all over the Internet, Sosa could not avoid the issue—although he tried, saying at first that his new, lightened skin was simply a side effect of a "skin rejuvenation" procedure. Faster than one can say little white lie, most people of color cried foul, claiming Sosa was just the latest celebrity to bleach his skin.

One week later, Sosa finally admitted that bleaching cream was to blame (or thank) for his new skin tone. He sat down for an interview on the Spanish-language show *Primer Impacto* and explained what he'd been using. "It's a bleaching cream that I apply before going to bed and [it] whitens my skin some." But he assured the interviewer that bleaching himself in no way implies self-hatred. "I'm not a racist," he said, smiling. "I live my life happily." Of course, one has to wonder what else Sosa would say, considering the man interviewing him was also Black, or "mulatto," as the journalist later referred to himself at the end of the Sosa segment. In fact, Sosa offered to give the interviewer some of his special cream if the reporter wanted to come on over to the light side. He didn't.

Given the context of anti-Black sentiment among much of the Dominican population, it makes sense that Sosa might be crippled with self-hatred because of his brown skin, which appeared even darker over the years from playing baseball for hours in the sun. It also makes sense that he would deny being racist, because most people never freely admit to that. Still, it is impossible not to speculate based on Sosa's choice to risk his health and his personal reputation—not only by bleaching his skin, but also by straightening his hair and wearing light-colored contacts—that he has issues with his Blackness. There is a saying in many Latin American societies that "money whitens"; in other words, the richer you are, the less noticeable your dark skin becomes. In Sosa's case, it looks like he took that adage literally, using his money to buy the best skin-lightening cream on the market.

From an unofficial examination of the public response to Sosa's whitening, it appears that white Americans were shocked by Sosa's transformation because they had no idea that anyone besides Michael Jackson—who was afflicted with a skin disease—could actually change from Black to white. But apart from their initial shock, white Americans seemed to care very little about the motivations behind Sosa's new look. One Chicago reporter compared Sosa's whitening treatments to women getting Botox and couldn't figure out what all the fuss was about. Black Americans, on the other hand, saw Sosa's erasure of melanin as a sure sign of self-hatred and they called him out on it. In comparison, Latinos were far more understanding. In a poll conducted by Univision in 2009, right after "Sosa Lite" debuted, 55 percent of viewers disapproved of Sosa's actions, but 45 percent approved. What's more, for every online comment I noticed crying foul over Sosa's skin transformation, there were two more requesting specifics on the cream Sosa used so they could try it themselves.

And that's probably the real genius behind this whole incident. Spurned on by Sosa himself, who admitted in a television interview that he was going to start selling his special "European" cream, rumors still persist—based on the fact that Sosa never went back to being Black—that Sosa's post-baseball career will include selling his own brand of bleaching cream. If that is in his plans, then his radical new look is a home run for advertising the product.

THREE

FAIR ENOUGH
Asian Americans and Color

White skin covers the seven flaws.
—Japanese proverb

The empress Wu Zetian holds the remarkable position in Chinese history as the country's only female emperor. Ruling from behind the scenes at first, as the favored concubine of the emperor Taizong, Wu Zetian eventually ascended the throne herself and ruled over China's vast empire from AD 690 to 705. Immortalized in the history books for being ruthless enough to murder her own infant daughter in order to capture the throne, but also for being a champion of women's rights, Wu Zetian's image is nothing if not controversial and confusing. Some historians want to classify her as a hero, others as a whore, but all can agree upon her legendary beauty, described by one poet as "so great that it overshines the moon." And what made Wu Zetian's beauty so remarkable? Why, her stunningly pale skin, of course.

Today, the average Chinese woman may not know what Wu Zetian did for China's agricultural system or how she worked to expand the rights of the peasant class, but she probably does know how the empress managed to keep her skin so white and youthful looking. Recipes abound for Wu Zetian's beauty potions and regimens. One reads, "Grind peach blossoms that have dried in the shade into powder and mix into a paste with the blood of a black chicken. The mask nourishes and whitens the skin and stimulates the metabolism." Other enterprising Internet marketers simply promise that *their* pearl creams for light skin use the exact same recipe that Wu Zetian used—and surprisingly, people buy it, as the pursuit of pale skin in China is as legendary as Wu Zetian.

And China isn't alone.

Even though Asia is an enormous continent with extremely diverse citizens, some commonalities are shared by many of the four billion–plus people who trace their heritage to that region of the world, particularly when it comes to notions of beauty and skin-color politics. As we travel back in history to examine the origins of the light-skin preference that is ubiquitous in many parts of Asia, I will focus on the Asian cultures most heavily represented and most influential in the United States—specifically, Chinese, Filipino, Indian, Korean, and Japanese cultures.

Contrary to what many might assume, in both East and South Asia, the adoration of light skin predates any contact with white Europeans. Moreover, desiring pale skin, even in today's global society, does not necessarily indicate a desire to be European. In fact, in a 2008 article—"Skin Lightening and Beauty in Four Asian Cultures"—the authors clarify that paleness and whiteness, while related, are not necessarily the same thing. Moreover, by tracing the desire for pale skin to before European contact, they assert that Asian people were not so victimized by their colonizers as to alter their own perceptions of beauty. Be that as it may, it would be impossible to suggest that Asians and Asian Americans today are indifferent to Western beauty ideals. And just as is the case in Black and Latino families, these beauty ideals are most often learned in the home. But let's not get ahead of ourselves.

Wealth and Whiteness

In ancient China, Japan, and Korea, pale skin—besides being a prerequisite for beauty—was an indicator of elevated economic status for both men and women. In other words, dark skin was the marker of the peasant class, whose work kept them outdoors toiling under a hot sun. Not only that, but dark skin was universally associated with, or, rather, became the physical embodiment of, all of the negative characteristics of an underclass: ignorant, dirty, poor, simple, uncivilized. In contrast, pale, pearly-white skin became the irrefutable badge of the intelligent, wealthy, pure, and civilized. It stood as proof that one was rich enough to remain indoors all day long.

For each country, the arrival points are slightly different as to exactly how and when pale skin became an established beauty norm and something for women to strive for. In Japan, historians date the trend to

AD 749, in the Heian era, when a noblewoman was restricted to staying indoors, at all times. Not only were these women not allowed to go outside, but the insides of their homes were quite dark. Some historians have even suggested that due to the low light levels indoors, women would heavily powder their faces to make themselves more visible to their husbands. As time passed, this need for heavy white makeup diminished, but the desire for pale skin remained. Later, in the seventeenth century, women started whitening their faces again as a symbol of beauty, in the style we now associate with geishas. To be beautiful, a geisha had to be pure white—and not just on her face, but all over her body. It has been said that a geisha's true beauty was actually determined by how pale and soft the skin was on her face and on the back of her neck. Of course, a Japanese woman didn't have to be a geisha in order to mimic the trends established by these world-renowned beauties. From the seventeenth century on, Japanese women knew that beauty implied having skin like "pounded rice" and would do anything to maintain it, from carrying umbrellas when out in the summer sun to dabbing nightingale excrement on the face because of its reported ability to whiten the skin. (Note: There are cosmetics today that still list bird poop as an ingredient for skin-lightening purposes.)

In China, the praise of "white jade skin" is evident in the earliest writings; a reference to the use of rice powder and crushed pearls to whiten the skin dates back to 1500 BC. According to *Racisms* author Francisco Bethencourt, the ancient Chinese also equated Black skin with uncivilized barbarians and all variations of dark skin were perceived as ugly and dirty. By the late nineteenth century, China had developed its own hierarchy of the world's people based primarily on skin color. The four main races, in order of dominance, were yellow (Asia), white (Europe), brown (South America), and Black (Africa), and a fifth race, the red race, represented Native Americans. As Darwin's theories of natural selection swept the globe, the Chinese were confident that the inferior, darker races would eventually be eliminated from the earth.

In Korea, a country whose national identity is deeply tied to Confucianism, pale skin for women was deemed a moral imperative from the beginning of the nation's history. "In Korea, flawless skin like white jade and an absence of freckles and scars have been preferred since the first dynasty in Korean history (the *Gojoseon Era*, 2333–108 BCE)," note the authors of the "Skin Lightening and Beauty in Four Asian Cultures" study. And while paleness was indeed associated with beauty in Korea, pale skin also indicated that a woman was doing her duty by staying indoors, studying her Confucian texts, and being a good mother and wife. So, for a woman, pale skin also became synonymous with purity and fine moral character.

This left no real options for the Korean woman who had to work outdoors. Not only did her darker skin brand her as a member of the lower class, but women with dark skin were also viewed as loose and promiscuous because, clearly, their dark skin was proof that they spent too much time frolicking in the streets instead of attending to their pious duties indoors. On the other hand, a man in Korea who had to work for a living and therefore might have darker skin was judged less harshly, since working to support a family was a prescribed duty for a Korean man. In other words, a darker-skinned man may have been of the lower class, but that didn't mean he was also morally bankrupt. Yet for a woman, the rules were clear and fixed: she was either pale and pure or dark and degenerate.

Colonial Influence in the Philippines and India

The Philippines offers a different historical narrative when it comes to skin-color politics because Spain colonized the Philippines and remained in power for more than three hundred years. The Spanish ruled this Pacific island nation from the mid-sixteenth century until the Spanish-American War, in 1898. Like her Latin American cousins, the Philippines contains a mixture of Spanish and indigenous populations—there are over 150 different native ethnic groups in the Philippines—as well as a significant Chinese population. Sprinkle into the mix other European groups who immigrated in the nineteenth century and you have the recipe for an incredibly diverse population. Still, the Filipino people are classified as Asian and, like most of their fellow Asians, prioritize light skin. But their skin-color politics are truly a blend of East and West.

Much as in Latin America, the Filipino penchant for pale skin is a response to seeing a power structure dominated first by white colonizers and then by the mixed-race people—the mestizos—with the lightest skin. "It may not be that Filipinos who yearned for lighter skin were wishing to be White," write Joanne Rondilla and Paul Spickard in their book *Is Lighter Better? Skin-Tone Discrimination Among Asian Americans,* "but certainly they were wishing to look like members of the Filipino upper class, who were mestizo." Rondilla and Spickard note that, since the nineteenth century, in the Philippines, mestizoness has been associated with those in power. Couple this obvious light-skin power structure with both a geographical proximity to mainland Asia and a significant Chinese population in the country, and it would be expected that a belief system in which light skin signifies beauty and class would also be in play. Sadly, this light-skin hierarchy was only exacerbated by the invasion and eventual takeover by the Americans after the war of 1898. The Americans brought with them not only a military presence but also the practices of segregation based on race and color, favoring the light and white over the darker-hued citizens of the Philippines.

Finally, we come to India. The preference for light skin in India is legendary. But as in most other Asian countries, with the exception of the Philippines, the distinction between light and dark in India goes far back, before eighteenth-century British colonization.

Scholars who have examined early Hindu texts have found mentions of skin-color differences and apparent conflict between the light skinned and the darker hued. But in reality, the conflict between the light-skinned Northern Indians (Aryans) and the darker-hued Southern Indians (Dravidians) was more of a turf war between North and South than one between dark and light. What's more, there are Hindu gods and goddesses with dark skin who have long been considered both beautiful and benevolent, crushing the theory that in India dark skin has always been associated with negative characteristics or inherent evil.

On the other hand, long before white Europeans arrived in India, a social hierarchy of castes was already in place, and that caste system seemed to relegate the darkest-hued Indians to the lowest level—the so-called untouchables. Still, it is a highly contested issue whether or not the caste system was *based on* skin color. Radhika Parameswaran is a professor at Indiana University's Media School, in Bloomington. A specialist in race, ethnicity, and caste in South Asia, Parameswaran confirmed that not only is this question about caste and color debated continuously; it is also a question with no true answer. "Unraveling the caste system and its associations with color is a thicket and a maze that no one can enter," she told me. Even though it is generally believed that upper-caste people have light skin and those in lower castes have darker skin, Parameswaran uses herself as an example that defies such a rigid binary system. "I'm from the South, but I'm dark skinned and upper caste," she said. "I betray the system." But the assumption about the correlation between caste and color is so ingrained in the people of India that in the end, Parameswaran admitted, perception will trump reality. "There's a perception that light skin means upper caste and that upper caste means you're better, so a lower-caste person with light skin could pass for upper caste and get those benefits," she explained. On the other hand, while growing up in India, she recalled, her extended family members were always concerned that she'd never find a man "from the community" to marry because she was too dark. Her upper-caste status could not erase her dark skin.

When the British arrived and colonized India in the mid-eighteenth century, they naturally gravitated to those Indians with lighter skin and European features, assuming their lighter skin meant they were closer to their own kind of people. Not only that, but the British took advantage of the caste system, making it a government-sanctioned method of organizing—and discriminating against—the Indian people. Projecting their own racist and colorist thinking onto the Indian population—one method the British used to distinguish between Aryan and Dravidian Indians was to measure the width of their noses—the British simply reinforced the idea that light-skinned Indians were more civilized and intelligent by bestowing more power and privilege on those in the upper castes who looked more European. Under colonial rule, light-skinned Indians were tapped for positions in the government and leadership roles in industry and education. Darker-skinned Indians were left with menial jobs and tasked with serving their new masters. So, whether or not a belief system that favored light skin over dark was already in place before colonization, the British took a giant step in institutionalizing colorism, leaving a lasting legacy of disregard of and discrimination against those with dark skin.

In short, to conclude that Asian cultures appreciate pale skin seems like a safe generalization to make. That being said, however, it should be noted that, historically, Asian people had many other criteria by which to assess a person's social status and all-around worthiness beyond skin color. To assume that all social stratification was based primarily on skin color would be to examine Asia though a Western lens, which besides being culturally insensitive, would also be inaccurate. In many Asian cultures, one's family bloodlines or religion would be far more relevant than one's skin color in determining how a person would be treated. In Japan, for example, while pale skin was almost universally prized, a person's ancestral origins were far more critical in predicting success in society. Indeed, one of the most historically discriminated against groups in Japan are the Burakumin. Their scarlet letter derives not from any physical characteristic but rather their theoretically impure blood, stemming from a history—approximately since the early seventeenth century—of working in trades associated with death, like butchering and undertaking. Because any profession associated with death is considered unclean in a country heavily influenced by Buddhism and Shintoism, the Burakumin could never escape the perception that they were dirty and low class, which left them ritually shunned and living on the margins of society even into modern times.

Survival of the Lightest

Skin color, or "race," is hardly the only—or even the most significant—trump card when discussing who gets relegated to the lowest levels of society in Asian cultures. At the end of the day, yes, skin color has always been important in Asia, but it certainly wasn't the sole factor in determining a person's dignity and worth. But then the West came calling.

The idea of separating mankind into distinct species or different races was a preoccupation of nineteenth-century Americans and Europeans. Both the scientific community and greedy governments across the European continent and in the United States were desperate to justify their quests to colonize new lands, enslave other people, and export their cultures all over the world. Discovering irrefutable proof that the white race was superior to all other races was the main goal, as it would make their continuous invasions into the so-called third world appear not only reasonable but inevitable.

Surprisingly, the European insistence that the white race was superior did not meet with great resistance in Asia. Instead, these new race theories were accepted by many Asian power brokers as modern and progressive ideas that could be utilized for their own gain. "The Japanese missions to the United States and Europe in 1860 and 1871–73 absorbed racial constructs concerning not only other peoples of the world but also internal minorities in the Western world," writes Bethencourt. In both China and Japan, the idea that the lighter races were more civilized and advanced provided both countries with the justification to discriminate against and invade Asian countries with darker populations, whom they declared to be barbaric and uncivilized. "Historically, much of Japan's imperial aggression in other parts of Asia rested on a discourse of racial superiority," said Fabienne Darling-Wolf, a professor at Temple University who has spent the past twenty years exploring Japanese culture, particularly as it relates to race and gender. In other words, these new race theories—now discredited as scientific racism—provided any nation with lighter-skin populations a scientific justification to abuse those nations with darker-hued citizens. Think of it as light-skin imperialism over the dark-skinned world. Light-skinned Asians were just as likely as their Western counterparts to support and propagate these pseudoscientific excuses for oppressing the darker "other."

Arriving in America

The first group of Japanese immigrants arrived in the United States on May 7, 1843. The first group of Chinese immigrants arrived a few years later, in 1849. Both groups were instrumental in building the transcontinental railroad. Unfortunately, upon the arrival of these immigrants, the US government had little idea how either the Chinese or the Japanese fit into the Black/white binary of racial organization. Just a glance at the US census categories appropriate for Asian Americans over the years demonstrates the government's confusion in determining where Asians fit in the racial order. "Racial classification was even more vexed with respect to Asian immigrants, who began arriving on the west coast just prior to the Civil War," wrote Harvard scholars Jennifer L. Hochschild and Brenna M. Powell in their article "Racial Reorganization and the United States Census 1850–1930: Mulattoes, Half-Breeds, Mixed Parentage, Hindoos, and the Mexican Race." The authors noted, "The census reflected the nation's perplexity and anxiety about this population, and provided the categories according to which the government eventually resolved it." Hochschild and Powell pointed out that the confusion about how to classify Asian Americans had less to do with their ethnic and geographical origins and more with how much privilege to bestow upon them. "For Asians, the crucial issue was not racial mixture," Hochschild and Powell wrote, "but rather the deeper question of what a race actually is and who would be allowed to join the insiders of American society rather than being excluded." Interestingly, for the 1890 census it was determined, amid much debate, that Chinese and Japanese were not of the same Asian race, because it was popularly believed—with some scientific racism to back it up—that the Chinese were inferior to the Japanese. Citing an 1877 government report on the issue, Hochschild and Powell noted that while the Chinese were described as an "indigestible mass in the community," the Japanese were favorably viewed as "Christian, democratic, cultivated, honest, intelligent . . . like the Frenchmen of the East," But neither the Japanese nor the Chinese, nor the other Asians who immigrated to the United States in the late nineteenth and early twentieth centuries, ever achieved the official government designation that would permit them into the upper echelons of white society. "Both [the Chinese and Japanese] remained unambiguously non-white and non-American," wrote Hochschild and Powell. "Thus both remained legally on the margins of American society, excluded from the mainstream by laws prohibiting naturalization, interracial marriage, certain forms of property ownership, and inheritance." But that didn't stop many Asian Americas from continuing to strive toward whiteness and all that whiteness entailed.

There are two well-known cases where Asian American men petitioned the US government to officially recognize them as white so that they could apply to be citizens and reap the benefits that came with such status. The first man was Takao Ozawa, a Japanese immigrant with light skin who had lived in the United States for twenty years. In 1915 he applied to become a naturalized citizen, but the law—written in 1790—said that option was available only to "free white persons." The Supreme Court denied Ozawa's request to naturalize on the grounds that Japanese people were not racially white, even if their skin color fell into that category. Supreme Court Justice George Sutherland wrote in his 1922 decision that "free white persons" referred to a person of what is popularly known as the Caucasian race. Apparently, "Frenchman of the East" wasn't good enough to qualify as an American in the West.

Less than one year later, an Indian man by the name of Bhagat Singh Thind embarked on his own quest for naturalization based on the fact

that light-skinned Northern Indians like himself are members of the
Caucasian, or Aryan, race. And since Justice Sutherland's denial of Ozawa's petition had been based on the fact that Ozawa was not a Caucasian, Thind figured he had a much better case to make. But he had no
such luck. Thind's petition was also denied and again it was Supreme
Court Justice Sutherland who explained the decision. Sutherland wrote
in his closing opinion,

> The immigration of that day [late eighteenth century] was al-
> most exclusively from the British Isles and Northwestern Eu-
> rope, whence they and their forebears had come. When they
> extended the privilege of American citizenship to "any alien, be-
> ing a free white person," it was these immigrants—bone of their
> bone and flesh of their flesh—and their kind whom they must
> have had affirmatively in mind. . . . It may be true that the blond
> Scandinavian and the brown Hindu have a common ancestor in
> the dim reaches of antiquity, but the average man knows per-
> fectly well that there are unmistakable and profound differences
> between them to-day.

In other words, Chief Justice Sutherland was saying that there was
not a single white man in America who would ever consider an Indian
person white, scientific evidence be damned. It was true that whiteness
was often defined as the literal color of one's skin. (Before Bhagat
Thind's petition, and in lower courts, a handful of Indian men had actually won the chance to naturalize based on their Aryan ancestry and
having skin so pale that their blue veins could be seen. Sadly, those cases
were overturned after Thind's loss in the Supreme Court.) However,
the Asian desire to be recognized as white was more than skin deep. Being accepted as white meant access to resources, respect, and better
schools (Asian kids weren't allowed in white schools in the Jim Crow
South). And sometimes it was about love.

In 1926, to bypass anti-miscegenation laws and to gain the approval
of his white girlfriend, Mildred, a Japanese American named Shima Kito
underwent eyelid surgery, a nose job, and a surgery to tighten his lower
lip. He was determined to literally turn himself into a white man. He
even reportedly changed his name to William White in order to make

his transformation complete. Kito's determination to rid himself of his Asian heritage was so exceptional the *New York Times* covered the story, under this headline: "Changes Racial Features: Young Japanese Wins American Bride by Resort to Plastic Surgery."

Since 1965, when Congress reversed the restrictions on Asian immigration, Asians have grown to be the second-largest immigrant group in the United States. And in that time, the native-born preference and appreciation of lightness has seamlessly merged with American racism and white-privilege politics, so that now the Asian American preference for pale skin may have little to do with distinctions of class and status in one's native land, and instead it may signify a closer relationship to those in power in the United States. Or perhaps it is simply the easiest way for Asians to widen the distance of association between themselves and other ethnic groups, like Blacks and Latinos. Maybe it's a combination of all three things. Rondilla and Spickard wrote in *Is Lighter Better?*, "The desire for light skin among [Asian American] women is a double-edged sword because, on the one hand, light skin is seen as beautiful in their native country. At the same time, when they come to the United States, the image of a typical American is usually of one who is White."

Kim Chanbonpin is a law professor at the University of Chicago. A Filipina American who was raised in a small suburb of Los Angeles, Chanbonpin has a personal interest in how colorism and the law intersect in the Asian American community. In particular, she is interested in charting the trend of Asian Americans becoming honorary whites, much like the Jews and Irish shifted from ethnic to white in the early twentieth century. It's a trend she finds troubling. "This movement toward an honorary white status is based on, at its heart, anti-Black racism," she said. "And in order for Asians to move up the skin-color hierarchy, they must step on the shoulders of Blacks and then not pull them up, but crush them heel to head."

Cracking the Asian Community

At a cocktail party in Manhattan, I found myself chatting with two Korean American women, both in their late twenties. As is often the case at cocktail parties with creative people, the subject of work came up. In general, I never brought up the subject of this book in social situations because explaining skin-color politics in mixed company isn't always a rewarding experience. Also, it's not something you can talk about in quick sound bites while sipping a fizzy drink and nibbling on tapas.

Still, I knew I would be searching for Asian subjects to interview in the near future, and these two Korean American women had distinct skin tones—one was light and one was dark—so I hoped they'd immediately "get" what I was talking about and offer to help me in any way they could. But that's not what happened.

Before I could even finish the explanation of what I was trying to do with the book, one of the women interrupted me to clarify. "Wait, when you say you're talking to Asians about skin-color differences, you mean South Asians, right? Because Chinese, Korean, and Japanese people don't really have skin-color differences." I looked at this woman, let's call her Kristi, and tried to discern if maybe she was literally color-blind, because her friend sitting right next to her was at least three shades darker than she was. We'll call the friend Sara.

"I don't mean to state the obvious, but you two are both Korean and you're totally different colors," I said cautiously, hoping I wasn't saying anything that would cause unease. But Kristi waved away my observation. "Yeah, but she just got back from Mexico." Sara didn't dispute this, she only laughed nervously.

I didn't want to get into a "how dark are you?" discussion with two women I just met, but it seemed clear to me that even under her tan, Sara was never going to be as white as Kristi, whose pale skin was practically translucent. I tried to point out again, gently, that indeed there was a color difference between the two women, but Kristi refused to acknowledge it, claiming that Sara was just tanned. But Sara prodded me to continue talking about the book.

I explained how I hoped to get people to open up about how color politics played out in their families and how that then impacted their family dynamics. Although Sara seemed interested in what I was saying, I found myself trying to convince Kristi that my work had merit. She looked completely unconvinced. Finally she just stopped me and asked with an air of annoyance in her voice, "Do you at least have a sociology background or something?" As if I needed some sort of credentials in order to bring up such a taboo topic. "Nope, I'm just a journalist," I said with a sigh. Clearly not the right answer. Kristi turned away from me then and started chatting up the guy on the other side of her at the bar. I was dismissed.

Sara and I kept talking. I mentioned that later on I hoped to create a video to accompany the book, and I would feature people from different ethnic groups talking about skin-color politics. "Oh, I'd love to do that," Sara said, who admitted she was an aspiring actress. "Unless you think I'm too dark." She laughed right after she said that, but it was an awkward laugh, for an awkward joke. I laughed with her and took the business card she held out to me, promising I'd call if and when the video came to fruition. But I couldn't get that last statement out of my head: "unless you think I'm too dark." Why did she say that unless she'd heard it before? Did she think she was too dark? Who jokes about being too dark besides people who've grown up deflecting such criticism? And Kristi seemed so oblivious to Sara's situation, so dismissive of the possibility that color mattered in her community. Or maybe she was defensive because she knew it was an issue and didn't want me digging through her culture's dirty laundry. Either way, I left that party knowing there were stories in the Asian American community to be told, but I was worried about how I was going to convince anyone to tell them to me.

The Beauty Myth

Meeting Kristi was the perfect portent of what was to come when I approached the Asian Americans in my network. I kept getting rejected when I asked them if they'd like to be interviewed for a book about colorism. Either they found nothing to share when they searched their family memories or they were defensive, bordering on offended, when I broached the subject of colorism in their family and community. I realized pretty quickly that using the term "colorism" automatically set many Asian Americans on edge, much as it had in the Latino community, because generally speaking, Asians don't think of themselves as having "racial" problems. And since colorism is such a close cousin to racism, I'm sure I was turning people off. But then I received a sign. Literally. It was a sign on the side of the road.

In 2014, a billboard appeared in Queens, New York, aimed at Korean Americans. Advertising a new face cream by the Korean brand ElishaCoy, the billboard posed a question in bold letters: "Do you wanna be white?" It featured an image of an Asian woman with pale skin looking happy and white. While in South Korea this question may not have raised eyebrows, in the United States it sparked a considerable amount of public commentary on Korean beauty ideals and if in fact Koreans were idealizing Eurocentric beauty concepts in their adoration of light skin. Thanks to ElishaCoy, I realized the conversation I was trying to have with Asian Americans should probably start with beauty, not colorism.

In fact, rather than even using the word "colorism," I started using the term "skin-color politics" and often began the conversation with a discussion of beauty when raising the subject of this book with Asian Americans. The more people I spoke with, from across the Asian American community, the more I realized that this issue was often couched in beauty talk, but it saturated every aspect of life. Before I jumped back into searching for subjects to interview, I decided to call upon the experts for advice. The first person I reached out to was Joanne Rondilla, the coauthor of *Is Lighter Better?*

These days, Rondilla is a lecturer at the School of Social Transformation at Arizona State University. Despite the fact that her book was published in 2007, it is still the only book on the market that focuses specifically on skin-tone discrimination in the Asian American community. For the book, Rondilla and her coauthor interviewed dozens of Asian American women from diverse ethnic backgrounds in an attempt to qualify and understand the seemingly universal desire for pale skin among women with nothing in common other than the fact that they call Asia their ancestral home. While Rondilla did manage to gather a great diversity of women to interview, she warned me of the pitfalls of bringing these types of questions to this particular community.

Rondilla had some key words of advice. First, she told me that, because I'm not a member of the Asian diaspora, it was very likely that people would be wary of opening up to me. "They may believe that you won't understand if you're not of that community," Rondilla said. She also reiterated the idea that some Asian groups would deny that colorism is a problem in their community because the word implies only skin color. "Koreans don't think they have a colorism issue, but they don't realize that colorism also includes body and beauty standards," Rondilla explained. She proceeded to tell me about the booming eyelid-surgery trend both in Korea and in the Korean American community. "I have students who told me that at age sixteen, eyelid surgery was a rite of passage in the family. It shows wealth," she said.

The eyelid surgery Rondilla was referring to is known medically as blepharoplasty, or, in lay terms, "double eyelid" surgery. The procedure is popular among all types of East Asian people, many of whom have a single eyelid fold. Having a double fold pulls the eyelid up, giving the eyes a rounder appearance. While many Asian beauty experts and scholars would argue that the surgery is just as common in Asia as it is in the West, suggesting that the look is not meant to be an imitation of white beauty ideals, it's an argument that's hard to believe considering the amount of Western influence in Asian popular culture. And here in the United States, where a white beauty standard is clearly the norm, eyelid surgery is one of the most common surgeries among Asian Americans, according to the American Academy of Plastic Surgeons.

In late 2014, Julie Chen, the well-known Chinese American newscaster turned daytime TV talk-show host, made headlines when she admitted on her show, *The Talk*, that she'd had eyelid surgery early in her career after a boss at the news station where she worked told her that her "Asian eyes" made her look "disinterested" when interviewing subjects on camera. Later, an agent reportedly told Chen she wouldn't represent her unless Chen had the surgery to make her eyes look bigger. While Chen admitted feeling mildly conflicted about her decision, she also admitted that her career did take off once she had the surgery.

So, for Asian Americans, pale skin or whiteness represents many things. Beauty, access, wealth. It's the old world and new world combined. "I don't think we should dismiss the notion that colonialism and Western beauty standards contribute to the obsession with pale skin," said Grace Hwang Lynch, a Taiwanese American blogger who writes about the Asian American experience on her popular blog, *HapaMama*. "I think we need to always be critically thinking about where these ideas come from and whether they are still valid," she said. As we've seen with every other ethnic group, it's complicated. I promised myself I'd keep all of this in mind as I journeyed into this community.

Mother Knows Best: Dark Daughter, Light Mother

Jessica Dela Merced was only twenty-four when she wrote, directed, and starred in the short film *Bleached* in 2010. A "dark comedy" about a

Filipina American high school student whose mother enlists her to be the before-and-after model for her new bleaching-cream company, the film is hilarious and haunting. At first the girl, played by Dela Merced, rejects the idea of bleaching her skin, but when she starts seeing results she begins to enjoy her new fair skin and the benefits it brings. But then something happens that makes her light-skin fantasies fall apart. Clearly the film is a cautionary tale about the physical and emotional dangers of skin bleaching, but it also, in its mere fourteen minutes of running time, provides a glimpse into how skin-color politics get passed along from mother to daughter. "Don't you want to be beautiful?" the mother asks the daughter in the film, implying that, without bleaching her skin, true beauty would elude the girl.

Rondilla agrees that it is often mothers, grandmothers, and aunties in Asian American communities who pass on the "light skin is good, dark skin is bad" paradigm to their daughters. Clearly this is a familiar pattern across cultures. And likewise, it is these same mothers who can cause the most pain when they voice displeasure with their daughters' dark skin. "The impact is equal if not greater when it comes from intimate circles," said Rondilla, who has her own wounds to heal around this issue.

Although their relationship was not as extreme as that of the mother and daughter in *Bleached*, Rondilla said it was her mother who instilled in her a sense of inferiority because of her skin color. "I realized that all this color-coded anxiety stemmed from my relationship with my mom and the women in my family—especially their notions of beauty and the ways they projected those ideals on to me," she wrote in her 2012 dissertation on colorism and Filipino beauty ideals.

Rondilla grew up in California and was only about seven years old when she first encountered colorism in her family. On a big family trip to the Philippines, Rondilla said, her place in the family was sealed. "That's when I realized I had no value in the family," she said. "I was teased and mocked constantly by my cousins because I was dark. My cousins would say, when we were in a room watching a movie, 'Joy, could you smile because we can't see you because you're so dark.'"

Rondilla related this terrible story to me over the telephone. We'd never met in person, but I had seen pictures of her and seen her on film. I had to interrupt her narrative because the story she was telling me didn't make sense. The woman I was picturing in my mind wasn't dark at all. I quickly pulled up her headshot on Google and, sure enough, she had a very light complexion, lighter than most Filipinos I know. I needed an explanation before she could continue with her story. Rondilla laughed at my question and explained. "When I walk down the street, I don't read as dark, but next to my mom, I do. She's pure vanilla, and I'm dark caramel." So, because her mother is light, Rondilla is dark. It's that simple and that damning. And because her mother was a former beauty queen in the Philippines—a title she claims she won because of her light complexion—skin color and beauty were closely entwined in Rondilla's home. "Growing up Filipino you get greeted by 'Look how fat you are' and 'Look how dark you are,'" she said. For Rondilla, the way to deal with the skin-color issues in her family and community was to make it the focus of her academic work. And she continues to do so. "There's still so much work to be done," she said.

Risa Patterson is another brown-skinned Filipina woman with a fair-skinned mother. Risa's children attend the same preschool as my daughter and we've often chatted on the playground. Risa never mentioned to me that she dealt with colorism in her home growing up, but then again, that's not exactly the type of conversation one has during pickup at preschool. I was just happy she was willing to talk to me about how the skin-color differences played out in her family when I asked her if I could interview her for this book.

I met Risa in her home on an early spring afternoon. We sat in her kitchen while her children dashed outside to play, taking advantage of the unseasonably warm temperature. Risa is a tiny woman, a fact that she says often keeps people from taking her seriously, as they assume she's much younger than she really is, which is forty-four. With her youthful face, nut-brown skin, and long, shiny black hair, she could indeed pass for someone more than a decade younger. Risa warned me that she didn't have too much time for the interview because she had to ferry one of her three children to music lessons. Also, she didn't think she had very much to share.

Risa's mother was the lightest in the family, while Risa, her older sister, and her father all had similarly dark skin tones. "My father once told the story of why he married my mom. He would say it was her soft, light skin. He liked that she was light," Risa began telling me. Of course, I didn't say anything, but I thought I knew how the rest of the story would go, considering Risa and Joanne Rondilla are close in age and both have immigrant Filipino parents. I assumed Risa would have been subjected to the same type of light-skin indoctrination as Rondilla—but I was wrong.

"Skin color didn't come up in my nuclear family," Risa said, surprising me. Despite the fact that her mother was much lighter than her daughters, Risa and her sister would compete to see who could get the better tan, with no interference from their parents. "When I was in high school, I was living predominately among white people, and my teen-aged friends were fair and everyone wanted a tan, so I felt I was ahead of the game," Risa said, laughing at the memory. When asked whom she emulated, in terms of beauty, it was neither her pale mother nor the white girls around her. "I wanted to be Janet Jackson because she was so beautiful. I also wanted to be Hispanic," she said, admitting that she liked being mistaken for Latina, which happened frequently when she was growing up. "I thought being Latina was better than being Asian."

When asked about this desire to be mistaken for Latina, Risa surmised that it was because she saw very few Asian beauty role models in popular culture, and because her mother's idea that light skin was more beautiful didn't correlate with Risa's sun-seeking peers. Although mother and daughter had different ideas about beauty, Risa said her mother never prohibited her from tanning and never said anything disparaging about Risa's darker complexion. "I think my mother has always respected the choices I've made in terms of how I want to look," she said. But she didn't give up her own ideas either. "I think my mother still has pride in her fair skin, but largely because her sister, who was darker, was the beautiful one, but my mom had the lighter skin. It kind of evened things out," Risa explained.

I shared with Risa some of the other stories I had heard of Filipina women who had mothers with fair skin, and the conflicts that raged in their homes, and then asked why she thought her own mother hadn't pressured her to conform. "I do have an aunt who would scold me in the summers for always being in the sun and looking too Black," Risa admitted. "Just last summer, at eighty years old, she looked me over from head to toe and said, 'Risa, why are you so Black?'" As for her mother, at first Risa didn't have an explanation for her accepting attitude around

skin color. She had to stop and think. Finally, Risa decided that perhaps
due to the fact that her mother had been quite ill as a child and had to
live away from home, she had developed a sensitivity to others in pain,
or to those who were different. "I just think my mother has that peace-
maker instinct in her."

I accepted Risa's explanation, and it reminded me that despite cultural trends and stereotypes, everybody has the power and potential to
go against the norm and create new traditions and ideals. But I also
wondered if the fact that Risa and her family lived in a predominately
white suburban environment, where there was little Asian influence of
any kind, had paved the way for a childhood free from the color wars.
Joanne Rondilla grew up in California surrounded by not only other
Filipinos but also many other Asians who also worshipped light skin. I
came up with this theory myself, but it is based on my own experience
and the experiences of other Black people interviewed for this book who
noted that living away from one's ethnic community means the issues
that plague your community—light-skin versus dark-skin hostilities—
can largely be ignored. It is a possibility, but as my next interview made
clear, it's not an ironclad theory.

Susie Kim, thirty-four, is a Korean American stay-at-home mother with
three young children. Born in Korea, she grew up in the San Francisco
Bay Area in mostly white neighborhoods with her parents, her paternal
grandfather, and her much younger brother. We spoke over the phone
while she was in the car with her three kids, a feat I found particularly
impressive, especially because our conversation went on for forty minutes before I heard a peep from anyone.

By her own admission, Susie grew up in a loving family, but the
light-skin politics were in full effect. "My mom always chastised me for
being out in the sun too much, and she would get on me for getting too
dark," Susie said. "I always felt the pressure to be light." Not only did
Susie's mother preach a consistent "lighter is better" mantra; she practiced what she preached. "I saw my mom constantly using cosmetics to
stay light and she never sunbathed or went out in the sun. But I was a kid
and like all kids I spent a lot of time outside, and I would get yelled at for
it. 'Don't do that, you're getting too dark,' my mom would say."

Part of the problem is that Susie is naturally darker than her mother,
which meant she would always fall short of her mother's expectations.

Susie said she took after her father in the skin-tone department, but his dark skin was never an issue for her mom. "As a child I realized I got my [skin color] from my dad and I always wondered, 'Why don't you give Dad a hard time?' But he's a man," Susie said, noting that there is definitely a gender difference in terms of skin-color politics. "It always made me laugh because if men get to be dark and you're marrying the dark men, how does that work?"

While Susie could laugh about the double standard when it came to gender and skin color, she couldn't laugh about how bad she felt about the messages she was receiving about her own complexion. "There was a time growing up when I would tell my mom that what she was saying about my skin wasn't right and that she didn't love me," Susie said. And the negative messages came from her extended family as well. Susie recalled a summer visit with cousins in Korea when she was a child. "We were playing and this boy cousin my same age yelled at me for looking like a Black person," Susie said. "That was the first time I realized it might be bad to be a Black person. That idea had never been introduced to me before." Interestingly, Susie's cousin was reprimanded by his mother, but not for calling Susie Black. "[My aunt] didn't come back and say it doesn't matter what color you are. She let that statement go. To me it was like, 'She does look like a Black person and that's bad, but you still shouldn't say it aloud.'"

By the time Susie was in high school, she began to challenge her mother's insistence that pale skin was a necessity in life. Her mother responded with frustration. "My mom was like, 'It's not my fault there are these flawed standards out there. I'm just talking about how things are.' I think maybe she felt like it was her job as my mom to help me navigate the system rather than push back against it," Susie said. And for a long time, Susie didn't push back. "I bought lightening creams and fretted over the freckles on my nose because my mom was always like 'don't get freckles,'" Susie said. "So even though I was irritated at my mom for judging me," she admitted, "I still put on sunscreen and bought stuff to even out my skin tone. I did a lot of things that were conflicting when it came to race and identity and being a woman."

Eventually, after going to college and living away from home, Susie was able to free herself from her mother's light-skin brainwashing. "Sometime in my early twenties I was like, 'Why am I doing this?' and I chilled out," Susie said. But it wasn't until she became a mother that she really began to examine the issues involved in skin-color politics. "In addition to our cultural norms I started to realize that capitalism was behind a lot of this obsession over light skin," Susie said. "Think about all of these companies making money on creating a hierarchy of skin color."

With three children and a white American husband, the skin colors in Susie's own household vary greatly. "We talk about skin color in a very matter-of-fact way," Susie said. "We talk about who's lighter and darker and who has dry skin, but I feel and I hope that it's simply a statement of fact rather than a hierarchy like I felt when I was younger."

After talking to Susie, I realized how little has changed from ancient times when Korean men with dark skin got a pass for being providers, but a woman had to be light and without freckles to prove both her beauty and her virtue. Add on to that anti-Black racism, and light skin remains a moral imperative for a Korean American woman. Susie suffered through that indoctrination, but she is breaking the cycle with her own children. Still, her mother holds fast to her beliefs. "She hasn't changed in any way," Susie admitted, but added that she has forbidden her mother from talking about light skin and dark skin with her kids. She doesn't want her mother to pass her prejudices on to her children. Based on Susie's confident attitude and the fact that she is so willing to talk about these issues now with her mom and her kids, I believe the light-skin adoration in this family will end with Susie's mother.

Dark Girls

In August 2012, the *New York Times* ran a photo essay with photographs that at first glance looked truly frightening. I thought I was looking at images from a horror movie, something like a remake of *Creature from the Black Lagoon*. But in fact it was a story about Chinese people at the beach. The images were so disconcerting because almost all of the beachgoers were covered in gruesome, yet colorful, rubber facemasks. Dubbed "facekinis," the contraptions looked like rubber ski masks with tiny holes for the eyes, nose, and mouth. Indeed, the beach looked like it had been invaded by rainbow-colored aliens. According to the article, Chinese women had taken to wearing facekinis because, while they enjoyed frolicking at the beach, they were desperate to protect their faces from the sun. Were they worried about getting a sunburn or skin cancer? Not really.

"I'm afraid of getting dark," one fifty-eight-year-old woman told the reporter as she took off her neon-orange mask. She then clarified her response: "A woman should always have fair skin, otherwise people will think you're a peasant."

Of course, not every Asian woman is afraid of getting dark. As it is in the African American community, dark skin can be visible proof of one's heritage. It can also be a source of pride, an act of rebellion, and even a marker of beauty.

For Ruby Park, twenty-six, a Korean American woman who grew up in the Baltimore-Washington metropolitan area, her dark skin has been a source of pride for her—and envy from others—throughout her life. "I am the color that white people wish to achieve when they get tans," she said. Growing up, Ruby said she and her younger brother played outdoors so much, and got so dark, that at one point her mother mistook an African American boy for her brother during an outing at a community swimming pool. "I wore my dark skin proudly and mocked light-skinned beauty standards," Ruby said.

Ruby said her mother expressed frustration at her dark skin and, not surprisingly, implored both of her children to wear sunscreen all the time, but she was not malicious in her critiques. "I don't remember ever being told outright that my skin tone was unacceptable," Ruby said. "My mother and my aunties tried to teach me to wash my face with rice water and milk to lighten my skin tone; however, my mother never pushed it very much when I refused and went outside to play in the sun." Interestingly, Ruby said her mother viewed her dark skin as a testament to her assimilation into their adopted country. "Part of her was sort of proud that her daughter was so headstrong and 'American,'" Ruby said. "Whenever we went to Korea and people commented on her very dark-skinned, English-speaking children, she played it off like, 'They're American, what can I do?'"

Despite her mother's lack of restrictions on Ruby's time spent in the sun and her pride in her "Americanized" children, Ruby recalled still being quite aware of the light-skin beauty ideal her mother prized. "I knew that I was not beautiful in the way my mother and her culture designated. I did not have fair skin, narrow and wispy hips, and flattened curves," Ruby said, noting she was always heavier than any Korean girl was supposed to be. "But I did know that my mother still considered me to be beautiful. She loved my eyes and my hair and my full lips. She loved my smile and my jovial personality. Most of all, my mother and my father were extremely proud that I was smart."

Today Ruby is married and a graduate student studying sociology. Due to warnings about skin cancer and other dangers from too much sun exposure, she spends less time in the sun than she did as a child, and she wears the sunscreen her mother always wanted. "At this point in my life," Ruby said, "I am comfortable in my skin both literally and figuratively."

I loved Ruby's story and her convention-busting attitude about color. Although one might assume that Ruby was just born with the strength to defy colorist attitudes in her community, really I think it was because her parents, especially her mother, were vocal in their support of Ruby's beauty and intelligence. Plus, Ruby mentioned one other thing that gave her the confidence to play in the sun. "My parents did not limit my outdoor activity as a child, partly because women in my mother's generation were cloistered indoors as soon as they hit puberty," Ruby said. "My mother attributes this as the primary reason why she and her contemporaries frequently suffer from illness. She did not want this for her daughter, so I spent most of my free time outdoors." So, Ruby's mother may have believed that white skin was beautiful, but it was not a limited vision of beauty. In her eyes, her dark daughter was beautiful too.

Sasha Roy, twenty-one, was born in Bangladesh and immigrated to the United States when she was four. Like most of the other Asian Americans I'd spoken to, Sasha recounted numerous childhood memories of a mother who was desperate to preserve her daughter's light skin. "My mom would let me play outside but she would slather on the sunscreen. And she would take me to the park but only during sunset," Sasha said. The message that light skin was preferable was reinforced not only by the extensive South Asian community in Sasha's Queens neighborhood, but also by the media messages imported through the Bengali newspapers and TV shows her parents frequently watched. But Sasha didn't want her light skin preserved.

"One of the things I remember when I was younger was that I was the lightest of all the South Asians in my school," Sasha recalled. And far from being a point of pride for her, it felt instead like a source of disconnect from her people. "I would be upset because all of my friends were actually darker than me and I wanted to be the same shade as them," Sasha said. "I always felt that it was a marker of how I was different, and how I was distinctly not Bengali."

Indeed, looking at pictures of Sasha one could easily mistake her for being Latina, given her toffee-colored skin and wavy dark hair. (Sasha actually mentioned she was often mistaken for Latina while growing up in Queens.) When she left for college in Massachusetts, Sasha deliberately started spending more time in the sun, hoping to darken up. She joined the South Asian student organization at her college but again found herself the lightest one in the group. "People didn't think that I was South Asian because I was so light skinned, and I was being teased for being light."

Today Sasha is a junior in college, studying the history of colorism, and she speaks knowingly about issues like white-skin privilege and anti-Black and -brown racism. Sasha's mother isn't happy about it. "She gets really tired of me talking about this," Sasha said. "My mom thinks I got radicalized about race in college, but she thinks it's just a phase." Sasha noted that whenever she points out something colorist her mother says or does, her mother dismisses her. Likewise, Sasha ignores her mother's warnings to stop riding her bicycle in the sun so much at school.

Considering her mother a lost cause in this war against colorism, Sasha is really happy to see many of her South Asian friends from childhood ignoring the older generation's continuous demands to stay out of the sun. In true millennial fashion, they are posting pictures of themselves on social media happily outdoors. "They're taking these beautiful pictures of themselves on the beach and they're embracing that," Sasha said proudly. She wants to be part of that movement of dark-skin love so badly, but she still hasn't found a way to love her own light skin. "I edit my photos a tiny bit on Instagram so my skin is a shade darker," she admitted. "I realize that is not a really great way to acknowledge my own light-skin privilege," she said. I agreed but didn't say so aloud because Sasha said she is working on acceptance; plus, she's only twenty-one. I was just happy to hear a South Asian young person championing the dark side of beauty and identity. Sasha's dilemma, as with the other people I spoke to who suffered from light-skin isolation, made it abundantly clear that light skin isn't the universal prize. Yes, there is a skin-color hierarchy in which those with the lightest skin rule from the top, but most people don't want to be a different color; most people just

want to belong to their assigned group. They want to fit in. They want
to be recognized members of their community.

Fair Enough in India

Before I officially started the research for this book, an Indian commercial for a vaginal bleaching cream called Clean and Dry Intimate Wash
caught my eye. The concept—bleaching one's lady parts—and the commercial itself were so absurd that not only had the commercial gone viral, but multiple US and British media outlets had picked up the story,
using the opportunity to explore India's obsession with light skin. Wrote
Lindy West for the feminist pop-culture blog *Jezebel*:

> As if it isn't bad enough that darker-skinned people are encour-
> aged to stay out of the sun and invest in skin-bleaching products
> like Fair & Lovely, and that white actresses are being imported
> to play Indian people in Bollywood movies, now everyone has to
> be insecure about the fact that their vaginas happen to be the
> color that vaginas are? Splendid! God, I was just saying the other
> day that my misogyny didn't have enough racism in it.

After that ridiculous entrée into the world of skin-color politics in
India, it seemed that everywhere I turned were public outcries and quiet
rumblings in the Indian American community highlighting this obsession with fairness.

In September 2013, it was the historic crowning of Nina Davuluri as
Miss America, the first Indian American to ever win the title. Davuluri
was born and raised in the United States and said she entered the pageant to change the face of Miss America. Though she planned to spend
her reign talking about STEM careers and body-image issues, the causes
near and dear to her heart, she ended up instead having to focus almost
all of her time in the media on the racist responses to her win. And those
racist responses came from a variety of sources.

Garden-variety white racists accused Davuluri of being everything
from a Muslim to a terrorist. Of course, they also suggested she wasn't
even American, so how dare she be awarded the title of Miss America?
Most of these detractors lodged their comments and complaints anonymously, via posts on social media. But there were other critics on social
media who also questioned Davuluri's right to the title.

Surprisingly, while certain segments of white America were trying to determine if Davuluri was American enough to be Miss America, certain Indian Americans were trying to determine if she was light enough to be a beauty queen. Yes, rather than wholesale support of one of their own who had broken the beauty queen glass ceiling, Indians and Indian Americans all over social media were saying Davuluri would never have won any beauty contest in India because her skin was too dark.

"I totally get it," Davuluri told CNN when asked about this issue. "When I was little it was always, 'Don't go out into the sun, 'cause you're going to get too dark.' I'd go to India on average every year growing up and (some of my family) would say, 'Oh, you'd be so much more beautiful if you were fair' or lighter. So I get it from that standpoint," she said.

Davuluri is a deep mahogany-brown color, which apparently would disqualify her from even being considered a national beauty on the Indian subcontinent. "In India, we prefer our beauty queens strictly vanilla—preferably accessorized with blue contact lenses," wrote journalist Lakshmi Chaudhry, poking fun at Davuluri's critics.

If Americans hadn't been aware prior to the 2013 Miss America pageant that light skin was so important to Indian concepts of beauty, then Davuluri brought it to the mainstream. Not just CNN but Time.com, *Buzzfeed*, and *New York* magazine covered the brouhaha over Davuluri's dark skin. So, while her win may have been a victory for diversity, it certainly was also a sad reminder that color still matters in the Indian community, both in the motherland and here in the United States—a disturbing idea that showcases how the light-skin ideology born in another country can still be nurtured and maintained here in the United States. Just ask former Louisiana governor Bobby Jindal.

In February 2015, Governor Jindal made headlines when a photo of what was identified as his official portrait went viral. In the painting, Jindal was portrayed with pale-white skin. For the record, Jindal's skin color is not white; it's brown. Not light brown. Not dark brown. Just brown. All over social media and in the traditional press, people questioned the governor's sanity and perceived self-hatred with this blatant attempt to whitewash his own image. Cultural commentator and humorist Luvvie Ajayi hit the nail on the head with the title of her blog post about the issue: "Was Brown Paint Busy When They Created This Bobby Jindal Portrait?"

As it turned out, the portrait wasn't "official." Reportedly, it had been a gift to the governor from an artist (perhaps one who had run out of brown paint?). Jindal deflected the whitewashing criticism, remarking at a press event, "You mean I'm not white? I'm shocked at this revelation." He then tried to make the issue about a liberal preoccupation with race instead of about his own questionable attitude about his color and Indian identity. "The Left is obsessed with race," he quipped and then quickly moved on to other issues.

But here's the problem with Bobby Jindal and his brown skin. The portrait-gate of 2015 is only the latest instance in which the then governor was accused of trying to de-Indian his identity. The actual official portrait that hung in his office also cast Jindal as a man with a peaches-and-cream complexion. What's more, Jindal had previously been accused of having his skin lightened for his official photographs. Born Piyush Jindal, the future governor changed his name to Bobby as a boy and converted from Hinduism to Catholicism after college. Coupled with his conservative politics and his insistence that he is not a hyphenated "Indian-American" but simply an American has led many to believe that Jindal wants to be white, or at least not brown.

In June 2015, after Jindal announced his bid for the presidency, a hashtag movement—#bobbyjindalissowhite—spread across Twitter. Both Indian Americans and Indians in India tweeted about how far away from Indian culture the governor and presidential hopeful had fled. Everything from his Catholic conversion to that infamous painting was mocked. Jindal had become the poster child for self-hatred.

The case of Jindal—while unique in that he is an Indian man trying to make a name for himself in an extremely white community, aka the Republican Party—provides a good example of how skin color is not solely a beauty issue and certainly does not only affect women. Jindal may feel that his dark skin color is an impediment to his being taken seriously as an American, a conservative, and a Christian, so if he can alter his image to look whiter (which, to Jindal, seems to translate as "more American"), even if it's just in pictures, why not give it a try?

A Respectable Asian

"I don't feel a lot of concern about my skin color," said Liz Tanaka, thirty-two, a Japanese American nursing student who grew up in Seattle.

"I know that being lighter comes in handy in the US because you look like an East Asian and people will assume you're fairly respectable, which they won't always if you look darker," she said. A child of divorced parents, Liz said that even though her father had the lightest skin in the family and her sister the darkest, skin-color issues didn't factor significantly into her memories of childhood. Yes, her sister tended to avoid the sun, but that really wasn't much of an issue living in Seattle. Mostly, Liz said, she remembers her mother teaching her that she should be kind to all people regardless of their skin color. Still, Liz learned lessons about color from her family that weren't so kind.

"I don't think my parents ever said [that light skin was better] but it was certainly implied that in the past it was," Liz said. "And I think that definitely influenced both my sister's and my thinking to some degree." For her sister that meant lusting after Liz's lighter skin. "She would say she envied me because I was a lot lighter, and she wished she was also that way, but our parents never said anything about it," Liz recalled. She also made it clear that her sister's desire for lighter skin was just one of many body-image issues she had. "She tended to be self-conscious about all aspects of her appearance," Liz explained.

But Liz also remembered hearing stories from both her mother and grandmother about the hierarchy of marriageable men. "The people on the bottom were Portuguese, Filipino, Mexican, and Black," she said. "My grandmother also said that when my grandfather first approached her she ran away because she thought he was Filipino. Of course he wasn't Filipino, and she married him, but she was still very concerned that he could be mistaken for a Filipino if he wore the wrong clothing." Apparently Liz's Japanese grandfather was from Hawaii and he was, in Liz's estimation, "pretty dark."

But, as she stated, Liz isn't really thinking about her skin color these days. She now lives in Los Angeles and enjoys getting a tan. But when she travels she can't help but be reminded of her light-skin advantage. "I travel in Asia a lot and fairer skin helps you there too," she said. "Frankly, it's the only part of my appearance that anyone will say anything nice about."

Liz's story is the perfect one to end this section because she exemplifies both hope and despair. On the one hand, she admits that the color of her skin barely registers as a positive or negative in her daily life in the United States, and yet, even though they didn't strongly enforce a light-

skin hierarchy, her parents managed to instill in their daughters an understanding of how light-skin politics work. What's more, that same
colorist thinking is reinforced every time Liz travels to Asia. She would
have to be a special kind of Jedi to deprogram herself of the subtle but
constant messages celebrating light skin she gets both in Asia and here
in the United States.

The Asian American community grows largely by immigration. And
thus the light-skin preference born in Asia is continuously re-imported
into the United States, infecting future generations. "There is definitely
a strong preference, verging on obsession, for fair skin in East Asia, and
recent immigrants hold on to these preferences," blogger Grace Hwang
Lynch confirmed. And clearly this is not just in East Asia. These same
ideals are imported by South Asian immigrants as well. So, how does
one block the importation of an ideology? Is it something that can be
done through border control? Probably not. Really, this a problem that
second-generation Asian Americans, like Sasha Roy, are already tackling
with tools their parents never dreamed of.

Girls on Film

Hwang Lynch believes conversations about colorism are already happening in the Asian American community, but she's not sure to what
effect. "In more socially conscious circles of Asian Americans, this obsession with fair skin is often critiqued, but I don't know if these messages are changing the minds of people who are already obsessed with
paleness," she said. As pointed out by both experts and regular folk, the
skin-lightening industry is such a ubiquitous force to be reckoned with
all over Asia that the fight against light-skin adoration has to be thought
of not as a single battle, but as a war. And the soldiers who need to take
on the fight include those in the academic world and the media. Joanne
Rondilla said she is seeing progress in academia, where more and more
students are undertaking research about colorism across the Asian diaspora. "But we need to spark more discussion using other outlets besides
academic ones," she said. That's exactly what filmmaker Jessica Dela
Merced did with her short film *Bleached*.

I spoke to Dela Merced over the phone to talk about her reasons for
making *Bleached*. Now twenty-nine years old and based in San Francisco,

Dela Merced admitted the film, her first, had been a response to what she saw all across Asia—from an app popular in India that allows people to see what they would look like with lighter skin to the booming skin-lightening business in places like Japan, South Korea, and the Philippines. "I knew most of the Asian community dealt with this issue, but it was never in the news," she said. By making this film, which definitely falls into the category of "dark comedy," she found a way to get people talking about the consequences of lusting after light skin. And talk they did. From film festivals to special screenings at universities, the film enjoyed a lengthy touring schedule all across the United States and even in the Philippines. Dela Merced was thrilled the film was screened in the Philippines and, while she doesn't consider herself an activist, realizes that getting *Bleached* shown in Manila—the epicenter of light-skin adoration for her community—was a step in the right direction for the Filipino American community as well.

I met another young Asian woman who was using film to tackle the issue of colorism, not only in her community, but around the world. Her name is Nayani Thiyagarajah. Born and raised in Toronto, Thiyagarajah's Tamil parents emigrated from Sri Lanka. At twenty-six, Thiyagarajah directed and produced a full-length documentary on colorism. *Shadeism: Digging Deeper* details the experiences of a handful of twentysomething Canadian women from different ethnic groups who all deal with colorism within their families and in their communities. The film does an excellent job documenting how colorism is a universal problem and how the experiences of a young Afro-Canadian woman mirror those of a woman with a Bangladeshi background, for example. Interspersed between the stories of these young people were talking heads from both the United States and Canada who could contextualize and explain how pernicious and dangerous colorism really is. Inspired by a conversation she had with a three-year-old cousin who was already talking about wanting lighter skin, Thiyagarajah said she had to make this movie because up until then she hadn't realized just how common colorism really was. Not to mention how dangerous.

I interviewed Thiyagarajah over Skype after meeting her in person at a conference on colorism, where a preview of her film was met with great enthusiasm. A passionate young filmmaker, who was much in demand after word that *Shadeism* had been accepted into the Zanzibar

Film Festival, Thiyagarajah was not easy to nail down for an interview. We eventually found an evening that worked for us both. I was settled in my office at Temple University, and she was at her home in Toronto. The first thing I wanted to know was whether in her own family—made up of a younger brother and two parents—she had ever experienced colorism. Surprisingly, she said no. "I grew up relatively privileged in that sense," she said. "I dealt more with body weight." Even though when I met Thiyagarajah I would have described her as having dark-brown skin, she had grown up in her family with the firm understanding that she had light skin, and she was praised for it. "I was told to stay out of the sun so I could keep my light skin," she said.

On the other hand, Thiyagarajah said, her brother had a completely different experience growing up in Toronto. He had darker skin than Thiyagarajah, and curlier hair, unlike Thiyagarajah's long, flowing locks. "I think he experienced prejudice and oppression in different ways than I did," she said. "If he got into trouble or had a lot of energy, people outside of the family would be quick to say he was angry or had ADHD and I don't think that was disconnected from his skin color." Thiyagarajah said as adults she and her brother have had conversations about the way he was treated. "He's been very real about the fact that people have commented on his darker skin," she said.

Based on her own observations of her brother, conversations with her diverse group of friends, and then the devastating conversation with her three-year-old cousin who could already articulate her yearning for light skin, Thiyagarajah decided to explore the subject through film.

In the documentary, Thiyagarajah profiles several young women who deal with colorism in their communities in Canada, and she also travels to India, Africa, and Jamaica to investigate how colorism manifests in other parts of the world. While the film itself was a challenge to make, often leaving Thiyagarajah and her crew emotionally drained, Thiyagarajah feels hopeful about the future overall.

"People in their own small ways are having the dialogue," she said, citing the growing number of media resources—from websites to live theater—taking on the issue of colorism. "I also see a lot more journalism covering this issue and that's a start," she said. "And social media has been huge." Now that the film is done, Thiyagarajah wants to create an accompanying educational curriculum, and she is seeking distribution channels. But she knows real solutions will not come only from great movies and a solid social media campaign. "These discussions need to happen in a systematic level in the government and in educational settings." She also reiterates that the billion-dollar skin-lightening industry must be curtailed in order for light-skin adoration to be diminished. In the meantime, Thiyagarajah said, "We want to reach a wide audience, not just in North America but across the whole world."

Dark Is Divine

The good news is that the whole world is waking up to this issue. And Asia is no exception, despite what may seem like its perpetual love of light skin. Thiyagarajah says she sees a growing awareness of colorism in the South Asian community in North America and across the diaspora. "They might not call it shadeism or colorism, but they can tell you about skin lightening and wanting light skin," she said. Indeed, across South and East Asia, sparks of activism are happening. India, for example, has a Dark Is Beautiful campaign meant to counter the prevailing attitudes that people with dark skin cannot be beautiful or successful. In Pakistan, activist Fatima Lodhi launched her Dark Is Divine movement in 2013, using a combination of social media, school outreach, and straight-up grassroots organizing. Lodhi is leading a youth-led movement to make South Asia a region where "the skin color of the women shouldn't matter at all." Hopefully the momentum from those movements will find its way to the South Asian communities in the United States.

"I'm a cheerful pessimist," said Indiana University's Radhika Parameswaran, who has witnessed the activism taking place in the country of her birth. "Resistance to colorism is happening all over India now with middle-class families who don't buy into the [skin-color] hierarchy," she said. "And it's the same in the Indian American community too." She points to Miss America 2014, Nina Davuluri, and Davuluri's parents: "I wouldn't rule out that her parents probably told her, 'Skin color doesn't matter; it's what you do that counts.' They dismissed the colorism and said she could do what she wants." And that's what Davuluri did, with no apology. "That's progress," said Parameswaran.

FOUR

BEIGE IS THE NEW BLACK
Mixed-Race Americans and Color

God made the white man, the devil made the mulatto.
—Eighteenth-century British proverb

The mixed-race community is hard to define culturally because the only element common among its members is generally a claim laid to two or more racial categories. But still, a growing group of mixed-race people in this country are creating structures, traditions, and an official community for themselves and others like them. For the purposes of this book, I have defined mixed-race families as those in which the parents come from different ethnic backgrounds and their children are obviously mixed.

It should come as no surprise that if color matters in single-race families, then it's going to matter in mixed-race families as well. Despite the assumption that two people who married across color lines may be immune to such a polarizing disease as colorism, nothing could be further from the truth. We all bring our racial baggage to the table, both to a marriage and to our newly formed families. Mixed-race families are no different. In some cases the colorism that manifests in a mixed-race family may even be worse, because of additional elements: a color hierarchy between parents, differing traditions and beliefs about color held by parents, and/or the burden of historical conflicts between the different ethnic groups represented in the home. How this plays out in everyday life is far from predictable.

Mulatto America

Even though America was founded on the principles of racism, where all men were not considered equal, it is abundantly clear that interracial relationships, both coerced and voluntary, have long been part of our historical legacy. Let the record show that as early as May 10, 1632, a white English captain, by the name of Daniel Elfrye, who was bringing African captives to Virginia, was chastised by his employer for getting too friendly with a Black woman on board ship. The official reprimand by the London Company stated that Elfrye "too freely entertained" a mulatto woman on his ship. And then, of course, we must note the relationships between white men and Indian women—romanticized by the marriage between Pocahontas and John Smith—as we debunk the myth that the United States of America was ever a nation of pure-blooded citizens. The earliest European settlers in what would become the United States—both Spanish and English—were mostly men. The fact is, then, if these settlers desired female companionship, it was statistically necessary that they be involved with African and Native American women. And in the early years of colonial life, when day-to-day survival was never guaranteed, nobody's priority list included keeping track of who was getting cozy together at night.

When white European women began to marry Black and Native American men, however, that was problematic. Indeed, the first recorded interracial marriage between a Black person and a white person in the British colonies was the 1681 union between an Irish servant named Nell Butler and a Black slave named Charles. They both lived in Western Maryland. Nell's British employer, Lord Baltimore, warned her against the union, but she went through with it anyway. Once the two became husband and wife, Butler became a slave, as did, some time later, the couple's children. Charles and Nell may have been the first to cross the color line legally, through marriage, but they certainly wouldn't be the last, despite the increasing number of laws restricting what was originally known as amalgamation but eventually, in the 1800s, became known as miscegenation. Really, the anti-amalgamation laws, enacted state by state from 1664 on, were a response to the race mixing going on all over the country. The fears of the white men in power—that their pure white race would be diluted, not to mention that they would lose their unpaid workforce if their African slaves married white people— had lawmakers doing everything in their power to keep the races separated and far from equal. But of course no laws can regulate love and desire.

Black people and white people fell in love and wanted to live together as husband and wife from the deepest swamps in the South to the
coldest climes of the North. And they were willing to be together despite the country's greatest attempts to keep them apart. There are stories of white men and women being so desperate to marry their Black
lovers that they swallowed some of their blood—then they would claim
to have Black blood in their veins, which, according to law, made them
Black too. Whether this was common practice or not, the idea of a white
person drinking their Black lover's blood to circumvent the law was
common myth and caught the attention of novelist Edna Ferber and
became a crucial plot point in her 1926 novel *Show Boat*. (And yes, that
is the book that the Tony Award–winning musical is based upon.)

Rather than go through the drama and mild distaste of ingesting
bodily fluids, some white people simply had their race changed on official
government documents—from white to Black—so they could marry a
loved one. Author Bliss Broyard describes just such an incident in her own
family's past, in *One Drop: My Father's Hidden Life*. Her white great-great-
grandfather, living in Louisiana, decided to marry his Black girlfriend, a
free woman of color. In order to sidestep the law that prohibited marriage
between races, he simply declared himself a "free person of color" on his
wedding certificate and the marriage was sanctioned. Ironically, years
later, Broyard's own father, the celebrated journalist and writer Anatole
Broyard, waited until he was on his deathbed to tell his own children that
he had been passing as white when in fact he was of African American
descent.

In nineteenth-century New York City, notoriously poor but remark-
ably diverse neighborhoods like Seneca Village and Five Points were
filled with interracial couples, living in both legal and common-law relationships. The poor and working class of all races didn't have the privilege
to believe in racial purity when choosing a mate. While it scandalized the
upper classes, Blacks and whites married and raised children in these
neighborhoods and several others like them across the nation. Some of
these interracial communities, like Five Points, were located in the midst
of an urban metropolis, while others, like the little-known fishing community on Malaga Island off the coast of Maine, were mostly hidden from
society's judgmental eyes. The interracial community of Malaga, though
poor, still boasted a stable community of Black, white, and interracial

families that made their living mostly from fishing and shipbuilding. But when a local developer decided to turn Malaga Island into a tourist destination in the early twentieth century, the people were forcibly removed from the island. They were portrayed in the press as "strange," "degraded," and "feeble minded" due to their interracial mixing. Today, descendants of the Malaga community continue to live with the shame that was cast upon them by the government of Maine and the local press back in the early twentieth century.

And then there are the stories of interracial couples in antebellum America who decided to avoid detection and prosecution by fleeing to remote areas and reinventing themselves as something other than Black or white. One of the most famous communities to succeed in this identity-reinvention scheme is the Melungeons of Appalachia. Until recently, most Melungeons believed their tawny skin could be attributed to their Portuguese or Native American ancestors, when in fact a 2010 DNA study revealed that most Melungeons can credit their tan skin to an African ancestor. Most researchers now agree that the Melungeons were actually founded by a small group of Black men and their white wives who fled the Virginia area for the hills of Kentucky where they could live in peace. The Melungeons weren't alone. The Lumbees of North Carolina and the Turks of South Carolina passed as Native American tribes, but as with the Melungeons, such origins were invented to mask their interracial roots. As a matter of fact, a funny epilogue from an earlier story is apt here. Remember the Platt family from Florida who claimed to be white with Irish and Native American heritage? Well, the Native American tribe they claimed allegiance to, the Croatoans, is believed to be one of those "mixed" tribes with African roots.

Suffice it to say, the laws of the land were far from effective in squashing romantic relationships between Black people and white, both before and after the Civil War. Publicly, we didn't believe in race mixing; privately, it was as American as apple pie. And as the country became more diverse with the arrival of Asian and Latino immigrants, the mixing continued—unabated, for the most part—even though interracial relationships between whites and Asians or whites and Latinos were also illegal. It was not until 1967—when a young interracial couple from Virginia, Mildred and Richard Loving, won the Supreme Court case that struck down all anti-miscegenation laws in the United States—that it became legal for people of different races to marry. Although the results of that decision didn't suddenly cause a huge spike in interracial marriages, June 12 is now a nationally recognized holiday, Loving Day, celebrating love across the color line.

Latino Mixing

In the Spanish-speaking Latino community, as we have already seen, postcolonial nations sought to whiten their populations—by inviting white Europeans to immigrate to their lands and by promoting interracial unions with that handy slogan *mejorar la raza*. It is obvious that the appreciation of lighter skin remained a part of the cultural heritage of Latinos who immigrated to the United States, but coupled with the added burden of being an ethnic other, the move to dilute their culture became a bit less enticing. Still, white people held the reins of power in the United States, so marrying a gringo could be seen as advantageous.

According to the classic assimilation theory, intermarriage between an immigrant group and the dominant population reduces social boundaries. But it also dilutes the ethnic identity of the resulting offspring. For some Latinos, this blending into white American culture through marriage was an easy way to assimilate and enter the middle or even upper class. Others chose to stick to their own kind and hold on to their traditions instead of whitewashing them. But the mixing of cultures didn't take place only between Latinos and whites. In states such as California, where the immigrant populations from Latin America and Asia grew in tandem, there is a long history of Latino and Asian mixing. From Mexicans marrying Filipinos (self-described "Mexipinos") in Los Angeles to the now almost extinct Mexican-Punjabi community based in Southwest California and Arizona, interracial relationships blossomed between multiple cultures and races, even before the Loving Decision of 1967 made them legal.

Hapa, Amerasians, Hafu

What can be said of Latino immigrants in this country can also be said of Asian Americans when it comes to interracial relationships, whether noting patterns or drawing conclusions. For newcomers, a certain status of assimilation comes with marrying a white American—but along with it comes a loss of ethnic identity. The reality is that many mixed-race

Asian Americans were actually brought to this country because of American soldiers, both white and Black, who met, married, and procreated with Asian women while serving in the Korean or Vietnam wars. These were some of the first mixed-race Asian American children many Americans encountered.

For some Asian women, the decision to follow their American husbands to the United States wasn't so much a choice as a necessity, as they felt their mixed-race children would not be accepted in their home country. This is the reason many mixed-race Asian American children were put up for adoption after the wars; for the most part, Asian women, especially without the help of the fathers of their children, would never be able to live with the social stigma of having a mixed-race—or, rather, not racially pure—child. Terms like "Hafu" (Japan) and "Amerasian" (Vietnam) were coined to refer to this generation of mixed Asian American kids and, as such, had negative connotations. These terms have recently been reintroduced into the popular American lexicon as young mixed-race Asian activists reappropriate the names for themselves.

Ironically, many people in East Asian countries today complain that the images being offered up as beauty ideals are in fact of mixed-race Asian women, creating a beauty standard that is impossible for any monoracial Asian woman to achieve. So the pendulum has swung, from the face of racial mixing being one of shame to it being the one to emulate, as mixed Asian features are desired today both here in the United States and in East Asia.

Mix Match

In May 2013, a white man was accused of kidnapping three little Black girls and then taking them shopping at Walmart. If that sounds ridiculous, it's because it is indeed ridiculous. The man in question didn't kidnap the girls—he was their father. Many media outlets in the United States, and even some abroad, covered the story of the Virginia-based interracial couple—dad is white, mom is Black—who found themselves under police investigation after a "concerned citizen" at Walmart alerted store security about the suspicious man and the little girls who didn't "match up." Indeed, by the time the man returned home from Walmart, the police were at his door waiting to question him about his relationship with the girls, a four-year-old and two-year-old twins. Of course the incident was quickly diffused when the police realized that the man had a Black wife, but it didn't stop the Internet from exploding. The mixed-race community in particular saw this incident as a ludicrous yet not wholly unexpected experience for an interracial family whose members are different colors.

As the mother of two children whose Blackness isn't exactly obvious, I must confess that what happened to the man in Virginia is a variation on a fear I've had since my daughter was born. It all started when a Chinese friend of mine told me about the time he lost his son at the local mall. He'd had both of his young children with him when, in a split second, he lost sight of his son, who was around four years old at the time. My friend said he was so panicked because he didn't know if he should stay in one place, hoping his son would find his way back to him, or dash through the mall on a quest for the boy. In the precious moments that it took him to decide what to do, a Good Samaritan brought his child back to him. Father and son both cried at being reunited.

"How did the woman know he was your son?" I asked my friend.

"Well, she saw a little Chinese boy wandering around crying and then she saw a big Chinese man looking frantic and she put two and two together," he said.

See, that would never happen to me if I lost track of my daughter in a mall. If a Good Samaritan found her and happened to notice the hysterical Black woman weeping and wailing outside of Macy's, that Samaritan would probably run the other way thinking she was protecting some little white girl from a crazy Black woman. Like the concerned citizen at Walmart said, my daughter and I don't match.

The thing is, in my regular life, matching is not such a big deal. I regularly wear mismatched socks, and sometimes I wear two different earrings if I can't find a pair. But there is something fundamental, something innately human, in the desire to match with your family members, to have visual evidence of your shared genetic makeup. Of course, sometimes that desire to match your child is of a more practical nature, like my fears about losing my daughter in the mall. Krystal Sital, a brown-skinned Trinidadian woman married to a Polish American man, penned an essay for *Salon* in 2015 about the frequency with which her relationship with her two light-skinned daughters is questioned in her suburban New Jersey neighborhood. Sital wrote,

At meet-ups, play groups and libraries, mothers with the same skin tones as their offspring (typically white) give me second and third looks. *Is she the baby sitter? Is she the mother?* Sometimes these questions are tossed into the conversation, sometimes these questions are at the crescendo of our exchange, and sometimes (believe it or not) people just open with them. I doubt my interrogator feels a fraction of my discomfort, never having to endure it several times a day.

She went on to explain that it's not only white women who wonder (aloud) if her children are hers, but brown and Black women as well. The funny thing, Sital wrote, is that despite having different-colored skin, she and her daughters share similar features: "Upon closer inspection, *my children really look like me.* There is absolutely no mistaking it. Still, no one bothers to look that closely."

Many people take the visual evidence of a genetic connection to a loved one for granted—people who are constantly told that they are the spitting image of their mother or father, or the two brothers who are three years apart but could easily pass for twins. In many multiracial families, this never happens, and that yearning for public confirmation of connection never ends.

Heidi Durrow, forty-five, the author of the best-selling novel *The Girl Who Fell from the Sky* and founder of the Mixed Remixed Festival—an annual celebration of the mixed-race experience through literature and film—knows exactly what I mean. When I interviewed her over the phone she recalled her earliest yearnings to look like her Danish mother. "I really struggled because I didn't look like my mom," said Durrow, a self-proclaimed Afro-Viking who has light-brown skin and curly, dark-brown hair. "My mom has blond hair and blue eyes. Her hair is straight and I just really wanted that," Durrow recalled. Although today Durrow is one of the most well-known and prolific advocates of the mixed-race experience—she even founded Mixed Race Experience Month in May 2007 to highlight kick-ass mixed-race individuals throughout history—her struggles with not matching her mother continue. And it's not because she wants the blond hair to meet some Western beauty standard. "I still want to look like my mom, because I want to look connected to her when we're out and about in the world," she said. "I don't know what it is, but I want people to see the connection. I want it to be palpable in the world."

Sharon Chang is a scholar and mixed-race activist based in Seattle. She is the author of the book *Raising Mixed Race: Multicultural Asian Children in a Post-Racial World* and has a background in childhood development. Much of her work deals with parenting mixed-race children, and she understands Durrow's yearning from childhood to match her mother. Chang said that at a very early age, children understand from the world around them that families are supposed to match, and this societal pressure can make children ultra-conscious of the difference in skin color or race between their parents and themselves. "We're in a society sorted by color, and they pick that up very quick," Chang told me in an interview over the phone. On the other hand, she said, parents struggle with this issue even more than children. "I definitely sense that desire to match coming far more from parents than children," she said. "When I did the research for my book, the strongest thread was parents yearning to look like their children because they get so much pushback in public and even from their own families," Chang explained, citing examples of mothers like Sital being asked if they're the nanny and fathers being questioned about their relationship with their own child.

Said Chang, "It's so disruptive to the [parent-child] relationship and when that intersects with this racial world we live in, it gets very complicated." Chang said she heard fears from mono-racial parents raising biracial children that if their child didn't look like them they might not be able to connect with or even love it. They worried the child wouldn't feel like theirs. These sentiments were expressed by both white and Asian parents from Chang's study on parenting mixed-race Asian American children.

The author Andrew Solomon explored this idea in his 2014 best seller, *Far from the Tree*. In the book he profiled families where the children's identities were horizontal to those of their parents. In other words, the children were so different from their parents that their fundamental identities did not match. These children had been born with Down syndrome or autism or were deaf, dwarfs, or geniuses. Solomon wanted to see how parenting would be affected by these grave and unexpected differences. Some eight hundred pages later, he concluded that, in most cases, parents not only found a way to love their extremely exceptional children but found their parenting experience to be transformative as well.

Not surprisingly, a similar thing happens in multiracial families. A white mother may not feel confident raising her Asian-looking child. A white father may feel inadequate in rearing his Black sons. Like me, a Black mother may feel loss when parenting her daughter who could pass for white. But through some sort of transcendent grace, quality parenting happens and the kids come out okay.

Light Girls

In the mid-2000s, when I was juggling my freelance writing career with my chosen profession as a mom, I decided to start a T-shirt company. As the mother of two mixed-race, bicultural, bilingual kids, I'd begun writing about the mixed-race experience from a Black mom's perspective and was participating in a lot of mixed-race activities and events, immersing myself in the community that I figured my children may someday feel compelled to join. One of the most common complaints I heard from individuals in this community was of being bombarded with that annoying question "What are you?" no matter where they went. I saw an opportunity to address that issue with a T-shirt that might serve as a conversation starter. Partnering with a friend who just happened to be an amazing graphic designer and former advertising executive, we launched whatrugear.com, debuting a colorful range of tees with logos like "Mixed to Perfection" and "Ambiguously Brown." The shirts were a hit in our decidedly diverse local community, and word spread around college campuses too. Sadly, my dreams of being a T-shirt mogul never materialized, but the lessons learned from touring the country promoting those shirts stuck with me. For the individual who does not fit into an obvious racial category, moving through life requires answering that "What are you?" question before any human relationship can ensue. And if you're the mixed-race child of a monoracial parent, usually that parent has no firsthand knowledge of how to proceed. I talked to three young people who fit into that category, to hear how they handled their ethnic ambiguity.

My first conversation was with one of my former students, a biracial woman who reads as white. She was raised by her Black mother and I was thrilled she agreed to be interviewed for this book. No longer living the collegiate life, Samirah Daniels dropped by my office after work one day in the early summer. Now twenty-four, she works as a social media manager for a popular Philadelphia restaurant. When she walked through my office door in a black T-shirt and jeans, her long, straight brown hair hanging far below her shoulders, I found myself scanning her almond-tinted skin, blue-gray eyes, and coral-pink lips for any obvious signs of Blackness but could find none.

Back when she was sitting in my classroom at Temple two years ago, I assumed Samirah was white. Her unique first name and the silver ring she wore in her nose had me guessing she might be of Middle Eastern background, but I never pried. It wasn't until she mentioned something in class about having hair issues and wanting to wear cornrows as a child that I realized, with some shock, that Samirah must be Black. Now, as Samirah settled into her chair, I confessed that these had been my first impressions. She brushed off my apology and told me she gets that all the time. She is used to being mistaken for a white girl.

Despite being read as white by most people, Samirah made it very clear that she identifies more with Black culture than with white. Not only because she was raised in Washington, DC, solely by her Black mother (her white father wasn't around), but also because she was always surrounded by her mother's extended Black family.

"If I had to choose, I would say I identify more as Black, even though I'm not perceived as Black," she said. "I was raised in a Black family. My culture is an African American culture and that's what I know. That to me is being Black." Samirah doesn't equate Blackness with skin color, but she was very practical and matter-of-fact when she explained that despite her own sense of Black cultural identity, she understands that she moves through the world being read as white. When asked "What are you?" by strangers—which she says happens at least once a day—her answer is "mixed" or "Black and white." She also understands that despite feeling culturally Black, she receives the advantages of being perceived as white. Samirah admitted it's complicated, but it seems very clear that she has decided to let those complications rest on others. "It's just more trouble to me a lot of the time to explain who I am, so I've sort of let people think whatever they want about me."

When Samirah was growing up, her mom didn't spend a lot of time talking about Samirah's African American heritage. In fact, Samirah doesn't remember talking much about race and identity or skin color with her mom as a child, but then again, she grew up in a neighborhood that was mostly Black and Hispanic, so Blackness was all around her. It didn't need to be taught. Inside the house, Samirah said, her mother didn't shy away from racial discussions or discussing topics of racial concern, but they weren't meant as instructive or to counterbalance her light skin. "We never really talked about my skin tone," Samirah said, even though her skin was even paler when she was a young child and her hair was red. Reflecting back on her childhood, she shrugged and said, "No, we never really had that conversation." This despite the fact that the outside world always had something to say about the white girl with the Black mother. "I feel like I have always had to explain who my mom is because when you look at us next to each other, it's like we don't really make sense," Samirah said. "When I was younger a lot of people thought that she wasn't my mom or that she was my babysitter." Samirah said that undoubtedly this was the most annoying thing about being a different color than her mom—the constant need to explain their relationship.

Even though Samirah is only twenty-four and just starting out in life, I decided to ask if she had ever thought about her future children and what color she imagined them being. To my surprise, she was ready with an answer. "Actually I think about this question all the time," she told me. "I have a serious boyfriend and we've been dating for five years, but he's white, so if we had kids they'd just be white and that bothers me." I asked her why it would bother her and at first she just said she wanted children that were visibly mixed like many of her cousins and family members. "Maybe it's because that's what I'm surrounded by and that's just what my family looks like," she said. But I pushed her a little more and she admitted something else.

"If my kids were growing up with someone who's perceived as white and a white father, it wouldn't give them my background," she began. "I grew up in this Black culture and I was surrounded by all these people who had these experiences and brought something to the table that was instructive and useful for me as a human." Samirah shrugged. "I don't know. Maybe I've been surrounded by too many overprivileged white kids in my life and I feel like there is just something about being different that is beneficial to your life."

After she said all this, Samirah looked relieved, a little defiant, and maybe a little hopeful. And she wasn't finished. "This is going to sound mean, but I also want my children to have some color because I feel like all little white children look the same." We both laughed, sharing a conspiratorial moment, and I knew then that Samirah must really see herself as Black if she categorized "white children" as the "other."

Although Samirah seems to have a healthy sense of who she is and doesn't spend a lot of time trying to "Blacken up" her appearance or speech, I can only imagine the yearning to have a child that would validate her Blackness. And I understood on a personal level the fear that having a white child would somehow signify an ending to her connection to her Black family.

That's what happened to my friend Patrice. Patrice is the daughter of a Black father and a white mother. She is so racially ambiguous, with almond-colored skin, thick brown hair, and brown eyes, that it took me almost six months after I first met her to verify that she was indeed biracial, although she identifies as Black. Patrice spent a lifetime being culturally misunderstood. Growing up and into early adulthood, she said, she'd get yelled at in certain neighborhoods for not speaking Spanish.

Patrice is now divorced from her children's father, who is white. Her two daughters look like average white kids. Not white with a little bit of something ethnic, but just garden-variety white American. I visited Patrice at the end of the spring, on a gorgeous sunny day in Brooklyn, to ask her if she ever wished her children were darker. She didn't even have to stop and think. "Absolutely," she said. Given Patrice's strong Black identity and progressive racial politics, I wasn't surprised by her answer, but at the same time, I was still prepared for a politically correct response where she would tell me that she loves her children exactly the way they are and color doesn't matter. But that's not what she said.

I asked her why she wished her girls had been born with more melanin. "Because it would make everything easier," she said.

"Easier for you, or easier for them?" I asked.

"Easier for everyone. It would just make it so we didn't have to explain ourselves all the time."

I understood, or at least I thought I understood, how soul crushing it must be to have to enter a space and let everyone know you're Black before they said something racist or assumed you were the enemy.

"I used to always announce to the world that I'm Black," Patrice said. "But I've stopped doing that because it's exhausting."

And while she raises her daughters without filters on her opinions and racial politics, she knows the two girls are perceived as white and for the most part identify as white. How could they not?

"My daughters don't have the lived experience of what it means to be Black. They don't even know how it feels to walk through the world with a Black mom because I don't read as Black," she said with a sigh.

This would be Samirah's reality, the one she already fears. This is Patrice's lament. And the more mixed people I spoke with, the more I heard yearnings of wanting to look like the person of color in the family rather than the white one. Despite the benefits of white privilege and the seemingly unanimous worldwide view that European beauty is the ideal, for many mixed people, looking white feels like the losing end of the stick.

Joy Huang Stoffers, twenty-three, can relate. The daughter of a Taiwanese mother and a white American father, Joy grew up in New Jersey. She recalls her father joking that she leaned toward the West, while her older brother leaned to the East, meaning while her brother could pass as fully Asian, Joy has often been mistaken for white. "I remember wanting to feel the same kind of affinity with a parent that my brother had with my mother based on appearance," she told me in our Skype interview from her apartment in England, where she is currently studying creative writing.

Not only did Joy's more Western features obscure her Asian heritage to the outside world, but inside the home, being pale and having inherited her father's Irish skin made her feel different. "My brother could get away with minimal sunscreen or none at all," Joy told me. "But it was always 'Lather her up all the time' with me," she said. "I was so jealous of my brother." The sunscreen and the attention paid to her pale skin by her mother—who had darker skin than Joy—made her even more aware of the difference between herself and her brother and mom. "There was more planning involved and more attention put on me [because of my skin color] and I wasn't an attention-craving kid," she explained. When the family took their semi-annual trips to Taiwan, again her pale skin brought unwanted attention, due to the popularity there of mixed-race features. Joy was often stared at and complimented on her beauty. "When I was really little I was like, all this attention is fun, but it got creepier as I got older," she said. "I had just enough of the foreign, but enough Asian. I was somewhere in between and that was fascinating [to them]."

Today, Joy said, she is comfortably mixed. "I look in the mirror and I see both sides in me," she told me. "Other people might not see that, but I see it and I feel that's more important." One of the ways she has worked through her identity issues is through her writing. Her debut novel, *Whasian*, is, not surprisingly, about a mixed-race Asian/white girl coming to terms with her identity. And Joy said she will continue to talk and write about this issue because people like her are often forgotten in identity debates. "The mixed-race bigotry is not discussed as often, and being biracial [can feel] like erasure," she said.

Erasure. That's a terrible feeling, because everybody wants to be seen.

Choose Your Own Identity

I thought it was quite remarkable that both Samirah Daniels and Joy Huang Stoffers had been able to craft their own ethnic identities, despite not having the same identities as their parents. It says something about the fluidity of identity in the twenty-first century. It also probably says something about this generation of millennials, who often seem unfettered by yesterday's rules of identity classification.

But what about the child who is darker than his mother or father? Can he, too, define his own identity? Or will the rules of race and color deter him? Julian Chang-Li, twenty-four and the child of two multiracial Black and Asian parents, makes his own rules when it comes to his identity. Julian is a musician who pays the bills with a day job in marketing. Based in Pittsburgh, he was raised in Miami by his Jamaican father and American mother. He also has an older brother. Julian's father was born in Jamaica, his mother in the Bronx, and while both parents identified as Black, they both had Chinese grandparents. On his mother's side, there are Filipino and Irish ancestors as well. "Yeah, we've got the whole melting pot going on in my family," Julian laughed when we spoke on the phone. As a result, Julian has brown skin, thick black hair, and dark eyes. He could be the poster child for racial ambiguity.

When Julian was growing up, his mother listened to Chinese music, his father loved Chinese cinema, and the entire family were members of the National Association of Chinese Americans. Julian said that because of his and his brother's dark skin, however, his mother raised them both with the understanding that how they thought of themselves might not match how the outside world perceived them. "My mother always confirmed that we were two Black boys in a society that really doesn't treat Black male bodies with respect," he said. By the time he left for college,

Julian was ready to challenge the system that did not recognize both sides of his identity.

"If you're a Black and Asian person, you're supposedly just Black, but that just negates your Asian-ness," he said. Despite having a skin tone darker than his mother and older brother, Julian says he feels more Asian than Black (ironically, his brother, who looks more Asian, identifies as Black), so he joined an Asian students' organization at college. Julian was immediately made to feel welcome by some, but there were others who challenged his right to be in the group, mostly because he had dark skin and wasn't "Asian enough." He explained, "I basically spent a super long time trying to prove my Asianness, in college." The high point in his quest was getting crowned Mr. Asian-American in 2013. The male-only pageant, sponsored by the Asian Students Association at his school is an annual event meant to counterbalance the limited stereotypes of Asian males in the media. For Julian, it was a monumental win. "It was never the South Asian guys that won," he told me. "It was always the fairest-skinned East Asian men, so I went in thinking I was going to lose. But out I came with the win." His pride was short-lived, however; Julian said many of the Asians on campus didn't accept the fact that he had won.

Two years after college graduation, Julian is active with several pan-Asian groups in Pittsburgh, and he continues to press against boundaries and limits when it comes to identity. "I personally think it's super weird that these definitions of race and what it means to be Asian and what it means to be Black come from a white perspective and there are no allowances for any in-betweens," he said. "It's like, pick your one category and stay there because 'the man' says so." These days Julian is okay straddling identity boxes. "I don't really identify with any federally recognized category," he said. "I just say I'm multiethnic. It's the best thing for me."

After speaking with the identity-bending millennials, I almost felt like I could safely declare that identity boxes have been obliterated, now existing just for show. Like the Choose Your Own Adventure novels I grew up with in the 1980s and '90s, these young people were proving to me that, at least in the multiracial community, there is obviously a level of choice now in deciding what identity to claim. Tiger Woods could be considered the patron saint of the Choose Your Own Identity movement. Back in the late 1990s, when Woods burst on to the scene and was

heralded as the first African American to win the Masters Golf Tourna-
ment, he was quick to correct the racial labeling. He was not going to be
categorized as African American, not when his mother claimed Thai-
land as her homeland. Woods, who had clearly given this much thought,
announced to the world that he was actually Cablinasian, a label that
incorporated his multiple ethnic roots—Black, white, and Native American from his father and Asian from his mother—from both sides of his
family. Not everyone was thrilled with the term, but more than a decade
later people still remember it, even if they don't use it.

"If Tiger Woods wants to be Cablinasian, I have no problem with
that," said Jesse Washington, forty-six, a prolific writer on race, identity,
and sports. The former Associated Press staffer, who covered the "race
beat" for AP, is himself biracial, the child of a Black father and a white
mother. But the reality is, no matter how often Woods repeats his preference for "Cablinasian," most people still refer to him as "the Black
golfer." Washington explained why. "We're layered with a set of social
customs and definitions that are particular to this country, like the one-
drop rule," he said, referring to the fact that if Woods is even partly
Black, then he theoretically qualifies for full Black status. "But remember, being Black and [being] biracial are not mutually exclusive." In fact,
that's how Washington explains his own racial identity. He often calls
himself a Black man with a white mother. "I never tried on a biracial
identity, for two reasons," Washington told me. "First of all, society always viewed me and treated me as a Black person, and second, my dad
had a very strong Black identity and he was the role model [for me]."
Washington exemplifies a very common experience for mixed-race people who tend to look like one race over the other. Like Samirah Daniels,
who passes as white, Washington passes as Black. Most people are
shocked when they discover his mother is white. In fact, according to
Washington, when he was growing up, most people assumed his mother
was Black because of the color of her children and husband. In other
words, she became Black by association.

There are, of course, limits to the "choose your own identity" game,
and not everyone gets to play. Right in the middle of my research for this
chapter, a white woman named Rachel Dolezal made national headlines
when it was discovered that she had actively tried to become Black by association. The single mother of two Black boys, one biological (technically,

he's biracial) and one adopted, Dolezal was born in Montana to two white parents. But in the past decade, she decided she identified more with Black culture than with white. So, she reinvented a genetic history and past for herself that included a Black father. Her racial ruse was so believable that she became the president of the local chapter of the NAACP in Spokane, Washington, where she lived. By darkening her skin with what appeared to be makeup and/or a spray tan, wearing traditionally Black hairstyles, and championing a lot of Black causes, her claim to Blackness probably would have gone unquestioned had her parents not outed her to the media.

Many people were furious with Dolezal for laying claim to a history and a culture that weren't her own, and perhaps even cheating actual Black people out of jobs and opportunities that she had earned under the false presumption that she was Black. While social media, particularly Black Twitter, exploded with outrage, I was struck by how simple it had been for Dolezal to pass as Black. Even when she hadn't bothered to add an extra layer of spray tan, with the right hairstyle, jewelry, and politics, her story was believable. Her claim of being a biracial member of the Black community seemed legitimate. After all, thanks to light-skinned, biracial celebrities such as Rashida Jones, Mariah Carey, and Meghan Markle, the public face of Blackness can indeed look quite white. But unlike those celebrities, Dolezal actually has no Black blood running through her veins. Somebody forget to tell her that if she didn't have the right materials, she wasn't allowed to play the "choose your own identity" game. At the end of the day, the only game Dolezal seemed to be playing was dress-up, in the kingdom of make-believe.

Secrets and Lies

Ironically, right before Rachel Dolezal hit the stage, I had seen *Little White Lie*, a documentary by a woman named Lacey Schwartz. The film represents Schwartz's exploration of her own racial identity. Growing up the only child of a middle-class Jewish couple in Woodstock, New York, Schwartz always wondered why she had brown skin and curly hair, unlike either of her white Jewish parents. Without dwelling on it, her parents told Schwartz that she took after her paternal grandfather, who was from Sicily. For most of her childhood, Schwartz grew up believing she was simply a white girl with brown skin and curly, bordering on kinky, hair. Her parents told her she was white, her extended family told her she was white, and all of her friends in their mostly white community accepted her as one of their own. It wasn't until she went off to Georgetown University—where the admissions department, based on a photo she submitted, assumed she was Black—did Schwartz begin to suspect the truth. And the truth was that Lacey Schwartz's mother had had an affair with a Black man who was her biological father.

The lie Lacey's mother told had far-reaching repercussions, including the dissolution of her marriage and the rupturing of the relationship between Lacey and her father. He never seemed to get over what he termed "the ultimate betrayal" by Lacey's mother. (Was that betrayal her affair, the lie, or the fact that her lover was Black?) Still, like Dolezal and her fabricated fantasy of a Black identity, Lacey Schwartz lived for almost two decades as if she were actually white, despite a skin color that betrayed the obvious. But, as she said in the film, "I wasn't trying to be white. I was white." Skin color be damned, Schwartz believed she was white and the rest of the world went along with it. Before her father knew the truth, he too felt nothing but love and adoration for his daughter, meaning the different colors between parent and child really meant nothing until racial categories were placed upon them.

By all accounts, Schwartz had a privileged and happy childhood up until her parents' divorce, when she was a teen. And yet, in the film she mentions all of the times she felt different growing up because of her skin color and describes how she yearned to be lighter so she would fit in. "It was embarrassing to be singled out. It made me feel ugly," she said. But, except for one conversation about that mysterious Sicilian relative when Schwartz was quite young, her parents never mentioned the color of her skin. They seemed to think that if they didn't mention it, it might go away. "But my darkness was always questioned by outsiders," Schwartz admitted in an interview. Ultimately, it was outsiders who forced Schwartz to confront her mother about the truth of her origins. And once she learned the truth, she was able to forge a new identity where her "dark skin" was no longer an issue. "Just like that, I was welcomed into the Black community," she said in the film. "My dark skin became light skin and the bad hair became good hair."

Based on the experiences of Dolezal, Schwartz, and Julian Chang-Li, it seems like racial identity *doesn't* depend on skin color. Instead, it can be created with a convincing hairdo, sufficient background knowledge, and a little white lie or two. But dig deeper—uncovering Julian's lack of acceptance by the Asian community, or the questioning of Schwartz's dark skin by outsiders—and one sees that at the end of the day, people are treated by others based on how they are perceived. For example, President Barack Obama said he chose to check African American on his census form in 2010 because that's how he is perceived. He said the American public views him as Black so it would be foolish to identify himself any other way. When he was running for president for the first time, Obama addressed this issue with talk-show host Charlie Rose. "If I'm outside your building trying to catch a cab, they're not saying, 'Oh, there's a mixed-race guy,'" Obama said. The president didn't deny or negate his white mother; he simply embraced a Black identity because fighting against other people's perceptions would be a losing and exhausting battle.

Sharon Chang understands the president's predicament and says many mixed-race people find themselves in the same situation. "There's that dissonance between self and imposed identification that a lot of racially ambiguous people deal with and it's very disorienting," said Chang. "The best thing we can do for mixed kids is to talk to them about that within our homes with conversations that begin with 'We need to talk about the way you look and the assumptions around the way you look,'" she said. Chang also noted that parents too often are afraid to get into these taboo topics with their kids, but avoiding the issue, like Schwartz's parents did—although her situation was unusual—can only end with children who have issues with who they are supposed to be. "Socialization of race and culture has to be comprehensive with children," agreed Vetta Sanders Thompson, a professor at the George Warren Brown School of Social Work at Washington University. "Parents have to talk about all aspects of race and color. Children need constant dialogue around these issues."

Mixed to Perfection

The author Emily Raboteau, thirty-eight, is the daughter of a white mother and an African American father. She stands as a perfect example of a biracial child whose parents never shied away from the topic of her ambiguous identity.

Despite Raboteau's tawny skin tone and relatively straight, dark hair, she unapologetically claims a Black identity, or sometimes biracial, which she views as a category of Blackness. Raised in the mostly white suburban setting of Princeton, New Jersey, Raboteau is one of four children. The second-oldest and the only daughter, she also describes herself as the lightest child in the family. Still, she said, she never thought of herself as anything other than Black. "I was raised to identify myself as African American and my first self-portrait, drawn in kindergarten, featured a face colored in with black crayon. That's how I understood myself," she said, adding that she never really perceived difference in the skin tone of her family members, even though they were all different shades. "I think that from a young age, I had a more nuanced understanding of Blackness than skin tone," she said.

Providing their daughter with Black and brown dolls and children's books featuring African American characters, Raboteau's parents were intentional in the way they raised their children, so that their cultural foundation, despite living in a mostly white environment and having one white parent, was solidly Black. Raboteau said that until she left for college, her sense of identity as a Black person was never shaken. "[It] was never something that confused or distressed me as a child," she said. "When I graduated from high school and went to college, leaving my nuclear family, that was the first time I felt a degree of confusion, because without the visual context of my family, most people did not perceive me as Black." Today, Raboteau can verbalize why Blackness shouldn't be equated with skin color and how definitions of race are useless. "Social scientists disproved racial difference over a century ago," she said. "Race itself is a false construct, and it has very little to do with skin color, though it has real consequences and implications." On the other hand, she said, Blackness is obviously a real category, but "it has more to do with a cultural feeling than anything connected to color."

Admittedly, it took Raboteau some time to come to terms with outsiders' assumptions in terms of her identity and how she would walk through the world. Her book *Searching for Zion* explores some of those feelings along with her decade-long quest to find not only a geographical location that Black Americans could call home, but a community for herself that she could claim as a biracial Black woman. "I didn't think of myself as the 'tragic mulatto' straight out of central casting," Raboteau wrote in *Searching for Zion*. "The role was an embarrassing cliché from a dusty, bygone era, but I struggled against it. . . . I belonged nowhere. I wasn't well. Was the sickness my own, my country's, or a combination of the two?"

Raboteau has since married, and that marriage brought her a lot of comfort and a chance to recreate her family. "I married another mixed person [because] it was important to me to marry somebody who would understand my cultural context and references on a very deep level," she told me. Today the couple has two children and everyone in the family is a different color. "This is not distressing or weird to me," Raboteau said. "My preoccupation is with teaching my children to be kind, self-loving, self-confident, and generous people who know something about history and culture and can move through the world with joy and grace."

Raboteau's explanations and confident sense of self-identity that had nothing to do with skin color bolstered the idea that "good parenting" can make a difference in a child's racial identity development. Skin-color differences, while apparent in Raboteau's home when she was growing up, never caused strife. Subsequently, in her household now, Raboteau is adequately prepared to raise her own children without fretting about variations in the shades of their skin.

Like Raboteau, journalist and author Soledad O'Brien grew up in a mixed-race household of different colors in which colorism was never an issue. But unlike Raboteau, O'Brien has a different explanation for why color talk never came up during her childhood.

O'Brien, one of six children, grew up in Smithtown, Long Island, a town that is 95 percent white. O'Brien's mother is Afro-Cuban, and her father is Irish by way of Australia. Despite the fact that O'Brien, her mother, and her siblings were varying shades of brown and her father white, she says skin color was a non-issue in her home. "Honestly, I don't really even remember a time when I thought my dad was a different color than us," she said. "It never really occurred to me." O'Brien attributes the lack of skin-color conversations in her family to one basic fact: nobody cared about it outside of their household. O'Brien explained that in an all-white town, race talk was irrelevant. "No one is going to have conversations about race because there was nothing to talk about," said O'Brien. While she admitted there were occasional annoying questions and comments about her hair or lips (yes, her lips), the potential conflict between light skin and dark skin never entered her consciousness. "We never talked about skin tone," O'Brien said of her family. "We never talked about people being darker or lighter." Although her parents never introduced any type of skin-color hierarchy to their children, O'Brien also credits her colorism-free childhood to the fact that no one else in their environment valued or devalued any particular skin color either. "You need a critical mass of people of color to even start any of these conversations," O'Brien explained. "And we didn't have any critical mass." Nor did she have any extended family to engage with on these issues. "My mother's Cuban relatives stayed in Cuba and my dad's Australian relatives stayed in Australia," she said. "I had no relatives." According to O'Brien, it wasn't until she left home that she had her first taste of skin-color bias. "The first time I thought about skin color was in college," said O'Brien, who attended Harvard University. "That was the first time I heard about the paper-bag test and I didn't understand what [it was]."

Today, O'Brien is married to a white man and has four children—two girls and two boys—of varying hues and hair types. The family lives in Manhattan and, not surprisingly, based on her own upbringing, color talk is not a part of O'Brien's parenting plan. While she doesn't avoid discussing critical issues around race and identity—consider her career—she refuses to engage in any discussion with her kids that suggests a hierarchy based on how someone looks. After declaring that she unapologetically throws away fashion magazines because of the damaging messages they provide to young girls, she said, "I don't want to be part of [any] conversation about skin color or hair texture or how skinny you are or how you look," she said. "We do not need to have any of those conversations."

Comparing Raboteau's and O'Brien's upbringings, there are similarities and differences, but the outcome—healthy mixed-race children raising healthy mixed-race children—seems to be the same. Both women grew up in mostly white environments and both women had one Black parent and one white. But while Raboteau's parents very intentionally raised their children with a strong Black identity, O'Brien's parents, perhaps because they were both immigrants in a new country, didn't emphasize race in the same way. As a result, Raboteau identifies as Black or biracial, while O'Brien says she is Black and Latina and Irish and Cuban. "Identity is so much more important to other people," O'Brien said when I asked how she likes to be identified. Rather than rejecting any identity label, she embraces them all. "I think you can be all of those things," she said, "and I don't struggle with it all."

Rejection

Of course, not every mixed-race child wants to be seen as Black or ethnic and not every parent wants his or her child to lean in to their colorful side. In September 2014, a man named Calvin Hennick penned an essay for *Ebony* with the headline "I Hope My Son Stays White." In the essay, Hennick, who is white, wrote passionately about how he hoped his infant son would stay light enough to pass for white even though the baby's mother is Haitian. While Hennick wrote with a decent amount of humility, it didn't take the sting out of his prayers for his child to reject his Blackness: "I want my son's skin color not to matter, but the truth is that it does," he wrote. "If he gets darker . . . there will be consequences for him. People will fear him. . . . It will only be worse if he wears a hoodie and sags his jeans, and so shamefully I also hope that he'll be 'culturally white,' following the trends of the suburbs and not the inner city."

Not surprisingly, Hennick's essay received a lot of angry comments from people who saw his fears as racist. What was surprising, however, was the amount of support from both Black and white readers who understood Hennick's point of view. It will be interesting to see how Hennick's son feels about his identity in the years to come, and whether Hennick's approach to keeping his son white will help or hinder the boy's development. The fact is, if his son chooses to identify as Black, Hennick clearly won't be the obvious role model to help him navigate that world. Indeed, if and when that happens, there is the distinct possibility that Hennick's son will rejects his father and embrace his Haitian heritage in full.

It kind of comes with the territory that children will reject their parents' teachings and values, determined to live life on their own terms. While that can be discouraging and difficult to accept for any well-meaning parent, it is certainly not unexpected. When a child rejects their parents' heritage, that's another story. That type of rejection feels both painful and deeply personal. But when children in interracial families choose to identify with one race or culture over the other, it's often not really a choice but rather a decision forced upon them based on the way they look and the environment they grow up in. I met a young woman whose situation illustrates this perfectly.

Angela Diaz, twenty-two, has a Puerto Rican father and a white mother of Irish, English, and German heritage. Her parents split up when she was five years old. Born and raised in Philadelphia, Angela lived with her mother and sister in the Germantown section of Philadelphia. When I met Angela in a small bookstore in Center City for our interview, I could guess why she had essentially rejected her mother's culture and instead chose to embrace a Puerto Rican identity.

She was dressed in tight black sweatpants and a red T-shirt with her college mascot emblazoned on the front, and her toffee-colored skin and long, black, curly hair, which she wore slicked back into a free-flowing ponytail, screamed Latina. Because of Angela's brown eyes and the urban slang with which she peppered her conversation, one would be hard-pressed to imagine that not only is her mother white but that Angela has an older sister with straight blond hair, green eyes, and not a speck of slang in her day-to-day vocabulary. "Technically we look a lot alike," Angela said when describing her sister. "We're just different colors. She's a white girl all the way, but I'm the stereotype of a Puerto Rican."

What's interesting about Angela's story is that for the first several years of her life, with her father out of the picture, she didn't know what culture to claim. She attended a public elementary school with a mostly Black population, and her ethnic identity came up several times, especially since her blond-haired, green-eyed sister went to the same school, which only added to the confusion regarding Angela's racial status. "My mom told me I was mixed, but people were like, 'What are you mixed with?'" Angela said, laughing at the memory. "I didn't know, so I said, 'I'm white and Black,' since my mom was white and all my friends were Black." It wasn't until Angela's dad returned from serving in the Navy, when she was around ten years old, that her identity came into focus. "When my dad came home, my whole world changed," she said. "I look just like him, and I realized I was Puerto Rican. Once he came home, I saw more of him and his side of the family."

Meeting her Puerto Rican relatives felt like a revelation for young Angela, who clearly loves her mother but can also admit that she felt alienated growing up in a household with a white parent and a sister who looked white. "I felt a sense of displacement," she said. Spending time in the Puerto Rican neighborhood her father grew up in, in New York City, Angela quickly decided that she had found the place where she belonged. "I feel like I really grew up in my grandma's neighborhood," she said. "Most of my fondest memories are there. That's what I consider home."

When it was time for Angela to apply to high schools, she deliberately chose a school that had a significant population of Latinos. Her sister, on the other hand, attended a high school with a majority-white student body. And while Angela spent every weekend and school break with her grandmother in New York, soaking up her culture, her sister stayed away. "My sister's blond-haired self stuck out in my grandma's neighborhood," Angela explained. "They'd call her *La gringa*, but I could fit in because I looked like everybody there." Meanwhile, back home in Philly, Angela said she stuck out amid all of her sister's white friends. So, in essence, due to their different colors, these two sisters grew up with completely different cultural identities. "At first glance I gravitate toward people of color," Angela confirmed. "My sister, it's white people."

For reasons that have more to do with the difficulty of life with a single mother who was also putting herself through school while raising two children than with the fact that her sister looked white, Angela said she and her sister didn't get along as children. By the time her sister went away to college, however, they had resolved many of their issues and are now really close. "On an intellectual level we connect so much better now," Angela said. "She's traveled a lot, I've traveled a lot. We've got a greater world view." The differences in how they present to the world haven't changed, though. "We dress and speak differently," Angela said. "I can [code] switch, but you hardly ever hear her use slang. We just carry ourselves very differently, but we're tight."

Another big difference between the sisters revolves around whom they love. "She's engaged to a white guy, which I could never be," Angela told me, not even bothering to mask her distaste at the thought. When I asked her why marrying a white man seemed so unpleasant, she was ready with her answer.

"I don't like light skin," she said. "I don't find it attractive." She was also forecasting into the future. "Also, I want my babies to have some color. If I marry a white guy and [my daughter] came out white, I don't know what I'd do." She joked, "She'd be my sister." But Angela wasn't joking about how important it was for her future offspring to share her color. Not because of some superficial color preference, but because she wanted to spare them the alienation she felt from her own mother and that her sister felt from their father and his family. "I don't want my kid to feel that way," Angela began. "I want them to look at me and think they look like Mommy and have a sense of belonging. When you don't look alike, you feel a disconnect. It's hard to get over it and that's a shame because it's just skin deep." In her next breath, Angela admitted that her kid could come out purple and she'd still love it no matter what. But she won't back away from the idea that color matters and that a child wants that connection to his parents. "I would just prefer my children to look like me."

Of course, looking like mom or dad isn't always the the key to a successful bonding experience between parent and child. For Mikah Castile, the fact that she *did* look like her biological mother—having inherited her pale skin and light hair—brought Mikah no closer to her mother and actually made her relationship with her father painful and fraught with tension.

Mikah, thirty-eight, is a special education teacher based in Rhode Island. Born and raised in New Jersey, she is the daughter of a Native American mother and a Jamaican father. She grew up identifying as Black, but due to her pale skin and almost red hair, lately she's been calling herself mixed—simply to avoid all the confusion the "Black" moniker seems to create in a doubting public. "I was raised by my Black father in a Black household and have always identified with being Black," Mikah said. But after she left home for college, people kept telling her she didn't look Black and seemed to require long explanations regarding her ethnic background. "I don't have time for that many conversations," she said. "I would rather cut to the chase, say I'm mixed, and move on." Although Mikah is now able to take other people's discomfort with her racial identity and thrust it back on them, it has been a long time coming.

Mikah was always the lightest child in the family. Before her parents divorced, when she was five, it was just Mikah and her older sister. Mikah said her sister took after their father and had brown skin and black, curly, "mixed girl" hair. Mikah, on the other hand, had kinky reddish-brown hair and skin almost as pale as her mother's. When they went out in public as a family, people always had questions. "With me it was always, 'What are you?'" Mikah said. "I guess it's because my skin is fairer and my hair is red, but my hair is just like my dad's. I look like him so I didn't understand why people looked at me that way." Inside the house, Mikah said, her parents never made any distinction between their daughters. "We were both the same in our parents' eyes," Mikah said. "They would tell us, 'You are both our daughters and the same.'" That all changed, however, after her parents divorced and Mikah's father married a Black woman, also from Jamaica.

"My stepmother made negative comments about how white my skin was," Mikah said, the pain in her voice coming through clearly over the phone as we spoke. "That was the first time I realized I looked white"—and, by extension, somehow flawed. "I overheard my stepmother say to a friend when my little sister was born that she was happy her daughter came out darker than me because she didn't think she could stomach having a child as white as me." Mikah paused to collect herself before she could continue her story.

Around the same time that her stepmother began making disparaging remarks about her skin color, Mikah started high school and she found herself at the receiving end of racial taunting by the Black boys at her school. "They made comments about how disgusting my skin color was and told me no Black man would ever find me attractive." Hurt, Mikah went home looking for support. Unfortunately, her biological mother offered little comfort. "My mom has her own issues, so she was really no help," Mikah explained, noting that her mother had become an on-again, off-again parent over the years. Her father simply had little sympathy. "My dad was the typical male. He was like, 'You're in school to study, don't worry about the other stuff.'" At least her older sister, who is six years older than Mikah, offered her a shoulder to cry on and words of support, telling Mikah to ignore the boys at school because they were probably just jealous.

Unfortunately, when Mikah's sister left home, things got worse between Mikah and her stepmother. Mikah confided in her father about her stepmother's emotional abuse, but her father refused to believe her and eventually threw Mikah out of the house when she was nineteen years old and in her first year of college. The years that followed were filled with anguish and pain for Mikah as the relationship with her father continued to deteriorate. While she watched him lovingly support, both emotionally and financially, her three other sisters—all of whom had darker skin—she had to beg him for a minimal donation to her schooling. At the heart of their conflict was Mikah's identity. Not only did Mikah's dad have a hard time sympathizing with Mikah—specifically, with the toll it was taking on her to prove her Black identity to a world that was hell-bent on seeing her as something other than Black—but he refused to take his daughter's complaints about his new wife seriously, as something other than sour grapes. "He didn't want to see what was there and that it was affecting me," she said. And then there was the part about her mother.

"I think my dad sees my mom when he looks at me," Mikah said. "My mom and dad had a rocky relationship, so I don't know if when he looks at me he just thinks I'm like her," she mused aloud. "He doesn't know what to do with me."

Listening to Mikah revisit her past made me want to cry along with her. I ached for the little girl who was demonized in her own family for being too light. I wished I could scoop little Mikah up out of the past and praise her for being her unique self, but luckily, Mikah has managed to heal herself. But not without a lot of pain and missteps. "In college I went to the extreme where I felt if I embraced hip-hop and R&B and knew all of these Black history facts, I could prove my Blackness," Mikah said. "I had to dress a certain way and hang out with a certain crowd. And I even had the [Janet Jackson] *Poetic Justice* braids." Mikah also admitted she would only date Black men, again to prove her Blackness. "Looking back," she said, "that was so stupid." It wasn't until Mikah moved to the West Coast for a job that she began to realize how fluid identity could be and how whom she chose to love didn't validate (or invalidate) her own racial identity.

Today Mikah is happily married to a man who is also mixed. "When I first met him I thought he was Black and white, but he wasn't." Mikah laughed. "He's white and Filipino, and he's so comfortable with who he is," she said. "We went out and had fun, and it wasn't about what we looked like; it was about how we got along."

Thanks to the intervention of her older sister, relations between Mikah and her father have improved, but the two have never truly sorted through their issues. "I know I'm still living with hurt and anger," Mikah admitted as we came to the close of our discussion. "We've kind of brushed it under the table and I've never confronted it." For now, rather than dwelling on the past, Mikah derives great pleasure in dreaming about the future with her husband and the children they hope to have soon. "I'd love to have a brown baby," she said. "In my mind I picture her having color, not being so fair, and I picture her hair being curly."

When we say good-bye, I find myself wishing with all my heart that Mikah's dreams come true.

Imitation of Life Syndrome

I haven't written much about my own daughter here, but I admit her color confounds me. Admitting that is painful but honest. One day she might read these pages and know that I felt conflicted about the lightness of her skin. I just always pictured that my daughter would have brown skin and kinky hair. I find myself looking at little brown girls the same age as my daughter and wondering what it would be like to have a mini-me, a girl child who was unmistakably mine. I can admit that I'm still holding on to hope that her melanin production increases and that her hair will continue to curl on a journey all the way to something resembling my own kinky tresses, or at least until it gets thick enough so I can recreate the hairstyles of my youth on her. Sometimes I stare at blond-haired, blue-eyed white women with biracial baby girls with brown skin and curly hair and wonder, do they feel the same way I do?

Like my friend Patrice, I won't lie. If my daughter were visually Black, or even just noticeably colored, my life would be easier. Easier in that we wouldn't have to wear matching T-shirts to prove to the rest of the world we are related. Easier in that my parenting lessons could come straight from my own personal experiences instead of having to reinvent them based on a new identity paradigm. Easier in simple things like braiding hair and not forgetting to slather on sunscreen before heading outside to play. I'm not even sure I know what lessons to teach a little girl who will be perceived as white when she walks through the world. Of course I know my job as a parent is to treat my children as individuals and not as mere extensions of myself, but parenting children who read as your physical antithesis is challenging in a country with rigid racial rules and categories. Considering all of the other trials and tribulations of parenthood, it would be a great relief if this part were easy.

Of course some might argue that my daughter's life will be easier if she can walk through the world being perceived as white instead of

Black, but that's not what I want for my children. I want them to experience the world as I do, as Black Americans. Not because I want them to know racism firsthand, but because I think it's affirming to be a part of the African diaspora. The writer Bonnie Tsui addressed this same issue in an essay in the the *New York Times Magazine* about how her mixed—Chinese and white—sons would choose to identify. She didn't want to force them to identify as Chinese, but she also realized that if they only viewed themselves as white, they'd be missing out on something she found important. "There is something about being a racial minority in America that I would want them to know," she writes. " In the experience of being an 'other,' there's a valuable lesson in consciousness: You learn to listen harder, because you've heard what others have to say about you before you even have a chance to speak." I want that for my children too.

It isn't lost on me that I have some privilege in my ability to publicly lament the lack of melanin in my daughter's skin. While I certainly don't make it a habit to complain about my pale-faced daughter, if I were to mention that I wished my daughter were darker, I might be chastised for being superficial—but many people would nod their heads in understanding. On the other hand, if a white mother with a brown-skinned, mixed-race child complained that her child's skin was too dark or that she wished the child's hair weren't so curly, she'd probably be considered insensitive, ignorant, or just plain racist. Something like this happened in 2014 when a white Ohio woman, Jennifer Cramblett, sued the sperm bank that accidentally sent her the sperm of a Black donor instead of a white donor, resulting in her giving birth to a biracial child. The woman sued the company for "emotional and economic losses," citing the facts that her daughter's brown skin made her stand out in their all-white town and that her curly hair required special visits to a Black hair salon in a Black neighborhood—a neighborhood Cramblett and her white partner felt uncomfortable visiting. Social media exploded with harsh words for and condemnation of Cramblett. While my initial reaction to this story was outrage, thinking mainly about how this little girl would feel when she is old enough to know her parents were "dissatisfied" with her skin color and hair texture, in an honest moment my hypocrisy was revealed. I understand why a white mother would want a white daughter. I understand wanting to be able to walk through life and not be stared at, questioned, or ridiculed for one's life choices. I understand wanting to fall back on tradition and the familiar when parenting. I understand wanting a little bit of easy as a mother.

But yearning for a daughter of the same color isn't only about lessening the burden of parenthood for me. There is also an element of fear. Fear of rejection. I call it the *Imitation of Life* syndrome, referencing the 1959 movie starring Lana Turner, Sandra Dee, and Juanita Moore. In the film, Moore plays a Black maid whose daughter, Sarah Jane, has such light skin she can pass for white. Sarah Jane continuously tries to pass but her mother's presence always exposes her ruse, eventually leading Sarah Jane to run away from home so she can live out her white-girl fantasies, not caring that she's broken her mother's heart in the process. Of course, it is no longer 1959, and Sarah Jane is a spoiled brat in the movie, so one would probably not think this film would influence my thinking. But I would hazard a guess that there are plenty of mothers—and fathers—like me who fear their children will reject them because they don't look alike racially. And the rejection may not be driven by anger or distaste; it may simply be easier for my daughter to pass as white than to struggle to prove her Blackness. Just as it was easier for Angela to see herself as Puerto Rican and Mikah to simply stop trying to be Black.

I know a white woman with a biracial teen daughter who presents as Black. The fifteen-year-old's skin is cinnamon brown, her hair is kinky, and her lips are full—yet her mom confessed to me that her greatest fear is that her daughter would reject her whiteness. At the time I thought this mom was delusional, considering there was nothing white for this beautiful brown girl to reject, but then I realized what she meant. She was afraid her daughter would reject *her*. This is a very real fear for those of us who can't see a version of ourselves in our children. White parents who adopt children of color probably share a similar concern. We live in a racially polarized world, where young people so often feel compelled by forces outside of the home to choose a racial team on which to play. And while I wish it were otherwise, it's probably just easier to join the team where, based on your looks, you'll fit right in. And once that choice is made, parent and child may find themselves playing on opposing teams.

More Than Just Skin Deep

The background noise to my writing this book was a continuous cacophony of outrage over the killing of unarmed Black men and women in the United States. After the shootings of Trayvon Martin and Renisha Mc-

Bride and Tamir Rice, the bodies kept piling up and I couldn't avoid the anger I was feeling. And yet I did avoid having The Talk with my sons because I still couldn't figure out how to address the way the world violentally mistreats Black bodies without also having to address the fact that one child looks Black and the other one doesn't. (My daughter was too young to be part of any of these Talks.) That is not to say we avoid the color conversation in our home. Not at all. Think about it—my entire writing career centers around Black hair and identity politics; clearly, race and color comes up at the dining room table. But The Talk is something different. I was conflicted over whether I needed to have The Talk with both of my sons or just the one who actually looks Black.

The Talk would require me to tell my older son that he is in danger of being killed because of the color of his skin, while his younger brother gets a free pass at being a kid. The Talk means that my younger son can wear a hoodie, while my older son should consider a cardigan when leaving the house. The Talk means telling my thirteen-year-old son that he should make sure he isn't too loud in public places, lest someone become offended by his Blackness, while my ten-year old son can feel free to express himself with the only real threat being an unkind glance or a stern talking-to by an irritated stranger. Yes, this inequity plays out every day in our society, where white kids get a childhood and Black kids get a target on their back, but how do you reconcile those discrepancies inside your own home, between your children? I reconciled them by avoiding The Talk altogether.

Make no mistake, we talked about the injustice of the loss of all of these innocent Black lives. We participated in Black Lives Matter campaigns, both online and in person. We talked about violence and racism in America. But I ended the conversation before it turned into The Talk. I felt ill equipped to handle it, to essentially admit that one son was destined to have a better chance at escaping a bullet than the other based on the color of his skin—something he didn't earn and over which I had no control. If that kind of inequality weren't enough to insert a wedge into their relationship, at the very least it would cause a crack in their belief that they are equals. One might take that realization as an excuse to hate the other. One might take it as a burden of lifelong guilt. I wasn't prepared to be the one who makes that happen.

The thing is, my boys probably know it already. They aren't stupid and they're not blind. And still, I clung to the hope that if *I* don't talk about it, if *I* don't acknowledge the fact that the difference in the shade of their skin is significant, then *I* could keep that Pandora's box of racial evil shut. And I could protect them both. These are my real concerns about my boys and their different colors. It's not just about sunscreen and hairstyles. It's really about the experiences they will have in the world, away from their father and me. On their own, outside the context and protection of their family.

Strength in Numbers

The self-declared mixed-race community is one of the fastest-growing ethnic groups in the United States. Based on census figures, the number of Americans identifying themselves as being of more than one race grew by almost 32 percent between 2000 and 2010. What's more, thanks to "Mixie" writers like Heidi Durrow, Sharon Chang, and Mat Johnson, not to mention creative artists and activists such as Laura Kina, Fanshen Cox DiGiovanni, and Kip Fulbeck, the mixed-race community is going public, no longer a group that needs to hide or melt itself into monoracial boxes. But members of the mixed-race family, with their different skin colors and hair textures, and their non-matching members, still need support. When a white man can shop at Walmart with his biracial daughters and not be stopped by police, and an Indian woman can take her light-skinned children to the park and not be asked how much she charges for child care, then we will know we've really made progress.

Author and activist Heidi Durrow thinks that progress is still a long way off, given how difficult it still is for people to believe a brown-skinned girl could have a mother with a peaches-and-cream complexion. "We still don't trust what we see because we are so wedded to ideas that don't match reality," Durrow said. Today's reality for the mixed-race family is that because we don't match, people get uncomfortable. And when people get uncomfortable they tend to respond in ugly ways. They stare, they ask stupid questions, they suggest something unnatural is at play. And that doesn't bode well for a family of many colors. One day, perhaps the garden metaphor—a garden with flowers of many colors is as beautiful as one with flowers of a single hue—will be universally applied to families like mine. So when people see a family of many colors, they may stop to take note, but then they will respond with a smile instead of a sneer. Personally, I'm looking forward to that day.

CONCLUSION

All great change in America begins at the dinner table.
—RONALD REAGAN*

At the end of the summer, the results arrived in my inbox. About six weeks earlier, in our living room, Manuel and I had spit into test tubes and then sent off our saliva specimens to a lab in California. I wanted to know once and for all why I gave birth to three children who are three different colors. I understood Nina Jablonski's analogy of interracial genetic roulette, but still it boggled my mind that my pale husband could produce a child as dark as my first son, while, at the same time, our two other children are so light they could almost pass for white. I wanted to know definitively if Manuel carried a substantial amount of African blood, which would explain Esai's color, and/or if I, despite my brown skin and super kinky hair, had a significant amount of European DNA floating in my gene pool.

As it turned out, neither theory was true. Not only do I have a minimal amount of European DNA—about half of the national average, at 12 percent—but Manuel's results showed that only 0.6 percent of his DNA came from sub-Saharan Africa (although, interestingly, his maternal mitochondrial DNA shows that his earliest female ancestor did come from West Africa). I understood this to mean that while my husband may look white, he is, in fact, historically Black. So, instead of unraveling the great mystery of my children's extreme skin-color variation, the science of it all left me more confused. I decided to call the company—23andMe—to see if someone there could further explain my results in a way that might make sense of my multicolored family.

And while I had them on the phone, I also wanted to ask them about my parents. I had asked my father to spit into a test tube as well, so I

*I never thought I'd quote Ronald Reagan, but when he's right, he's right.

could see what specific genes I had inherited from him and not from my mother. As it turned out, once my father's DNA was entered into the system and attached to my records, it was clear that my mother had passed on the majority of my European ancestry, while my father had provided a mere 4 percent. I took that to mean that my dark-complected mother is actually the reason I have skin lighter than hers; it was not the work of my Lionel Richie–looking dad. So, all of those admonitions her mother had given her—to make sure she married someone light skinned so her children wouldn't hate her—were quite unnecessary. She had us covered. But, again, I felt I should talk to an expert to confirm my pseudoscientific theories and understandings. So, I placed the call.

It took a few weeks to get the scientists from 23andMe on the phone, but once I did, they were only too happy to answer all of my questions. I spoke with Dr. Joanna Mountain, senior director of research at the company, and Dr. Katarzyna Bryc, a population geneticist. Of course, asking Mountain and Bryc to break down their incredibly complicated work into a simple explanation that I could process over the telephone was neither fair nor realistic, but they made a solid effort. The first thing they told me was that looking at mom and dad is not the best way to predict the phenotypic outcomes of children. "It might be helpful to think about the children's grandparents, because each child gets roughly a quarter of their DNA from each grandparent," said Mountain. "And they may or may not get variants that are associated with lighter or darker skin from each grandparent." In other words, what we pass on to our children in our DNA goes way back beyond what we see in ourselves. Each child is essentially a repository for our ancestral history.

Then there is the issue of the many different genes that are actually involved in determining skin color. Unlike, say, eye color, which is determined by two genes, skin color is influenced by more than a hundred, so there isn't a simple dominant/recessive pattern of predictability. "Imagine if there are a hundred different genes or genetic markers that have influence on skin color and one child happens to get the darker version of sixty of those and the lighter version of forty," Mountain explained. "And another child happened to get the darker version of thirty-five and the lighter version of sixty-five. That's going to impact their appearance." Just like Jablonski's genetic roulette metaphor, how each combination of genes is going to manifest really is like a roll of the dice.

Both Mountain and Bryc had a chance to examine my DNA results before our phone call, but neither had any stunning moments of discovery that would explain my children's particular color presentations. And honestly, they didn't find the fact of their three different colors all that unusual either, considering how these things work. In fact, Mountain shared her own personal experience of having two blue-eyed children even though both she and her husband have brown eyes, and Bryc mentioned that both she and her brother have red hair even though she can't locate any relative on her family tree with red hair. So, I took that to mean that phenotypic variance is just part of the human experience and my brown, tan, and beige children are evidence of what happens when two people with wildly different ancestries come together. But my husband, Manuel, and I may *not* be all that different.

When I mentioned to Mountain and Bryc that Manuel's maternal haplogroup was L2b1a—one of the most common haplogroups for African Americans—they were both surprised. I felt vindicated somehow. For all of those times I'd claimed my husband wasn't really white, wasn't this the proof that I was right? "This L2b1a on the maternal side is very interesting," Mountain said, as I waited for her to put two and two together and discover Manuel's true Black identity. But I was getting a little too excited.

Mountain and Bryc wouldn't confirm that Manuel is, in fact, a Black man trapped in a white man's body, but they did admit that it was likely he had more African ancestry than his official results indicated. "The thing about our reference samples from Spain is that they are from people more recently from Spain," Mountain explained. "So [the test] is not picking up ancestry that is that deep. So he could have ancestry from Africa that's not being picked up." In other words, Manuel's mother's incredibly curly hair might actually be a thank-you note sent down through the generations by an ancestor from the motherland. And that same ancestor might be responsible for Esai's beautiful brown skin. Or, Esai could have simply received more genes for dark skin from me than his two siblings did. Like everyone kept telling me, skin color is a crapshoot.

So, did a scientific explanation make me feel any more confident about rearing my tricolored children? Not really. I now understand how the DNA was dealt, but that doesn't mean I know how to deal with some very real issues. But I know I am not alone in this conundrum about color and its effects on parenting and family life. As I've chronicled in these pages, so many people from so many different communities are struggling with these very same issues. And while their conversations may not be in loud voices or in the public domain, people *are* beginning to talk about it.

Colorism Is Coming out of the Closet

On April 21, 2015, Pulitzer Prize–winning novelist Toni Morrison published her eleventh book, *God Help the Child*. Morrison is a master storyteller who has mined the African American experience for inspiration throughout her career, and *God Help the Child* was no different. Lula Ann, the protagonist, is a dark-skinned Black woman with a light-skinned mother. The novel begins with a confession by Lula Ann's mother:

> It's not my fault. So you can't blame me. I didn't do it and have no idea how it happened. It didn't take more than an hour after they pulled her out from between my legs to realize something was wrong. Really wrong. She was so black she scared me. Midnight black, Sudanese black. I'm light-skinned, with good hair, what we call high yellow, and so is Lula Ann's father. Ain't nobody in my family anywhere near that color.

As the story continues, we learn how Lula Ann's dark skin prevented her mother from ever truly loving her. She took care of Lula Ann, but did not love her, did not mother her, and in turn we watch Lula Ann grow into a tragic figure. While Morrison seems to be using the story of Lula Ann and her mother to comment on many social ills in modern society, it cannot be denied that at the heart of the drama is this unrelenting issue of colorism. While one could argue that many of Morrison's novels make mention of colorism, this latest book addresses it head on, laying the blame for Lula Ann's miserable life on the fact that her light-skinned mother rejected her because Lula Ann was too damn dark.

Thanks to Morrison and countless other artists and activists, not to mention plain old fed-up citizens, the issue of colorism is finally coming out of the closet. From Morrison's latest novel to on-screen offerings by young filmmakers like Nayani Thiyagarajah and Jessica Dela Merced, cultural products addressing this issue are being created for public consumption from a wide range of sources and on multiple platforms. There are websites and Tumblr accounts devoted to colorism research, podcasts on which guests discuss colorism in the media, and even comics and zines challenging the prevailing notion that light skin is better than dark skin. But is it enough? Is it enough that Black people and Latino people and Asian people are having these conversations in their own communities, perhaps unaware that the same hurt is being felt in neighborhoods on the other side of town? Would it matter if conversations about skin color took place between communities instead of only among those of the same ilk? I don't have all the answers, but as I come to the end of this writing, I feel I have come to some useful conclusions about color politics and the family.

Colorism Is a Global Issue and a Global Moneymaker

I suspected this going in. But after speaking with experts from around the world and reading the latest research findings, it is extremely disheartening to find that the skin-color hierarchy favoring light skin over dark is a worldwide injustice. What's worse, it is an injustice that does not appear to be on the agenda of any national government or major international organization. While there are a handful of grassroots movements all over the world—from the Dark and Lovely campaign in India to a Black history initiative in Colombia—grassroots efforts aren't really an equal adversary to colorism's greatest sponsor, the global skin-lightening industry.

What I discovered in the reporting of this book is that the world-wide skin-lightening industry is a powerful partner in keeping women and men believing that they need light skin to succeed in the world. With projections that this industry will reach a value of $23 billion by 2020, it is understandable that those in the skin-lightening business are keen on keeping the insecurities, fears, and low self-esteem based on skin color alive around the world. And it's not just garden-variety bleaching creams sold on drugstore shelves that represent this industry. There are also the upscale face creams, lotions, and spa treatments that promise to keep skin light, bright, beautiful, and youthful looking, as well as lightening products for one's armpits, elbows, feet, and genitals.

The advertisements and messaging for these products are so ubiquitous in our daily lives we're not even aware of the many overt and covert ways we are told to lighten and brighten our skin. With slogans that promise beauty, success, and, even better, luck with the opposite sex, these products and the people selling them are undoing any progress made by grassroots activists. Short of ripping ads out of magazines or turning off the TV every time an ad for BB creams shows up on the screen, how does one person destroy a multibillion-dollar industry? Actually, that's the easy part. Stop buying the products!

But if you don't already buy skin-lightening creams, how can you participate in this moral boycott? Do the research. For example, the company (Unilever) that makes Dove products—ironically, the products that claim to celebrate a woman's "real beauty"—is the same company that peddles one of India's most famous skin-lightening products, Fair and Lovely. So, you might want to put that body wash back on the shelf if its manufacturer is conspiring to make people of color slaves to lightening products. Fewer products, fewer ads, fewer messages that light is right—and then grassroots organizers and activists may have a fighting chance to combat global colorism. Because at the end of the day, light skin isn't all that it's cracked up to be.

Light Skin Is Not the Perfect Prize

Contrary to the hundreds of years of history that seem to suggest light skin is a universal imperative for health, wealth, beauty, and power, my reporting seems to indicate that people universally crave something different: to belong. The novelist Mat Johnson, who frequently writes about race and identity, addressed this issue in his 2015 novel *Loving Day*. The book's protagonist, a light-skinned biracial man who yearns to find acceptance in a racial group, says in the opening chapter, "People aren't social. They're tribal. Race doesn't exist but tribes are fucking real." Based on the stories gathered for this book, I would have to agree. At the end of the day, people want to immediately be seen as part of a group, a recognized member of a tribe. Any tribe. The longing I catalogued in these pages was expressed by people who wanted to belong—to their parents, to their family, to their community. It wasn't a specific color they lusted after, it was a simple desire to be an obvious member of a group. Nobody wants to be an outlier, a lone wolf looking in at the pack. The deepest desire I heard from people had nothing to do with color. It was, at its most basic, a desire for a visually recognizable belonging to one's designated tribe, to the family. If their family color was white, they wanted to be white. But if their family color was dark, dark skin was the dream.

And as for the most-coveted shade of skin, I was surprised to find that, across cultures, light wasn't it. Over and over again, people from every ethnic group spoke of their desire for a child with more color, or of their own wish for more color. In the intimate spaces of home, where the outside world could not intrude, many a mother admitted her yearning for a baby with brown skin, be it to satisfy her notions of beauty or to guarantee that the baby would be a recognized member of her family. From the light-skinned African Americans who desired more melanin so they might claim the title of authentically Black, to the mixed-race Asian Americans who felt alienated from the Asian community because of their perceived "otherness," a universal desire for white or light skin I did not find.

In the end, the real winners in the skin-color game seemed to be those with medium skin tones, neither too light nor too dark. I found that some shade in between the two extremes of dark and light allows children and their parents to avoid many of the conflicts of colorism. (Again, nobody really wants to be an outlier.) In her article examining colorism in the African American community, "Revisiting 'Color Names and Color Notions,'" JeffriAnne Wilder calls this safe middle shade the "perceived sanctuary of brown skin." This idea is reiterated in studies focusing on other cultures as well. The middle ground is often the safest space. While this is neither a tip nor a suggestion for defeating colorism, it is a reminder that when we talk about color differences and colorism, we should not assume that light skin is the panacea for all that ails us as a community or within a family. Instead, the magic bullet would be to find a way to make everyone feel accepted.

Everyone Has a Story to Tell, but Not Everyone Wants to Tell Their Story

I went into this project with two major assumptions: First, because skin color is both obvious and arbitrary, it is easier for people to talk about than race is. Second, only certain people—people of color and the people who love them—would have stories to share about colorism. I was wrong on both counts.

I have almost a thousand friends on Facebook. Many of them have children who are different colors, via birth or adoption. Before I had even officially started doing research for this book, I paid attention to the family pictures on Facebook in which family members were different colors, and I'd make mental notes that I was going to contact these people at some point if I ever actually wrote this book. When that time came, I was shocked by the responses I received upon asking people if we could talk about how color differences impacted their family. Some people stopped speaking to me, others gave me frosty responses indicating I'd broached a line of decency, and some simply ignored my repeated requests. I was genuinely surprised at the nerve I had struck. Clearly, talking about skin color, despite the fact that it is as obvious as the nose on one's face, is difficult and painful for many people. One Asian woman admitted that she didn't want to talk to me about this topic because it would require her to revisit issues she had no desire to think about at this point in her life. An African American acquaintance, whom I assumed would have lots to say on this topic given the fact that each member of her nuclear family is a different color, also politely refused to talk to me with the excuse that she just didn't want to "go there." She wished me well, though, as did the Asian woman.

So, after talking to people who were willing to share their stories around the color differences in their families, I realized how painful an issue this really is. Children feel unloved by their parents because of their color. Siblings are estranged because of their color. People feel disconnected from their own family and community because of their color. Parents are passing on generational pain because of their color. Yes, skin-color differences cause pain. And just because colorism isn't a "real" word, bandied about in households across America, it is sitting right there in the middle of the living room daring anyone to acknowledge it.

So, I was wrong. Talking about color differences isn't easier than talking about race. It's just as hard, just as awkward, just as shameful, just as painful. But why wouldn't it be? Racism and colorism in the United States were both cut from the same, suffocating white-supremacist cloth. Which brings me to assumption number two.

I assumed white people would have few experiences with colorism. I assumed that unless they were intimately involved with a person of color, their understanding of the issue would be limited to an academic one at best. But I was mistaken.

Color Matters to White People Too

Many white Americans understand what it's like to have dark and light family members, and they have first-hand experience with discrimination too. The anthropologist Nina Jablonski admits this is why she started her research into skin color. She introduces her book *Living Color* with an anecdote about her own brush with colorism due to a North African ancestor who left his mark on her family. "In rural upstate New York, where I was raised in the 1950s and '60s, I was one of the most darkly pigmented kids in my school," Jablonski writes. "I didn't understand fully why my relatives avoided talking about our African ancestor or our color, but I realized that it embarrassed them. Some years later, I learned that my mother's brother, a decorated World War II veteran, had been called a 'nigger' by a superior officer while serving overseas . . . [and] my mother and her darker siblings had suffered color discrimination while growing up."

For other white people, the range of skin colors in the family doesn't necessarily lead to overt discrimination, but a certain disruption in family life still occurs. I was surprised by the number of white people who shared with me their experiences of being in a white family with different colors, once I told them about my research. There was the pale-skinned, green-eyed Israeli American who told me his father faced discrimination because other Israelis thought his dark skin marked him as a Muslim—and not only that, but when father and son were together, people never believed the two were related. Then there was the Italian American girl with sandy brown skin and thick curly hair whom I actually mistook for biracial (Black and white). She corrected my mistake and told me that, no, she's not biracial, just white. When I told her what my book was about, she mentioned that everyone in her nuclear family—her parents and three sisters—looks like she does, with a stocky build, light-brown skin, and thick, curly hair. Everyone, that is, except for one sister. "She's tall, skinny, and blond," she said. "Nobody believes we're sisters, and none of us know where she came from."

The stories from white people kept coming and it became apparent to me that they understood all of the issues I catalogued in this book. The questioning of kinship. The yearning to belong. The annoying questions. That surprised me and yet also inspired me in that while white Americans may be unaware that they are part of the colorism problem, they are not so far removed from the issue that they can't be active participants on the path to progress. In fact, it's probably in their best interest to halt all forms of discrimination based on skin color and perceptions of racial purity because a large percentage of white Americans are not all that pure. In December 2014, Dr. Bryc of 23andMe was the lead author on a study that found that approximately 3.5 percent of all white Americans have at least 1 percent of African ancestry. That officially counts as at least one drop! In the South, that 3.5 percent jumps all the way up to 13 percent in the state of South Carolina and 9 percent in Georgia and Alabama. This is why darkly pigmented children are born to white parents. Remember the Platt family in Florida.

Suffice it to say, white people understand color bias and colorism; however, they are not only victims of colorist behavior, but also its perpetuators. As mentioned in the introduction of this book, white people are just as likely to exhibit colorist behavior as their counterparts in the African American, Latino, and Asian American communities. This should come as no surprise to anyone, considering white Europeans essentially created the concept of a skin-color-based hierarchy. Lance Hannon of Villanova University wrote a compelling article titled "White Colorism," published in 2015, that addressed this issue. Hannon argues that "a full accounting of white hegemony requires an acknowledgment of both white racism and white colorism."

Hannon isn't suggesting that white people discriminate against one another based on whose skin is closer to pure ivory, but rather that white people reinforce the light-skin/dark-skin hierarchy entrenched in the African American and Latino communities, as members of those communities do themselves. He makes a compelling case that while white Americans are just as likely to associate light-skinned Blacks and Latinos with positive characteristics and dark-skinned Blacks and Latinos with negative ones, the current conversations about colorism almost totally exclude white Americans and their role in the perpetuation of the problem. "There is very little research with a dedicated focus on white prejudice regarding skin lightness," he wrote. "Furthermore, at the time of this writing, there are no sociological studies explicitly centered on white colorism."

It seems obvious that white Americans must be part of the solution to a problem that they helped create and continue to perpetuate. What might not be so obvious is that white people understand this issue on an intimate level that until now has never been shared. Now would be a good time for white Americans to share their stories and to listen to other people's as well.

Love *and* Good Parenting Can Conquer All

I used to follow a blog called *Anti-Racist Parent* that featured great commentary on parenting and race. The blog's focus was on raising emotionally and psychologically healthy kids in a world consumed with racism. Predictably, many of the blog's loyal readers were raising kids of color. In 2009 the editors of *Anti-Racist Parent* made the bold decision to change the title of the blog to *Love Isn't Enough* because, they explained, they wanted it on record that kids needed more than love to prepare them for the racism they would face in life. "One thing is for sure, simply loving a child is not enough to ensure his or her well-being—at least not 'love' in the passive way that people too often think of it," wrote blog editor and author Tami Winfrey Harris about the change. In addition to loving one's kids, Winfrey Harris said, parents need to "guide, protect, and teach" their children about race and racism. The same can be said about color and colorism.

Going back to the wisdom of Margaret Beale Spencer of the University of Chicago, she said children could be raised to resist the negativity of colorism found in the outside world. But, like Winfrey Harris, she categorized that type of parenting as work. Hard work, which must begin early and never end. "You have to do [the work] consistently from the time you start talking to your child because we don't know in terms of their cognitive development exactly when things click in," Spencer said. Obviously, love is part of this equation too, but loving our children of different colors isn't enough to make them understand that what makes them different doesn't diminish their status in the family or at school or anywhere else they might find themselves. That is a lesson that parents must reinforce, in both words and actions. Sharon Chang, the author of *Raising Mixed Race*, agrees and stresses the importance of constant communication around color and identity. "There's a big difference between those kids whose parents tried to talk to them and who were very honest with them and those [whose parents] avoided [these conversations]," Chang said. The parents who avoided the conversation left their kids grappling with these issues on their own. "And if you have to find the answers for yourself," Chang warned, "it can be overwhelming, bewildering, and exhausting."

Spencer had another important point to drive home. "Colorism is an adult problem that, unfortunately, a child experiences," she said. It took me a moment to process that message, but I then realized the obvious truth in her statement. Children do notice color differences but they have to be taught a color hierarchy. If adults didn't reinforce these insidious colorist notions—in their words and their actions—children wouldn't fall victim to a colorist mindset. They wouldn't grow up limited by a colorist doctrine, nor would they pass such ideals on to their own children. Think about Soledad O'Brien's experience or my friend Kia Walker's. Clearly, colorism would still exist in the outside world, but good parenting can serve as an effective vaccination to the disease.

After doing the work to write this book and talking to so many experts in the field, I realized that, in my own household, my children's variation in hue was an issue in my mind but not necessarily in theirs. All of my concerns about the differences in skin color between my sons are ones I've predicted without any actual evidence that a problem even exists. The worries I had about my daughter not being dark enough to join the Black girl tribe have yet to materialize. She's only four, for goodness' sake. As Spencer said, these are adult problems I was projecting on to my children.

Thankfully, I am not deterred by challenges and I love my children more than anything in this world. I am willing to put in the work. Instead of separating my boys into different categories of dark and light, I will raise them while honoring their differences without suggestion that one color is better than the other, either in my estimation or in the world beyond the walls of our home. And instead of fixating on the lightness of my daughter's skin, and lamenting that it isn't like mine, I will see the beauty in its sun-kissed shade of perfection. Without using color as a litmus test for acceptance, I will continue to raise my children as members of my tribe, albeit members with a Spanish father.

I've learned from the people who shared their stories with me that acknowledging color differences is important but it does not need to be defining. In fact, the people who seemed to be the least affected by the skin-color differences in their family were the ones whose parents never made color an issue. They didn't ignore it; they simply did not allow it to interfere with the message that their children were loved exactly in the skin they were in. So, that's where the shift in my parenting must occur. I will celebrate my children's unique colors and contextualize difference in a positive way for them and for myself. And as for The Talk, I've reimagined it as A Talk and it sounds a lot like the conversations we've already been having. Just as I'd want any parent to raise their children with an awareness of the unfair way people of color are often treated in this country, I will share the same information with my children. There is no need to separate my parenting lessons into different color categories. What I teach one is what I will teach the others. And I will teach them all that while, yes, color matters in some ways, it doesn't have anything to do with determining their value on this earth.

And to be quite honest, I may be being a little too hard on myself. I may be overstating the depth of my fears and the way they influence my parenting. I've had to focus on them while writing this book, but I don't spend the majority of my days or nights gnashing my teeth over the difference in pigment between my kids. In fact, my husband thinks we're doing a great job raising confident kids who are proud of their mixed heritage and unfettered by the range of color in their skin tones. I wanted to believe him, but I know in my heart that I have been conflicted and don't know if, as with Lisa Washington, my issues have seeped into my children's psyches. So, rather than wondering if they harbored any pain or discomfort about the color of their skin, I just asked them about it as I came to the end of writing this book. The recent conversation at the lunch table with my eleven-year-old son went like this, as his older brother listened in from the next room.

ME: Do you think you and your siblings are different colors?
ADDAI: Yeah. I'm like the color of sand and Esai is like your color and Aida looks white.
ME: Does that bother you?
ADDAI (*screws up his face and thinks for a minute*): No, not really.
ME: When you're out in public, what do people say about you and your brother looking so different?
ADDAI: Actually, most people think we look like twins. Right, Esai?
ESAI (*yells from the living room*): Yeah, they think we look like twins.
ME (*slaps palm on forehead*): Twins?
ADDAI: Yeah, twins.

Clearly I've been worrying for nothing all along.

And there you have it. Color talk at home around the kitchen table. No filters. No fears. This is how we do it from now on. If change is going to happen, it's happening right here first.

Sidebar: Color Names for Colored People

The biggest challenge in writing a book about skin-color variations is finding the proper language to describe the actual color of human skin. As mentioned in the chapter on African Americans, Black people have their own terminology to reference different skin tones, but many of those terms are offensive. And so I chose to rely on a combination of food and wood references to describe the hue of many of the Black people I wrote about on these pages. (I apologize if I offended anybody by likening his or her skin tone to a noble tree or a fragrant spice.)

But what about non-Black people? What are the appropriate words to describe people of Asian, Hispanic, mixed-race, and Native American descent? What about white people? Their skin isn't actually the color of milk. There's some real variety in Caucasian skin tones and it can get awkward trying to find the right words to describe them.

While there are some default words used to describe skin color, many of them are offensive and outdated, while others barely come close to describing anything approximating human flesh.

Here's a list of common words meant to describe human skin colors. Read them and understand my challenge.

RED: Refers to the skin color of Native Americans. (Author's note: I've never seen a red Native American person in my life. In fact, the only truly red people I've ever seen are pale-skinned white people who spend too much time in the sun without enough sunscreen; *see* English and German tourists on their first day of vacation in the South of Spain.)

YELLOW: Refers to the skin color of Asian people. (Author's note: Asia is a continent with 4.4 billion people at last count. They don't all have the same skin color and I don't think anybody is actually yellow. True yellow skin is usually a telltale sign that a person is jaundiced and should seek medical attention right away.)

WHITE: Refers to the skin color of Caucasian Americans and Europeans. (Author's note: As mentioned above, most white Americans are not actually white. Chalk is white. The only time white people actually look like chalk is when they have been "scared to death" and "all the color has drained from their face." Or, of course, when they are in fact, dead.)

BLACK: Refers to the skin color of African American people and other members of the African diaspora. (Author's note: Black is a beautiful color, but most Black Americans are not actually black. They're most often some shade of brown, ranging from dark to light. Calling a Black person "Black" used to be considered offensive, but since the Black Is Beautiful movement, the word, often with a capital "B," as I have done here, has been embraced and reappropriated as a word denoting pride and power by many in the African American community.)

BROWN: Refers to the skin color of Latino people. (Author's note: Seeing as how Latinos can be Black, white, Asian, or mixed, it seems rather ridiculous to assign a single color to such a diverse group. And yet, when referring to Latino people, brown is the default color for description. Tell that to Cameron Diaz or Sofia the First. Oh, wait—Sofia isn't a Latina. But still, the point is that Latinos come in every color, not just brown.)

OLIVE-TONED: Generally refers to people whose ancestors hail from around the Mediterranean Sea. (Author's note: Think Spaniards, Italians, Greeks, and various people from the Middle East. I always thought this was a nice way to describe people who looked darker than Northern Europeans.)

SWARTHY: Generally refers to people whose ancestors hail from around the Mediterranean Sea. (Author's note: Think Spaniards, Italians, Greeks, and various people from the Middle East. I always thought this was an offensive and mildly sinister way to describe people who looked darker than Northern Europeans.)

DUSKY: Generally refers to white people whose ethnic origins are suspect. (Author's note: People with a "dusky skin tone" might be hiding some Negro ancestor in their genetic closet, thus explaining their slightly brownish skin; *see* the "dusky" Platt family from Florida. Many now consider this term offensive and outdated.)

TAN OR TANNED: Generally refers to white people who have darkened their skin in the sun, from its original color to one that resembles a lightly toasted marshmallow. (Author's note: The actual dictionary definition of tan is a "yellowish-brown color," but it also can be used by Black people who have darkened their skin in the sun, thus making the phrase "tanned skin" useless and arbitrary without context.)

It is probably best to concede that human beings come in an infinite number of unique shades and colors and that trying to lump them all together under one color category is pure folly. That would be as foolish as suggesting all vegetables are green. As a writer it is definitely a challenge to find the precise language to capture a person's true colors, but in our daily lives I think our collective goal should simply be to appreciate the great variety in the human rainbow.

ACKNOWLEDGMENTS

Same Family, Different Colors has been a passion project from day one—and day one was way back in 2001, when my son Esai was born and we immediately became a family of different colors. From that moment on I became hyperaware of other families like mine and started contemplating a way to bring these families together. I didn't have a specific agenda; I just wanted to talk to other people who experienced the same stares, questions, and assumptions because of their family makeup. The mother in me wanted community, and the journalist in me just wanted to ask questions.

Fast-forward ten years, two more books written and two more children born. I finally got the courage to explore this idea about skin-color differences and families in book form. But as is often the case with writers, I doubted that anyone would care to read it and started to pursue other ideas. But, thanks to my do-or-die writers' group, WordSpace writers, I received the encouragement I needed to write not the right book for a fickle market, but the right book for me. So, all thanks go to Miriam, Meredith, Hilary, Tamar, Andrea, Jude, Ellie, and Eileen for their sage advice, unfailing encouragement, and threats to kick my butt when I wanted to give up. Without these women by my side, this book would still be just a notion, floating in the abyss of abandoned ideas in my mind.

I also want to thank my colleagues at Temple University's Department of Journalism for supporting this project by providing me with time away from campus to work on the book and for providing the world's best research assistant, Lora Strum, who made the research and reporting for this work a hundred times less stressful, thanks to her smarts and technical skills. And special thanks must go to my former Temple student Darian Muka for helping me out in the final stretch. Go Owls!

The research for this book was generously supported by a fellowship from the Penn Humanities Forum and the Andrew W. Mellon Foundation. That fellowship included a yearlong forum at the University of Pennsylvania, where I was lucky enough to be in conversation with the most interesting group of scholars, all engaged in research on color. I learned so much during that year, and much of what I learned landed in these pages. So, thank you Chi-ming Yang and Jim English for including me in such an impressive group.

Even with all of my research and good intentions, this book wouldn't exist if complete strangers—and some good friends—hadn't agreed to share their stories with me. I was overwhelmed by the number of people who wanted to talk about colorism in their families and communities. More importantly, I was overjoyed. Not only did the variety of stories make this book a better read, but also it indicated to me that this book is truly necessary.

On that note, I must thank Cecelia Cancellaro and Tanya McKinnon for helping me get this book in shape for the market and into the right hands. Thank you to Gayatri Patnaik and the entire Beacon Press team, who believed in me and in this book. I am so proud to be a Beacon author and so thankful this work will be shared with the world.

And finally, I have to thank my family. My husband and children not only served as the inspiration for this book, but they also helped me talk through so many ideas and concepts about skin color. Plus, they were kind enough not to complain during the last six months of writing when I would disappear for days and weeks to work on the book—particularly when I went off to the woods to spend a week at the wonderful Highlights Foundation Retreat to create the first real draft. I still dream about my time at Highlights and give thanks to the wonderful founders and staff who have created a perfect haven for writers to write. Thanks to the Laughing Lodge Ladies as well, who saved me from that horrible spider.

And to my parents, Morris and Quincy. They get the final thanks because without their continuous support of my writing career, I wouldn't be penning these words. Thank you, Mom and Dad, for believing in me, supporting me, and babysitting my kids. I love you.

SOURCES

The author conducted interviews, from 2014 to 2015, with the following people: asha bandele, Yaba Blay, Katarzyna Bryc, Kim Chanbonpin, Sharon Chang, Fabienne Darling-Wolf, Heidi Durrow, Marita Golden, Sandra Guzmán, Dash Harris, Tanya Hernández, Elizabeth Hordge-Freeman, Margaret Hunter, Yvonne Latty, Grace Hwang Lynch, Jessica Dela Merced, Thomas Morton, Joanna Mountain, Soledad O'Brien, Radhika Parameswaran, Emily Raboteau, Joanne Rondilla, Margaret Beale Spencer, Joy Huang Stoffers, Christina Sue, Nayani Thiyagarajah, Vetta Sanders Thompson, Jesse Washington, and Jeffri-Anne Wilder.

INTRODUCTION

Kwame A. Appiah, "Can I Call My Nonbiological Twins Black Because My Husband Is?" *New York Times Magazine*, January 27, 2016.

Associated Press, "Study of Immigrants Links Lighter Skin and Higher Income," *New York Times*, January 28, 2007.

David Batchelor, *Chromophobia* (London: Reaktion, 2000).

Steve Berry, "Suspicion of 'Nigra' Blood Racked Family," *Orlando Sentinel*, February 10, 1991.

Derrick Clifton, "There's a Big Issue Missing from How We Talk about Race—One New Study Proves It," *Mic*, March 2, 2015, http://mic.com/articles /111578/there-s-a-big-issue-missing-from-how-we-talk-about-race-one -new-study-proves-it.

N. D. B. Connolly, "Skin Trouble," *Talking Points Memo*, July 6, 2015, http:// talkingpointsmemo.com/primary-source/platt-segregation-ebony.

Joni Hersch, "The Effects of Color on Native Americans, Latin Americans and Immigrants of Color," panel presentation, Global Perspectives on

Colorism Conference, Washington University School of Law, St. Louis, April 3, 2015.

Margaret L. Hunter, *Race, Gender, and the Politics of Skin Tone* (New York: Routledge, 2005).

Nina Jablonski, "The Colors of Human Skin," lecture, Penn Humanities Forum, University of Pennsylvania, Philadelphia, November 19, 2014.

———. *Living Color: The Biological and Social Meaning of Skin Color* (Berkeley: University of California Press, 2012).

Achal Mehra, "Fair and Ugly—Indian Americans and Skin Color Politics," *New America Media*, March 1, 2010, http://newamericamedia.org/2010/03 /fair-and-ugly---indian-americans-and-skin-color-politics.php.

Itabari Njeri, "Colorism: In American Society, Are Lighter-Skinned Blacks Better Off?," *Los Angeles Times*, April 24, 1988.

Carolyn Purnell, "Color, Chromophobia, and Colonialism: Some Historical Thoughts," *ApartmentTherapy*, March 5, 2013, http://www.apartment therapy.com/color-chromophobia-and-colonialism-some-historical -thoughts-185710.

Jay Scott Smith, "Americans Rank Mixed Race People Ahead of Blacks Socially," *The Grio*, December 21, 2011, http://thegrio.com/2011/12/21 /americans-rank-mixed-race-people-ahead-of-blacks-socially.

Andrew Solomon, *Far from the Tree: Parents, Children and the Search for Identity* (New York: Scribner, 2012).

Scott Stump, "Cheerios Ad with Mixed-Race Family Draws Racist Responses," Today.com, June, 3, 2013, http://www.today.com/news/cheerios-ad-mixed -race-family-draws-racist-responses-6C10169988.

Frank J. Sulloway, *Born to Rebel: Birth Order, Family Dynamics, and Creative Lives* (New York: Vintage, 1997).

Desire Thompson, "Georgia Police Explain Why They Ignored 911 Call," NewsOne.com, September 17, 2015, http://newsone.com/3185257 /georgia-police-ignored-911-call-about-white-baby-with-black-family.

Shankar Vedantam, "Shades of Prejudice," *New York Times*, January 18, 2010.

Tanzina Vega, "School's Discipline for Girls Differs by Race and Hue," *New York Times*, December 10, 2014.

Alice Walker, *In Search of Our Mother's Gardens* (New York: Mariner/Harcourt, 2003).

CHAPTER 1: THE DARKER THE BERRY

Africans in America Resource Bank, "Conditions of Antebellum Slavery," http://www.pbs.org/wgbh/aia/part4/4p2956.html.

Francisco Bethencourt, *Racisms: From the Crusades to the Twentieth Century* (Princeton, NJ: Princeton University Press, 2014).

Yaba Blay, *(1)ne Drop: Shifting the Lens on Race* (Philadelphia: BlackPrint, 2014).

Howard Bodenhorn, "The Economic Consequences of Colorism and Complexion Homogamy in the Black Community: Some Historical Evidence,"

American Economic Association, August 2004, https://www.aeaweb.org
/assa/2006/0107_1015_1804.pdf.

Ayana D. Byrd and Lori L. Tharps, *Hair Story: Untangling the Roots of Black Hair in America*, rev. ed. (New York: St. Martin's, 2014).

Michael E. Dyson, "Me and My Brother and Black America," CNN.com, July 24, 2008, http://www.cnn.com/2008/US/07/23/bia.michael.dyson/index .html.

———. "Two Brothers, Two Paths: Shades of Race," *Anderson Cooper 360* blog, CNN.com, August 9, 2008, http://ac360.blogs.cnn.com/2008/08/09/two -brothers-two-paths-shades-of-race.

Brian Gilmore, "Rose-Colored Views of an All-Black School," *Washington Post*, September 2, 2007.

Lawrence O. Graham, *Our Kind of People: Inside America's Black Upper Class* (New York: HarperCollins, 1999).

Ronald Hall, Kathy Russell-Cole, and Midge Wilson, *The Color Complex: The Politics of Skin Color in a New Millennium*, rev. ed. (New York: Anchor, 2013).

Angela P. Harris, "From Color Line to Color Chart: Racism and Colorism in the New Century," *Berkeley Journal of African-American Law and Policy* 10, no. 1 (April 2013): 52–69.

Jennifer L. Hochschild and Vesla Weaver, "The Skin Color Paradox and the American Racial Order," *Social Forces* (December 2007): 643–70.

Margo Jefferson, *Negroland* (New York: Pantheon, 2015).

Obiagele Lake, *Blue Veins and Kinky Hair: Naming and Color Consciousness in African America* (Westport, CT: Greenwood, 2003).

Antoinette M. Landor, "Does Skin Tone Matter? Exploring the Impact of Skin Tone on Colorism Within Families, Racism, and Racial Socialization Among African American Adolescents," PhD diss., University of Georgia, 2012.

R. L. Lewis-McCoy, "The Willie Lynch School of Social Thought," Ebony .com, February 3, 2012.

Malcolm X with Alex Haley, *The Autobiography of Malcolm X* (New York: Random House, 1964).

Itabari Njeri, "Colorism: In American Society, Are Lighter-Skinned Blacks Better Off?," *Los Angeles Times*, April 24, 1988.

Kathy Peiss, *Hope in a Jar: The Making of America's Beauty Culture* (New York: Metropolitan/Henry Holt, 1998).

Sarah J. Shoenfeld, review of *The Paper Bag Principle: Class, Colorism, and Rumor and the Case of Black Washington, DC*, by Audrey Elisa Kerr, *H-Net*, August 2007, https://www.h-net.org/reviews/showrev.php?id=13464.

Patricia Smith and Charles Johnson, *Africans in America: America's Journey Through Slavery* (New York: Harcourt Brace, 1998).

Margaret Beale Spencer, "Shadeism Among Blacks, Bi-and Multi-Racial Americans in the United States," panel presentation, Global Perspectives on Colorism Conference, Washington University School of Law, St. Louis, April 2, 2015.

JeffriAnne Wilder, "Everyday Colorism in the Lives of Young Black Women: Revisiting the Continuing Significance of an Old Phenomenon in a New Generation," PhD diss., University of Florida, 2008.

———. "Revisiting 'Color Names and Color Notions': A Contemporary Examination of the Language and Attitudes of Skin Color Among Young Black Women." *Journal of Black Studies* 41, no. 1 (September 2010): 184–206.

JeffriAnne Wilder and Colleen Cain, "Teaching and Learning Color Consciousness in Black Families: Exploring Family Processes and Women's Experiences with Colorism," *Journal of Family Issues* 32, no. 5 (December 2011): 577–604.

CHAPTER 2: *MEJORANDO LA RAZA*

Fouad Ajami, "'A Cursed and Pernicious Seed': The Destruction of the Moriscos," *World Affairs* (May/June 2010), http://www.worldaffairsjournal.org /article/cursed-and-pernicious-seed-destruction-moriscos.

Julia Alvarez, "Black Behind the Ears," *Essence*, February 1993.

Mike Barnicle, "The Man Who Watched Walter Scott Die," *Daily Beast*, April 13, 2015, http://www.thedailybeast.com/articles/2015/04/13/the-man-who -watched-walter-scott-die.html.

Francisco Bethencourt, *Racisms: From the Crusades to the Twentieth Century* (Princeton, NJ: Princeton University Press, 2014).

Eduardo Bonilla-Silva and David R. Dietrich, "The Latin Americanization of US Race Relations: A New Pigmentocracy," In *Shades of Difference: Why Skin Color Matters*, edited by Evelyn Nakano Glenn (Stanford, CA: Stanford University Press, 2009).

Anna Brown and Mark Hugo Lopez, *Mapping the Latino Population, by State, County and City*, report for the Pew Research Center's Hispanic Trends Project (Washington, DC: Pew Research Center, 2013).

Ana Campoy, "Mexico Has Started Counting Its Afro-Mexican Population," *Quartz*, December 10, 2015, http://qz.com/569964/mexico-has-started -counting-its-afro-mexican-population/.

Nayeli Y. Chavez-Dueñas, Hector Y. Adames, and Kurt C. Organista, "Skin-Color Prejudice and Within-Group Racial Discrimination: Historical and Current Impact on Latino/a Populations," *Hispanic Journal of Behavioral Sciences* 36, no. 1 (2014): 3–26.

D'Vera Cohn, "Census History: Counting Hispanics," Pew Research Center: Social and Demographic Trends, March 3, 2010, http://www.pewsocial trends.org/2010/03/03/census-history-counting-hispanics-2.

Marta I. Cruz-Janzen, "Out of the Closet: Racial Amnesia, Avoidance, and Denial—Racism Among Puerto Ricans," *Race, Gender and Class Journal* 10, no. 3 (2003): 64–81.

Susan Deans-Smith, "Casta Paintings," *Not Even Past*, 2005, https://noteven past.org/casta-paintings.

Mandy Fridmann, "Rodner Figueroa escribe carta a Michelle Obama pidiéndole disculpas y acusa a Univision de humilliarlo," *HuffPost Voces*, March 3, 2015, http://voces.huffingtonpost.com/2015/03/12/rodner-figueroa-carta -michelle-obama-disculpas_n_6857160.html.

———. "Univision Host Rodner Figueroa Fired over Racist 'Planet of the Apes' Comment Towards Michelle Obama," *Huffington Post*, March 12, 2015, http://www.huffingtonpost.com/2015/03/12/rodner-figuero-fired _n_6854678.html.

Fans of Feidin Santana Facebook page. Accessed April 8, 2015. http://www .facebook.com/Fans-of-Feidin-Santana-973312652681155.

John M. Gonzales, "The Hispanic Color Divide," *New York Newsday*, July 15, 2003.

Ronald Hall, Kathy Russell-Cole, and Midge Wilson, *The Color Complex: The Politics of Skin Color in a New Millennium*, rev. ed. (New York: Anchor, 2013).

Jennifer L. Hochschild and Brenna M. Powell, "Racial Reorganization and the United States Census 1850–1930: Mulattoes, Half-Breeds, Mixed Parentage, Hindoos, and the Mexican Race," *Studies in American Political Development* 22, no. 1 (Spring 2008): 59–96.

Margaret L. Hunter, "The Persistent Problem of Colorism: Skin Tone, Status, and Inequality," *Sociology Compass* 1, no. 1 (2007): 237–54.

———. *Race, Gender, and the Politics of Skin Tone* (New York: Routledge, 2005).

Vanessa E. Jones, "Pride or Prejudice? A Formally Taboo Topic Among Asian Americans and Latinos Comes Out into the Open as Skin Tone Consciousness Sparks a Backlash," *Boston Globe*, August 19, 2004.

Sabia McCoy-Torres, "Excluding the Afro from Enrique Iglesias' Video en Español," *Latino Rebels* (blog), January 8, 2015, http://www.latinorebels .com/2015/01/08/excluding-the-afro-from-enrique-iglesias-video-en -espanol.

"Mercury Found in Skin-Lightening Cream Smuggled from Mexico." *Fox News Latino*, February 22, 2012, http://latino.foxnews.com/latino/health /2012/02/22/mercury-found-in-skin-lightening-cream-smuggled-in -from-mexico.

Claudia Milian, *Latining America: Black-Brown Passages and the Coloring of Latino/a Studies* (Athens: University of Georgia Press, 2013).

Ruben Navarrette Jr., "Why Isn't Disney's Princess Sofia Latino?," CNN.com, October 26, 2012, http://www.cnn.com/2012/10/25/opinion/navarrette -disney-hispanics.

Tiffany O'Callaghan, "What Could Have Made Sammy Sosa's Skin Lighter?," Time.com, November 10, 2009, http://healthland.time.com/2009/11/10 /what-could-have-made-sammy-sosas-skin-lighter.

Richard Prince, "Professor Asks, Where Are Diverse, Homegrown Hispanics?," *Richard Prince's Journal-Isms*, Maynard Institute website, October 16, 2013, http://mije.org/richardprince/new-fusion-features-light-skinned -latinos#Fusion.

Frances Robles, "Behind Closed Doors: Colorism in the Caribbean," interview by Michelle Martin, *Tell Me More*, NPR, July 16, 2007.

Enrique Rojas, "Sosa: Cream Has Bleached Skin," ESPN.com, November 10, 2009, http://espn.go.com/mlb/news/story?id=4642952.

Emily Rome, "'Sofia the First': Disney's First Latina Princess?," *Entertainment Weekly Online*, October 16, 2012, http://www.ew.com/article/2012/10/16 /disney-princess-sofia-the-first-latina.

Primer Impacto Univision, interview with Sammy Sosa via YouTube, November 11, 2009, https://www.youtube.com/watch?v=Qk-aC1F0S5M.

CHAPTER 3: FAIR ENOUGH

Luvvie Ajayi, "Was Brown Paint Busy When They Created This Bobby Jindal Portrait?," *Awesomely Luvvie* (blog), February 3, 2015, http://www .awesomelyluvvie.com/2015/02/bobby-jindal-official-portrait.html.

Francisco Bethencourt, *Racisms: From the Crusades to the Twentieth Century* (Princeton, NJ: Princeton University Press, 2014).

Eduardo Bonilla-Silva and David R. Dietrich, "The Latin Americanization of US Race Relations: A New Pigmentocracy," in *Shades of Difference: Why Skin Color Matters*, edited by Evelyn Nakano Glenn (Stanford, CA: Stanford University Press, 2009).

Kim Chanbonpin, "Understanding Color Distinctions in Asia," panel presentation, Global Perspectives on Colorism Conference, Washington University School of Law, St. Louis, April 3, 2015.

Lakshmi Chaudhry, "Miss America Nina Davuluri: Too 'Indian' to Ever Be Miss India," *FirstPost*, September 16, 2013, http://www.firstpost.com /living/miss-america-nina-davuluri-too-indian-to-ever-be-miss-india -1111477.html.

Kat Chow, "Is Beauty in the Eye(Lid) of the Beholder?," *Code Switch* (blog), NPR. November 17, 2014, http://www.npr.org/sections/codeswitch/2014 /11/17/363841262/is-beauty-in-the-eye-lid-of-the-beholder.

Fabienne Darling-Wolf, "Sites of Attractiveness: Japanese Women and Westernized Representations of Feminine Beauty," *Critical Studies in Media Communication* 21, no. 4 (December 2004): 325–45.

Mike Dash, "The Demonization of Empress Wu," Smithsonian.com, August 10, 2012, http://www.smithsonianmag.com/history/the-demonization-of -empress-wu-20743091.

Annabel Fenwick Elliott, "'Do You Wanna Be White?' Korean Skincare Brand Sparks Backlash by Posing Controversial Question on a Billboard in New York," *Daily Mail Online*, July 8, 2014, http://www.dailymail.co.uk/femail

/article-2684956/Do-wanna-white-Korean-skincare-brand-sparks
-backlash-posing-controversial-question-billboard-New-York.html.

"Empress Wu Zetian," *Biographies: Female Heroes and Rulers*, Women in World History Curriculum, http://www.womeninworldhistory.com/heroine6 .html.

Aidan Foster-Carter, "Adopting, Adapting: Korean Orphans," *Asia Times Online*, July 17, 2012, https://www.atimes.com/atimes/Korea/DG17Dg01 .html.

Ronald Hall, Kathy Russell-Cole, and Midge Wilson, *The Color Complex: The Politics of Skin Color in a New Millennium*, rev. ed. (New York: Anchor, 2013).

Jennifer L. Hochschild and Brenna M. Powell, "Racial Reorganization and the United States Census 1850–1930: Mulattoes, Half-Breeds, Mixed Parentage, Hindoos, and the Mexican Race," *Studies in American Political Development* 22, no. 1 (Spring, 2008): 59–96.

Geoffrey Jones, *Beauty Imagined: A History of the Global Beauty Industry* (Oxford, UK: Oxford University Press, 2010).

Vanessa E. Jones, "Pride or Prejudice? A Formally Taboo Topic Among Asian Americans and Latinos Comes Out into the Open as Skin Tone Consciousness Sparks a Backlash," *Boston Globe*, August 19, 2004.

Dan Levin, "Beach Essentials in China: Flip-Flops, a Towel and a Ski Mask," *New York Times*, August 3, 2012.

Eric P. H. Li et al., "Skin Lightening and Beauty in Four Asian Cultures," *Advances in Consumer Research* 35 (2008): 444–49.

Jack Linshi, "Why a Bobby Jindal Portrait Sparked a Racial Controversy," Time.com, February 5, 2015, http://time.com/3695541/bobby-jindal -indian-immigration.

Bianca London, "Donkey Milk Baths, White Wine Showers and Sperm Whale Wax Facials: The Bizarre Beauty Secrets of Ancient Goddesses Revealed," *Daily Mail Online*, April 2, 2015, http://www.dailymail.co.uk/femail/article -3019931/Donkey-milk-baths-white-wine-showers-sperm-whale-wax -facials-bizarre-beauty-secrets-ancient-goddesses-revealed.html.

Maureen O'Connor, "Is Race Plastic? My Trip into the 'Ethnic Plastic Surgery' Minefield," *The Cut*, July 27, 2014, nymag.com/thecut/2014/07 /ethnic-plastic-surgery.html.

Joanne L. Rondilla, "Colonial Faces: Beauty and Skin Color Hierarchy in the Philippines and the US," PhD diss., University of California, Berkeley, 2012.

Joanne L. Rondilla and Paul Spickard, *Is Lighter Better? Skin-Tone Discrimination Among Asian Americans* (Lanham, MD: Rowman & Littlefield, 2007).

"Skincare Tips from Empresses and Concubines," "Kaleidoscope: Health," *Cultural China*, http://kaleidoscope.cultural-china.com/en/7Kaleidoscope 5334.html.

Anna Sohn, "Korean Beauty: The Documentary," *Asia Society*, July 1, 2013, http://asiasociety.org/korea/korean-beauty.

Paul Taylor, D'Vera Cohn, Wendy Wang, Kim Parker, Cary Funk, and
   Gretchen M. Livingston, *The Rise of Asian Americans*, report for the Pew
   Research Center's Social and Demographic Trends Project (Washington,
   DC: Pew Research Center, 2012).

Lindy West, "Your Vagina Isn't Just Too Big, Too Floppy, and Too Hairy—
   It's Also Too Brown," *Jezebel*, April 11, 2012, http://jezebel.com/5900928
   /your-vagina-isnt-just-too-big-too-floppy-and-too-hairyits-also-too-brown.

Justin Worland, "Here's Bobby Jindal's Response to Controversy over His
   Portrait," Time.com, February 9, 2015, http://time.com/3701081/bobby
   -jindal-portrait-2016-presidential-election.

Seimu Yamashita, "Colorism and Discrimination in Japan's Marriage Scene,"
   Japan Sociology (blog), January 30, 2014, http://japansociology.com/2014
   /01/30/colorism-and-discrimination-in-japans-marriage-scene.

CHAPTER 4: BEIGE IS THE NEW BLACK

Bliss Broyard, *One Drop: My Father's Hidden Life—A Story of Race and Family
   Secrets* (New York: Little, Brown, 2007).

Jonathan Capehart, "From Trayvon Martin to 'Black Lives Matter,'" *Washington Post*, February 27, 2015.

Ta-Nehisi Paul Coates, "Is Obama Black Enough?" Time.com, February 1,
   2007, http://content.time.com/time/nation/article/0,8599,1584736,00
   .html.

Roberta Estes and Wayne Winkler, "For Some People of Appalachia, Complicated Roots," interview by Maria Hinojosa, *Tell Me More*, NPR, July 11,
   2012.

Dana Ford and Greg Botelho, "Who Is Rachel Dolezal?," CNN.com, June 17,
   2015, http://www.cnn.com/2015/06/16/us/rachel-dolezal.

Benjamin Gottlieb, "Punjabi Sikh-Mexican American Community Fading into
   History," *Washington Post*, August 13, 2012.

Kristen Gwynne, "How Racism Turned an Interracial Family's Trip to Walmart into a Kidnapping Investigation," *AlterNet*, May 22, 2013, http://
   www.alternet.org/how-racism-turned-interracial-familys-trip-walmart
   -kidnapping-investigation.

Calvin Hennick, "I Hope My Son Stays White," *Ebony*, September, 2, 2014,
   http://www.ebony.com/news-views/i-hope-my-son-stays-white-403.

Mat Johnson, *Loving Day* (New York: Spiegel & Grau, 2015).

Rebecca Chiyoko King-O'Riain, "Multiracial," in *Keywords for Asian American
   Studies*, ed. Cathy J. Schlund-Vials, Linda Trinh Võ, and K. Scott Wong
   (New York: New York University Press, 2015).

Travis Loller, "Melungeon DNA Study Reveals Ancestry, Upsets 'A Whole
   Lot of People,'" *Huffington Post*, May 24, 2012, http://www.huffington
   post.com/2012/05/24/melungeon-dna-study-origin_n_1544489.html.

Emily Raboteau, *Searching for Zion: The Quest for Home in the African Diaspora*
   (New York: Grove, 2013).

Sam Roberts and Peter Baker, "Asked to Declare His Race, Obama Checks 'Black,'" *New York Times*, April 2, 2010.

Meredith Rodriguez, "Lawsuit: Wrong Sperm Delivered to Lesbian Couple," *Chicago Tribune*, October 1, 2014.

Rob Rosenthal and Kate Philbrick, *Malaga Island: A Story Best Left Untold*, 2009, radio and photo documentary, WMPG-FM/Salt Institute for Documentary Studies, Portland, ME, http://www.malagaislandmaine.org.

Lacey Schwartz, *Little White Lie*, 2014, documentary film, Truth Aid, Montclair, NJ, http://www.littlewhateliethefilm.com.

Krystal A. Sital, "'Are You the Nanny?': The Awkward Encounters of a Mixed-Race Family in the Suburbs," *Salon*, May 25, 2015, http://www.salon.com /2015/05/25/are_you_the_nanny_the_awkward_encounters_of_a_mixed _race_family_in_the_suburbs.

Andrew Solomon, *Far from the Tree: Parents, Children and the Search for Identity* (New York: Scribner, 2012).

Tina Susman and Matt Pearce, "Rachel Dolezal Throws Doubt on Her Biological Parents: 'I Haven't Had a DNA Test,'" *Los Angeles Times*, June 17, 2015.

Stephan Talty, *Mulatto America: At the Crossroads of Black and White Culture* (New York: HarperCollins, 2003).

"Targeted By Security," Fox5DC (WTTG-TV), May 20, 2013.

Bonnie Tsui, "Choose Your Own Identity," *New York Times Magazine*, December 14, 2015.

Colin Woodard, "Malaga Island: A Century of Shame," *Portland Press Herald*, May 20, 2012.

Gary Younge, "Tiger Woods: Black, White, Other," *Guardian*, May 29, 2010.

CONCLUSION

Katarzyna Bryc et al., "The Genetic Ancestry of African Americans, Latinos, and European Americans Across the United States," *American Journal of Human Genetics* 96, no. 1 (January 2015): 37–53.

"The Global Skin Lighteners Market: Trends, Drivers and Projections," *Global Industry Analysts*, January 2015, http://www.strategyr.com/MarketResearch /Skin_Lighteners_Market_Trends.asp.

Lance Hannon, "White Colorism," *Social Currents* 2, no. 1 (2015): 13–21.

Toni Morrison, *God Help the Child* (New York: Knopf, 2015).

JeffriAnne Wilder, "Revisiting 'Color Names and Color Notions': A Contemporary Examination of the Language and Attitudes of Skin Color Among Young Black Women," *Journal of Black Studies* 41, no. 1 (September 2010): 184–206.

Tami Winfrey Harris, "Change Is Afoot: Love Isn't Enough Debuts Monday," *Love Isn't Enough* (blog), October 16, 2009, http://loveisntenough.com /2009/10/16/change-is-afoot-love-isnt-enough-debuts-monday.

Adames, Hector, 72, 91

African Americans: Black as a cultural construct, 139, 141, 142, 145–46, 148, 149, 155, 161; Black Is Beautiful message, 28–29, 50–51; class-based divisions in colonial American, 20–21; colorism in families (*see* Black families); colorism in the community, 27, 58–60; color tests in churches, 21, 26–27; complicity in reinforcing colorist ideals, 19–20, 27, 28, 29–30; Creole population, 22–23; discrimination within the Black community, 34–35; economic consequences of "complexion homogamy," 26; free mixed-race people of color in the colonies, 20–21, 22–23; importance of skin color in pre–civil rights America, 27–28; light-skin isolation within the Black community (*see* light-skin isolation); light-skinned Black elites in the nineteenth century, 23, 25–26; linguistic creations about skin color, 63–64; origins of colorism, 19; parents' need to racially socialize their children, 29–30, 161; presumptions made about light-skinned persons, 23, 26, 80; procreation between Blacks and whites in colonial America, 21–22; purpose of laws forbidding interracial relations, 21; slavery and (*see* slavery in America); standards of beauty amongst, 27, 29

African Methodist Episcopal (AME) Church, 26

Afro-Latino category, 76, 88, 89, 90, 92

Ajayi, Luvvie, 122

Alabama, 22

Alexander, Adele Logan, 24

Amerasian, 134

Anti-Racist Parent (blog), 173

Appiah, Kwame Anthony, 8

Asian American families: generational changes in preference for light skin, 112, 114, 116–17, 119, 120, 125; light-skin isolation,

120–21; light-skin privilege and, 124; males and skin-color isolation, 127; parenting style's influence on color awareness, 112, 114–15, 116–17, 124; parenting style's influence on self-acceptance, 112, 118–19; skin color and perceptions of a woman's worth, 117, 118; standards of beauty and, 112–13, 116, 117, 118–19

Asian Americans: American soldiers in East Asian countries and, 134; Asia's embracing of race theories, 99, 103–4, 105, 107; assignment of social stratifications to Asian immigrants, 105–7; awareness of colorism in the South Asian community, 120, 125–28; basis of the desire to be light-skinned, 107; changes in beauty standards due to mixed-race women, 134; Chinese history and colorism, 99; Chinese women's use of face protectors, 117–18; colonial influences in the Philippines and India, 100–102; colorism in families (*see* Asian American families); colorism's connection to beauty standards, 110–11; communities' influence on color issues, 115, 116, 119; community and media messages favoring light skin, 109–10; community's discomfort with discussing color differences, 108–9, 110; continuous importing of a light-skin preference, 125; cultural fixation with pale skin, 97–98, 99–100, 101–2; denial of US citizenship to non-Caucasian people, 105–6; double standard regarding gender and color, 116; European racism and, 103; generational changes in preference for

light skin, 112, 114, 116–17, 119, 120, 125; history of a connection between wealth and whiteness, 98–102; immigrants' arrival in the United States, 104; India's obsession with light skin, 121–23; intermarriage's effect on social-boundaries, 133; Japanese Americans' view of skin color, 123–25; Japanese history and colorism, 98–99, 103–4; Korean history and colorism, 99–100; legend of Empress Wu Zetian, 97; light-skin privilege and, 102–3, 104, 106–7, 124–25; messages celebrating light skin, 109–10, 112, 119–20, 125–26; opportunities for changing the dominance of colorism, 125–26; a public figure's attempts to appear white, 122–23; responses to a beauty pageant win, 121, 122; skin color tied to a woman's worth, 99, 100, 117, 118; standards of beauty, 109–10, 112, 116, 117, 118–19; use of film to tackle the issue of colorism, 125–28; US government's classifications for Asians, 104

bandele, asha, 51–52
Banks, Curtis, 63
Baseball Hall of Fame, 94
Batchelor, David, 17–18
Bethencourt, Francisco, 67, 68, 69, 99
Black America. *See* African Americans
"Black" as a skin-color descriptor, 177
Blacker the Berry, The (Thurman), 27
Black families: dark-skinned Blacks' desire to be light skinned, 35, 38,

45–46; a dark-skinned parent's anger over light-skinned privilege, 34–35, 37; experiences of siblings with different skin tones, 37, 39, 43–47, 61; growing up in a family that placed importance on skin color, 36, 43; growing up in a family where color was a non-issue, 30–33, 39–40, 48–51; growing up in a family with a parent hurt by color differences, 33–35; hair texture and the perception of beauty, 33, 36; having The Talk with different-colored sons, 161–62; individual's comfort level with their skin color or hair texture, 33, 35, 36–38, 39, 47; influence of birth order on how parents treat their children, 42; a light-skinned parent's identity as Black, 32; need for anti-colorism conversations within, 41–42, 58, 60; parents' need to racially socialize their children, 29–30, 161; perpetuation of a skin-color hierarchy in the home, 36, 43, 49, 51; perpetuation of a skin-color hierarchy outside the home, 43–44, 46; positive-parenting tactics, 32–33, 35, 40–41, 51, 61–62; role of the nuclear family in the solution to colorism, 41, 42, 58, 62; skin color and the perception of beauty, 35, 36, 38, 40, 47; society's expectation that family members match, 31–32, 39, 46
Black Is Beautiful message, 28–29, 50–51
Black No More (Schyler), 27
Black Power movement, 29, 37, 74
blanqueamiento, 69–71
Blay, Yaba, 30, 59

Bleached (Dela Merced), 111–12, 125–26
bleaching creams. *See* skin-lightening creams
blepharoplasty, 111
Blue Vein Society, Nashville, 26
Bodenhorn, Howard, 26
Bonilla-Silva, Eduardo, 71, 72, 80
Bon Ton Society, Washington, DC, 26
Brown, James, 28
"brown" as a skin-color descriptor, 177
Brown Power movement, 74
Broyard, Bliss, 131
Bruch, Sarah, 10
Bryc, Katarzyna, 164–65, 172
Burakumin, 103
Burroughs, Nannie, 27
Butler, Nell and Charles, 130

Cablinasian, 8, 145
Calderón, Tego, 92
casta paintings, 68–69
caste system in India, 101–2
Castile, Mikah, 155–58
Catholicism in the New World, 66, 67
Census Bureau, US, 73
Chang, Sharon, 137, 148, 173
Chang-Li, Julian, 143–44
Changonpin, Kim, 107
Chaudhry, Lakshmi, 122
Chavez-Dueñas, Nayeli, 72, 91
Cheerios commercial, 6
Chen, Julie, 111
Chicago Cubs, 94
Chicano movement, 74
China, 97–99, 117–18. *See also* Asian Americans
Christian churches, 21, 26–27
Chromophobia (Batchelor), 17–18

civil rights movement, 12, 28, 29, 50,
    60, 62
Clamorgan, Cyrian, 23
colonial America, 20
Color Complex, The, 21–22, 23, 24,
    26
Colored Aristocracy of St. Louis, The
    (Clamorgan), 23
Colored Methodist Episcopal (CME)
    Church, 26–27
colorism: bleaching creams use (*see*
    skin-lightening creams); conversa-
    tions' role in finding a solution to,
    59–60, 166–67; depth of the issue,
    11, 13, 41–42; discrimination
    within the Black community, 34–
    35; disparities engendered by,
    9–10; framework of this study,
    12–13; grassroots efforts against,
    167, 168; interracial and intra-
    racial characteristics of, 9; in in-
    terracial marriages (*see* mixed-race
    Americans); intra-community (*see*
    African Americans; Asian Ameri-
    cans; Latinos); legitimacy as a
    word, 8; light-skin bias across cul-
    tures, 9–10; light-skin bias in the
    media (*see* media); light-skin privi-
    lege and (*see* white privilege);
    methodology for researching, 13–
    14, 15; need for anti-colorism
    conversations, 41–42, 58, 60; ori-
    gins of, 19; parenting style's role
    in ending, 173–75; racism and,
    8, 12, 15, 16; scope of its impact,
    10, 41; social hierarchy based on,
    15; study's focus on the family,
    13–14, 15
Color of Love, The (Hordge-Freeman),
    41
Cotton Club, Harlem, 28
Cramblett, Jennifer, 159
Creole community, 22–23

Croatoans, 132
Cruz-Janzen, Marta, 80

Daniels, Samirah, 138–41
Dark Girls, 59
Dark Is Beautiful campaign, 128
Dark Is Divine movement, 128
Darling-Wolf, Fabienne, 104
Davis, Asha, 44–47
Davis, Lana, 44–47
Davuluri, Nina, 121–22, 128
DeFina, Robert, 10
Dela Merced, Jessica, 111–12, 125–
    26
Diaz, Angela, 153–55
Dietrich, David, 71, 72, 80
Dolezal, Rachel, 8
Dominican Republic, 72–73. *See also*
    Latinos
Don't Play in the Sun (Golden), 29
Du Bois, W. E. B., 15, 28
Dukes, Bill, 59
Durrow, Heidi, 136, 162
"dusky" as a skin-color descriptor,
    177
Dyson, Everett, 43–44
Dyson, Michael Eric, 43–44

East Hyde Park, Chicago, 26
Ebony, 11
Elfrye, Daniel, 130
ElishaCoy, 109–10
eyelid surgery, 111

facekinis, 117
Fair and Lovely, 168
Far from the Tree (Solomon), 13, 14,
    137
Ferber, Edna, 131
Figueroa, Rodner, 76, 90

Filipino Americans, 107, 112–15, 126, 157

General Mills, 6
Girl Who Fell from the Sky, The (Durrow), 136
God Help the Child (Morrison), 166
Golden, Marita, 29, 42, 59, 60
Green, Linda, 35–38
Guevara, Charles, 80–82
Guzmán, Sandra, 78–80

Hafu, 134
hair texture: attempts by Blacks to change, 27; characterization of, as being Black, 78, 147, 158; desirability of straight, 78, 136, 159; perceptions of beauty and, 27, 33, 36; perceptions of race and, 11, 22, 25, 146, 156, 165
Haiti, 72–73
Hampton Normal and Agricultural Institute, 26
Hannon, Lance, 10, 172
Harris, Dash, 76–77, 92
Hennick, Calvin, 152
Hernández, Tanya, 70
Hersch, Joni, 10
Hidden Brain, The (Vedantam), 9–10
"Hispanic" as term, 74
Hochschild, Jennifer L., 42, 104–5
Hope in a Jar (Peiss), 27
Hordge-Freeman, Elizabeth, 41, 42
Howard University, 26
Hunter, Margaret, 10, 66, 74, 86, 89, 92

Iglesias, Enrique, 90
"I Hope My Son Stays White" (Hennick), 152

Imitation of Life syndrome, 160
Implicit Association Test (IAT), 9
India: colonial influences in, 101–2; light-skin isolation, 120; media messages favoring light skin, 119, 168; a public figure's attempts to appear white, 122–23; skin politics in a beauty pageant, 121–23, 128. *See also* Asian Americans
In Search of Our Mothers' Gardens (Walker), 8–9
Is Lighter Better? (Rondilla and Spickard), 101, 107

Jablonski, Nina, 2, 16–18, 163, 171
Jackson, Michael, 96
James, Christopher, 52–54
Japan, 98–99, 103–4, 124. *See also* Asian Americans
Jefferson, Margo, 27
Jefferson, Thomas, 17
Jindal, Bobby, 122–23
Johnson, Mat, 168
Johnson, Sarah, 30–33, 35

Kant, Immanuel, 16–17
Kanter, Nancy, 89–90
Kim, Susie, 115–17
Kito, Shima (William White), 106
Korea, 99–100, 107–10, 118–19. *See also* Asian Americans

labels for skin color, 64
Landor, Antoinette, 58
La raza cómica, 71
Latina magazine, 78, 80
Latining America (Milian), 74
Latino families: anti-colorism progress in the Latino community, 80, 92; cultural identity of light-

skinned people, 82, 84–85; cultural value placed on light skin, 75, 77, 84, 86, 89–90; emotional impact of skin-based parental favoritism, 78–80; experiences of a dark-skinned male, 80–82; experiences of a light-skinned male, 83–85; family members' influence on perceptions of the worth of color, 77, 78, 81, 92; intra-family color awareness, 78–79, 81, 82; light-skin isolation within the Latino community, 85; parenting style's influence on self-acceptance, 83, 87–88; potential for discrimination change to begin in the home, 75, 92; reluctance to talk about colorism, 86; results of a pigmentocracy in Latin America, 72; self-esteem of dark-skinned people, 79–80, 87–88; self-identity of outliers in the family, 81–82, 84, 88; skin-color isolation, 81–82, 83–85; society's expectation that family members match, 81, 82–84, 87

Latinos: Afro-Latino pride movement, 92; anti-Black sentiment in the culture, 65, 76–78, 89; beauty standards in the community, 78–79; *blanqueamiento* promotion by colonizers, 69–71; Brown Power movement, 74; *casta* paintings' impact, 68–69; categorizing of Mexican Americans, 73–74; colorism in families (*see* Latino families); color labels in the *casta* system, 68, 69; cultural value placed on light skin, 75–76, 77, 86, 89–91; definition of, 65; depth of the dialogue about color, 91; discrimination concealment strategies of governments, 91–92; Dominican Republic and anti-Black

sentiment, 72–73; influence of appearance on a person's level of success, 74; intermarriage's effect on social-boundaries, 133; interracial relationships in the Spanish colonies, 67; leaders' attempts to deracialize their national identity, 72; message of the mainstream media in the United States, 88–90; Mexico's color-code ranking of the population, 71–72; perspective on Blackness, 75, 76–78; prevalence of brown-skinned people in newly independent countries, 71; racism in the Latino media and community, 76, 90–91, 96; rejection of Black identity in the community, 91; signs of progress in ending colorism, 80, 93; skin-color privilege for light-skinned outliers, 84, 85; skin-color transformation of Sammy Sosa, 94–96; Spain's importing of African slaves to the Americas, 66; Spain's social hierarchy resulting from blood-purity laws, 67–68, 69; Spain's use of Christianity as a means of unifying its diverse population, 67; Spanish Conquistadors' rationale for rape, 66; theory that mixed-race peoples are superior, 71–72; use of bleaching creams, 75

Latty, Yvonne, 86–88, 90
Light Girls, 44, 59
light-skin isolation: emotionally negative experiences of light-skinned children, 51–52, 54; identity-issues felt by light-skinned Blacks, 53–54, 55, 57, 85; impact of skin tone on parenting practices in Black families, 57–58; for an Indian, 120; within the La-

tino community, 85; making peace
with the past and, 54; a man's expectations for his children's view
of color, 54; need for anti-colorism conversations within Black
families, 58, 60; a parent's desire
to protect her dark-skinned child
from society, 56, 57; society's re-
actions to mixed-color families,
55–56, 57; some light-skinned
parents' desire for authentically
Black offspring, 55; of a young
South Asian American, 120–21
Little White Lie (Schwartz), 146–47
Living Color (Jablonski), 16–18, 171
Lodhi, Fatima, 128
Logan, John R., 75–76
Louisiana, 22, 25
Love Isn't Enough (blog), 173
Loving, Mildred and Richard, 132–33
Loving Day (Johnson), 168
Lumbees of North Carolina, 132
Lynch, Grace Hwang, 111, 125

Malaga Island, Maine, 131–32
Malcolm X, 43
Martinez, Enrique, 82–84
Maryland, 21
McCall, Willis V., 11
media: Black Is Beautiful message,
29; depictions of interracial families, 6; messaging celebrating light
skin, 59–60, 88–90, 109–10, 112,
119–20, 125–26, 167–68; obsession with light skin in India, 121–
23; racism in the Latino media
and community, 76, 90–91, 96;
reinforcing of light-skin politics,
89; skin-lightening industry, 27,
29, 126, 128, 167–68; use of film
to tackle the issue of colorism,
125–28

Mehra, Achal, 9
mejoranado la raza, 69–70. *See also*
Latinos
Melungeons of Appalachia, 132
mercury poisoning, 75
Mexican Americans, 73–74
Mexico, 71–72. *See also* Latinos
Milian, Claudia, 74
Mississippi, 22
mixed-race Americans: American soldiers in East Asian countries and,
134; anti-amalgamation laws, 130;
anti-miscegenation laws, 131;
changes in Asian beauty standards
due to mixed-race women, 134;
claiming of a racial identity without a genetic basis, 146; colorism
in families (*see* mixed-race families); communities' hiding of
interracial roots, 132; free mixed-
race people of color in the colonies, 20–21, 22–23; historical
legacy of interracial relationships,
130; intermarriage's effect on
social-boundaries, 133; interracial
communities in the nineteenth
century, 131–32; legalization of
interracial marriage, 132–33; millennials' position on identity,
144–46; number of Americans
identifying as mixed-race, 162
mixed-race families: Black as a cultural construct, 139, 141, 142,
145–46, 148, 149, 155, 161; children's desire to identify with a
monoracial parent, 138–42; cultural identity's precedence over
color identity, 139–40, 144, 145,
147, 154, 155; dealing with other
peoples' discomfort with a chosen
identity, 144, 155–56; definition
used, 129; elements of colorism
in, 129; feeling of a constant need

to explain the parent/child relationship, 140, 141; having The Talk with different-colored sons, 161–62; individual adoption of a cultural identity based on color, 153–54; individual discomfort with intra-family color awareness, 142–43; individual identity's relation to skin color, 143–44, 149–50; individual rejection of identity labels, 143–44, 152; individual struggles of children who don't match their parents, 136–37, 138, 140, 147; parenting style's influence on self-acceptance, 148, 150, 156–58, 159; parents and the reality of white privilege, 152, 161–62; parents' desire for their mixed-race children to experience their culture, 140, 142, 159; parents' desire to match their children, 137, 158, 159–60; parents' fears of not being able to connect with their biracial children, 137–38, 140–41, 152, 155, 160; safety concerns of parents, 135–36, 161–62; society's equating of skin color with race, 148, 149; society's expectation that family members match, 6–7, 134–36, 138, 140, 145, 151, 153, 162; society's upholding of the division between dark and light, 161, 162

Mixed Remixed Festival, 136
Morrison, Toni, 166
Morton, Thomas, 8
Mountain, Joanna, 164–65

Negro (Harris), 76–77
Negroland (Jefferson), 27
New Latina's Bible, The (Guzmán), 78
New Orleans, 22

Obama, Barack, 8, 148
Obama, Michelle, 76
O'Brien, Soledad, 88–89, 150–51
"olive-toned" as a skin-color descriptor, 177
One Drop (Broyard), 131
Organista, Kurt, 72, 91
Ozawa, Takao, 105

Parameswaran, Radhika, 101–2, 128
Park, Ruby, 118–19
Parrish, Charles, 63
Patterson, Risa, 113–14
Peiss, Kathy, 27
Philippines, 100–101, 124, 126. *See also* Asian Americans
pigmentocracy, 10, 28, 71, 72, 85
Platt family, 11, 132
Pocahontas, 130
Powell, Brenna M., 104–5
Puerto Rican Americans, 153–54. *See also* Latinos
Purnell, Carolyn, 18

Raboteau, Emily, 148–49
Race, Gender, and the Politics of Skin Tone (Hunter), 10, 66
"Racial Reorganization and the United States Census 1850–1930," 104–5
Racial Subordination in Latin America (Hernández), 70
racism: among Koreans, 117; Asia's embracing of race theories, 99, 103–4, 105, 107; Black parents' need to racially socialize their children, 29–30, 161; categorization of immigrants to the United States and, 73; colorism and, 8, 10, 12, 15, 16, 19, 172; European determination to prove the white

race was superior, 103; future of race as a category, 8, 15; institutionalization of, 17; in the Latino community, 76, 80, 90–92, 96; parenting style's influence on ending, 173; responses to a beauty pageant winner, 121; social hierarchy in Spain and, 68; society's expectation that family members match, 6–7, 11

Racisms: From the Crusades to the Twentieth Century (Bethencourt), 67, 99

Raising Mixed Race (Chang), 137

Rawles, Calida, 62

"red" as a skin-color descriptor, 176

"Revisiting 'Color Names and Color Notions'" (Wilder), 169

Rodriguez, Juan, 68

Rondilla, Joanne, 101–2, 107, 110, 112, 115, 125

Roy, Sasha, 119–21

Same Difference (Rawles), 62

Santana, Feidin, 93

Schwartz, Lacey, 146–47

Schyler, George, 27

Scott, Walter, 93

Shadeism (Thiyagarajah), 126

Show Boat (Ferber), 131

Sital, Krystal, 135–36

skin color: attempts to change (*see* skin-lightening creams); challenges for family's with different skin colors, 5–6; colorism and (*see* colorism); color names and the meanings behind, 176–78; complicated nature of inherited genetic variances, 164–65; discomfort when talking about intra-family differences, 170; evolutionary basis of differences in, 16; expecta-

tion that family members match, 1–2, 4, 5, 6–7, 11; future of race as a category, 8, 15; genetics of, 2, 163–65; historic and artistic symbolism of white versus color, 18; importance to white people, 170–72; individuals' desire to be an obvious member of a group, 168–69; Kant's influence on acceptance of color-based stereotypes, 16–17; logical fallacy of judging people by, 17; parenting style's role in ending colorism, 173–75; parents' expectations for their offspring's appearance, 3–4, 5; peoples' comfort with making comments about differences, 4–5; pervasiveness of color-based discrimination in the West, 17–18; preferences common to all groups, 169; public nature of skin-color differences, 6–7; publics' discomfort with interracial families, 6; ranking of dark and light across cultures, 18; resorting to avoidance rather than acceptance or confrontation, 5; role in perceptions people have, 2, 3, 4–5; significance of color versus race in interactions, 5, 7–8; terminology used only by Black people, 63–64; white privilege and (*see* white privilege); why skin color matters, 7. *See also* African Americans; Asian Americans; Latinos; mixed-race Americans

skin-color politics in communities. *See* African Americans; Asian Americans; colorism; Latinos; mixed-race Americans

"Skin Lightening and Beauty in Four Asian Cultures," 98, 100

skin-lightening creams: Asian cultural fixation with pale skin,

97–98, 99–100, 101–2; fighting the industry, 168; Filipina Americans use of, 112; health risks from, 75; industry's success, 126, 128, 167–68; Korean Americans use of, 109–10; Latinos' use of, 75; obsession with light skin in India, 121, 126, 128; reaction to the use by a public figure, 95–96; use of creams in the 1920s, 27

slavery in America: basis of a preference for light-skinned slaves, 24; color-based hierarchy within the slave population, 19, 23–25; legalization of slavery, 21; number of light-skinned Blacks that were slaves, 23; origins of colorism, 19; realities of light-versus-dark skin on a plantation, 24–25

Smith, John, 130

Sofia the First, 89–90

Solomon, Andrew, 13, 14, 137

Sosa, Sammy, 94–96

South Carolina, 25

Spellman College, 26

Spencer, Margaret Beale, 40–41, 58, 173

Spickard, Paul, 101–2, 107

Stoffers, Joy Huang, 142

Sue, Christina, 70, 91

Sugar Hill, Harlem, 26

Sulloway, Frank, 14

Sutherland, George, 105, 106

"swarthy" as a skin-color descriptor, 177

Talented Tenth, 28

The Talk, 161–62, 174

Tanaka, Liz, 123–25

"tan/tanned" as a skin-color descriptor, 178

Telemundo, 90

Thind, Bhagat Singh, 105–6

Thiyagarajah, Nayani, 126–28

Thomas, Cassidy, 60–62

Thompson, Vetta Sanders, 148

Thurman, Wallace, 27

Tsui, Bonnie, 159

Turks of South Carolina, 132

Tuskegee Institute, 26

23andMe, 163, 164, 172

Unilever, 168

Univision TV, 76, 90

Vasconcelos, José, 71

Vedantam, Shankar, 9–10

Virginia, 21

Walker, Alice, 8–9

Walker, Kia, 38–41

Walker, Lauren, 33–35

Walt Disney Company, 89–90

Washington, Jesse, 145

Washington, Lisa, 54–58

Weaver, Vesla, 42

West, Lindy, 121

Whasian (Stoffers), 143

whatrugear.com, 138

White, Walter, 28

"white" as a skin-color descriptor, 177

"White Colorism" (Hannon), 172

white privilege: Asian Americans and, 106–7, 124–25; class-based divisions in the American past, 20, 22–23, 25, 59; deriving of benefits from, 120, 140, 142; in India, 102; in Latin America, 72, 84; parents and the reality of, 6, 152, 161–62; pigmentocracy in the United

States, 11, 28, 71, 72, 85; presumptions made about light-skinned persons, 23, 26, 80; skin color and, 5, 8, 106
Wilder, JeffriAnne, 29, 30, 59–60, 169
Willie Lynch letter, 25

Wilson, Joseph, 23
Winfrey Harris, Tami, 173
Woods, Tiger, 8, 144–45
Wu Zetian, 97

"yellow" as a skin-color descriptor, 176